Theatre Workshop

This book is the first critical analysis, by someone outside the Company, of the work of Joan Littlewood, Ewan MacColl and Theatre Workshop, including the Company's unique actor training programmes.

'Who was Joan Littlewood? Why was she so famous? What was Theatre Workshop?' Robert Leach provides answers to these questions. Writing with the needs of Theatre Studies students in mind, Robert Leach sets the Company's aims and achievements in their social, political and theatrical contexts, and explores the elements which made its success so important.

Robert Leach is a theatre scholar and a practising theatre director; he teaches acting at the Cumbria Institute for the Arts; he has taught drama at the universities of Edinburgh and Birmingham. He was a close friend of Ewan MacColl during the latter's lifetime. His many successful theatre books have concentrated on revolutionary and political theatre, most recently *Makers of Modern Theatre* (2004).

Exeter Performance Studies

Exeter Performance Studies aims to publish the best new scholarship from a variety of sources, presenting established authors alongside innovative work from new scholars. The list explores critically the relationship between theatre and history, relating performance studies to broader political, social and cultural contexts. It also includes titles which offer access to previously unavailable material.

Series editors: Peter Thomson, Professor of Drama at the University of Exeter; Graham Ley, Reader in Drama and Theory at the University of Exeter; Steve Nicholson, Reader in Twentieth-Century Drama at the University of Sheffield.

Also published by University of Exeter Press

Theatre Workshop

*Joan Littlewood and the Making of
Modern British Theatre*

Robert Leach

UNIVERSITY
of
EXETER
PRESS

For Joy

First published in 2006 by
University of Exeter Press
Reed Hall, Streatham Drive
Exeter EX4 4QR
UK
www.exeterpress.co.uk

Reprinted 2010

British Library Cataloguing in Publication Data
A catalogue record for this book is available
from the British Library.

Hardback: ISBN 978 0 85989 759 4
Paperback: ISBN 978 0 85989 760 0

Typeset in 10.5pt Aldine
by JCS Publishing Services

Mixed Sources
Product group from well-managed
forests and other controlled sources
www.fsc.org Cert no. SA-COC-002112
© 1996 Forest Stewardship Council
FSC

Printed in Great Britain by Short Run Press Ltd, Exeter

Contents

Illustrations

For permission to reproduce illustrations 7, 8 and 9, thanks are due to Theatre Royal, Stratford East; for illustrations 3 and 4, to Peter Rankin; for illustration 5, to Jean Newlove. Illustrations 1, 2, 10, 11 and 12 are from the author's collection. Illustration 6 is by Joy Parker.

Preface

I am one of those who saw *Oh What a Lovely War* when a student, and found that the experience made a difference for the rest of my life. *Oh What a Lovely War* worked on me and many like me in two dimensions: first, it enlightened us, changed our attitudes to the First World War and, as a consequence of that, helped us to re-think the narratives of history and of our own times; second, it unveiled a kind of theatre that we had never conceived of before.

It invited us to ask: who was this company that was so extremely original, so unlike anything else in the theatre of the time? Where did it come from? What was its secret? Questions that have never been properly answered.

There are probably a number of reasons for this. The company, Theatre Workshop, was an embarrassment to the arts establishment, being unconventional and original. The Arts Council never subsidised it properly, and were therefore happy for it to be forgotten. The theatre establishment, meanwhile, did not on the whole wish to understand, being more concerned with the power games of huge national companies with huge national subsidies. Theatre Workshop's politics concerned the real world, and were radically left wing, which was generally disapproved of. Besides which, Theatre Workshop's leader, Joan Littlewood, was a woman, and could therefore be ignored by the men in charge. She was disrespectful, and would swear when she was angry. And, at least in her later years, it seems she did little to assist researchers or those who might have wanted to understand what Theatre Workshop was.

Thus, no analytical study of the roles played by Joan Littlewood and Theatre Workshop in making modern British theatre has appeared until now. This book is therefore a first attempt to rectify this omission.

For want of such a study, a number of legends have been allowed to grow up. For instance, I know at least three actors who claim that they auditioned for Joan Littlewood at the Theatre Royal, Stratford East, and tell the story of how they approached the building and saw the char scrubbing the doorstep. They asked this woman where the auditions were and were directed to the dressing rooms. Imagine their surprise on entering the stage to perform their audition piece, when they saw sitting in the stalls that very same charwoman whom they had accosted as she scrubbed the front doorstep. It was, of course, Joan Littlewood. 'You did your audition out there' was the punchline of all these stories.

Could all my informants have had the same (unlikely) experience?

Then there are the stories of her rehearsals in which she would cry to an actor performing falsely—'I don't believe you!' And it is certain that she was fiendish for 'truth' on the stage. But that cry was actually Stanislavsky's, which has by a kind of osmosis been transferred to her in this apocrypha of 'Joan stories'.

Joan's Book, Littlewood's published memoir, may itself be part of that apocrypha. I have been warned by several of her closest associates from Theatre Workshop to treat its contents with extreme caution. They flatly deny that some of the occurrences recorded in *Joan's Book* ever actually happened. Or, it wasn't like that, they protest. I am inclined to think they are telling the truth.

Yet Theatre Workshop remains probably the single most outstanding and original company in twentieth-century British theatre history. This is partly because so much of its practice was new. For instance, Theatre Workshop insisted on its actors constantly training in their art, and undermined the 'star' system. It used a resident playwright. It battled for adequate subsidy and against censorship. It radically re-evaluated the classical repertoire, and it applied classic drama to contemporary life. It introduced the ideas of major European theorists, from Appia to Stanislavsky and Laban, to Britain and developed a technique of performance, probably derived from Meyerhold and Mikhail Chekhov, which relied on honest spontaneity, something still extremely rare in British theatre.

Theatre Workshop's achievements were in large measure due to the fearlessness and brilliance of its leader herself, Joan Littlewood. But beyond her, other members of the company also made significant marks in different, often underestimated, ways, including Ewan MacColl, Jean Newlove, Harry H. Corbett, John Bury, Howard Goorney and Gerry Raffles, whose name now attaches to the square upon which the Theatre Royal, Stratford East, stands. This book attempts to investigate and critique the work of all these, and the others who made Theatre Workshop what it was.

In completing this work, I have been assisted in many ways by many people and organisations, which I am glad to acknowledge. I received a generous research grant from the British Academy and considerable additional financial help from Cumbria Institute of the Arts, for which I am extremely grateful. I would also like to thank David Bishop, archivist at the Charles Parker Archive, Birmingham; Patrick Clark of the Arts, Languages and Literature Department of Birmingham City Library; Patrick Ward, supervisor of the Working Class Movement Library, Salford; David

Horsfield, Chris Keable and Valerie Moyes at Ruskin College Library, Oxford; Patrice Fox and Richard Workman at the Harry Ransom Humanities Research Center, at the University of Texas in Austin; and the staff at the Theatre Museum, the Victoria & Albert Archive and Library Reading Room, Blyth House, London.

I am also greatly indebted to four people who gave me a good deal of their time and support over years, and who are now no longer alive to see the fruits of our conversations and correspondence: Ewan MacColl, especially for three days spent at Birmingham University discussing his theatre, its roots and aspirations, and for time also at his cottage in southern Scotland; Clive Barker, whose generosity in talking though ideas, discoveries and memories was unmatched; Charles Parker, for sharing his thoughts, especially on the subject of documentary; and Philip Donnellan, with whom I created 'The Red Megaphone' in November 1990. Their friendships were stimulating, and their ideas challenging. They each informed my understanding, but clearly none of them is in any way responsible for any mistakes in this book.

For permission to use the illustrations in this book, I am grateful to the Theatre Royal, Stratford East; Peter Rankin; and Jean Newlove.

I would also like to thank: all those who took part in 'The Red Megaphone' at the Midlands Arts Centre, Birmingham, in November 1990; the casts and crews of my own productions of *Johnny Noble* and *Landscape with Chimneys*; Murray Melvin, for answering my questions, encouraging me, and using his position as archivist at the Theatre Royal to supply some of the most striking photographs in this book; Howard Goorney, for answering my questions, especially during the 'Red Megaphone' weekend in November 1990; Peggy Seeger, for pointing me to Ewan MacColl's plays and granting permissions; Georgia Edmondson, for obtaining photographs; Claire Altree, for stimulating conversations and meaningful insights into the plays of Ewan MacColl; John Topping, for reading and commenting on an early draft of this book; Olga Taxidou of Edinburgh University, for obtaining documents as well as for her continual intellectual challenges; Professor Maggie Gale of Birmingham University, Bella Merlin of Exeter University and Karen Bassett and Charles Mitchell of Cumbria Institute of the Arts, for support; Professor Peter Thomson for his critical support of this project; and Simon Baker and Jessica Cuthbert-Smith for firm but friendly editorial support.

Perhaps most important to the making of this book has been the support and interest given to it by Jean Newlove, keeper of the flame of Laban, a brilliant performer, choreographer and teacher, and a barely acknowledged but profound influence on Theatre Workshop's style and achievements. Her friendship over the years has been extremely important.

Finally I would like to thank my wife, Joy Parker, for her unswerving support, and for the picture of the icosohedron, without which the book would be completely indecipherable!

Chronology

Year	Politics and society	Theatre, arts and culture	Theatre Workshop
1926	General strike	Cambridge Festival Theatre founded	
1927	First NUWM Hunger March	Tom Thomas, *The Ragged Trousered Philanthropists* Piscatorbuehne, Berlin: Toller, *Hoppla, wir leben!*; Tolstoy, *Rasputin*; Hasek, *The Good Soldier Schweik*	
1928		Moscow Art Theatre visits London Sherriff, *Journey's End*	
1929	Labour Government elected: MacDonald PM	Griffith, *Red Sunday*, Arts Theatre Hackney Red Radio debut, *Strike Up!*	
1930			
1931	MacDonald rejects Labour, forms 'National' government, wins election	*The Spirit of Invergordon* Moussinac, *The New Movement in the Theatre* BBC Radio: *Crisis in Spain* *Red Stage* first published	May Day: Red Megaphones debut performance
1932	Unemployed total: 3.5 million F.D. Roosevelt US president 200,000 attend Hunger March rally Lancashire cotton industry strike	Group Theatre founded 1st National Congress of Workers' Theatre Movement	Red Megaphones support striking cotton workers
1933	Hitler Chancellor of Germany	Terence Gray resigns from Cambridge Festival Theatre WTM activists at Moscow Workers' Theatre Olympiad	
1934	Gresford Colliery disaster British Union of Fascists founded	Left Theatre founded	Red Megaphones dissolved Joan Littlewood in Manchester, meets Ewan MacColl Theatre of Action formed: *Newsboy*, *Waiting for Lefty*

Year	Politics and society	Theatre, arts and culture	Theatre Workshop
1935	Peace Pledge Union formed National Government wins election Italy invades Abyssinia Comintern calls for 'united front'	BBC Radio: Brecht-Weill, *The Tupenny-Ha'penny Opera* 'Grand Re-opening' of Theatre Royal, Stratford East	Toller, *Draw the Fires*, Manchester
1936	First Moscow 'show trial' 'The Battle of Cable Street' Outbreak of Spanish Civil War	Auden & Isherwood, *The Dog Beneath the Skin*, Group Theatre Unity Theatre, Left Book Club founded	Chlumberg, *Miracle at Verdun*, Peace Pledge Union Theatre Union founded
1937	Japan invades China	M. Slater, *Towards Tomorrow*, Wembley Stanislavsky, *An Actor Prepares*	da Vega, *Fuente Ovejuna*, Manchester
1938	*Anschluss*: Germany annexes Austria By-election victory of 'Peace' candidate, Bridgwater, Somerset		Hasek/MacColl, *The Good Soldier Schweik*, Manchester
1939	Franco's Fascists take power in Spain Germany occupies Czechoslovakia Germany invades Poland: World War	Pilgrim Players founded	
1940	Chamberlain resigns: Churchill PM German 'Blitz' on Britain	CEMA founded: grants £150 to Pilgrim Players	Theatre Union, *Last Edition,* banned
1941	Germany invades Soviet Russia Japan attacks Pearl Harbor	Adelphi Players founded	MacColl/Littlewood, *Classic Soil*
1942	Beveridge Plan published		Theatre Union disbanded
1943			
1944	Education Act Battle of Stalingrad Normandy landings	Compass Players founded	
1945	Death of Roosevelt: Truman US president End of Second World War Labour government elected: Attlee PM Hiroshima and Nagasaki atom bombed	David Horne takes lease of Theatre Royal, Stratford East Adelphi Guild Players founded	Theatre Workshop formed, Kendal, then touring MacColl, *Johnny Noble*, Molière, *The Flying Doctor*; Lorca, *Don Perlimplin*
1946	Labour government begins to build British atom bomb Coal industry nationalised	Rattigan, *The Winslow Boy* CEMA becomes the Arts Council	MacColl, *Uranium 235* Theatre Workshop perform at Butlin's, Filey

Year	Politics and society	Theatre, arts and culture	Theatre Workshop
1946 cont			Arts Council rejects Theatre Workshop application for subsidy Littlewood meets Rudolf Laban
1947	Fuel crisis Cripps becomes chancellor of exchequer	Rodgers & Hammerstein, *Oklahoma!*, London Stewart, *Men Should Weep*, Glasgow Unity Unity Theatre, *Golden Boy*, S. Wales tour First Edinburgh People's Festival Gorelik, *New Theatres for Old*	Jean Newlove joins Theatre Workshop Theatre Workshop tours West Germany Theatre Workshop propose Theatre Centre, Liverpool Nelson Illingworth teaches voice
1948	Communists seize power in Czechoslovakia National Health Service founded Berlin blockade	McLeish, *The Gorbals Story*, Glasgow Unity Society for Theatre Research founded National Theatre Conference Fry, *The Lady's Not for Burning*	Theatre Workshop temporarily disbands MacColl, *The Other Animals* Theatre Workshop tours Czechoslovakia and Sweden
1949	Communists seize power in China USSR tests nuclear bomb		Littlewood, *Alice in Wonderland* Theatre Workshop first appear at Edinburgh People's Festival
1950	Labour win election with reduced majority Outbreak of Korean War	Theatre Royal, Stratford East, becomes 'tryout' venue for new musicals	Theatre Workshop temporarily disbands New policy: one-night stands as far as possible
1951	Conservative Government elected Burgess and MacLean flee to Moscow Timothy Evans hanged		MacColl, *Landscape with Chimneys* Theatre Workshop tours Sweden
1952	George VI dies; accession of Elizabeth II D. Eisenhower US president Britain explodes its own atom bomb		MacColl, *The Travellers Uranium 235* at Embassy Theatre, Swiss Cottage
1953	Death of Stalin Conquest of Mt Everest Coronation of Elizabeth II End of Korean War	*Plays and Players* founded	Theatre Workshop takes lease of Theatre Royal, Stratford East Shakespeare, *Twelfth Night*; Houghton, *Hindle Wakes*; Jonson, *The Alchemist*; etc.

Year	Politics and society	Theatre, arts and culture	Theatre Workshop
1954	Commercial television in Britain	David Scase appointed Director of Manchester Library Theatre Tynan appointed *Observer* theatre critic English Stage Company formed	Shakespeare, *Richard II*; Marston, *The Dutch Courtesan*; Shaw, *The Devil's Disciple*; Ibsen, *An Enemy of the People*; Anon, *Arden of Faversham*; MacColl/Hasek, *The Good Soldier Schweik* Arts Council gives Theatre Workshop £150 subsidy
1955	Churchill resigns as PM Conservatives win election: Eden PM Ruth Ellis hanged	*Waiting for Godot*, Arts Theatre *Richard II*, Old Vic	Jonson, *Volpone* Paris Theatre Festival: *Volpone*, *Arden of Faversham* Brecht, *Mother Courage*
1956	First Aldermarston march Khrushchev denounces Stalin's 'Cult of Personality' Introduction of Premium Bonds Visit of Bulganin and Khrushchev House of Commons votes to abolish hanging Suez: Britain, France and Israel invade Egypt USSR invades Hungary	Osborne, *Look Back in Anger*, Royal Court Unity Theatre, *World on Edge* Berliner Ensemble visits London	Marlowe, *Edward II*; Behan, *The Quare Fellow* Tour of Scandinavia: *Arden of Faversham* Theatre Workshop temporarily closed Arts Council subsidy: £500 Paris Theatre Festival: *The Good Soldier Schweik*
1957	Eden resigns: Macmillan PM Sputnik launched	Rattigan, *Variation on a Theme*	Shakespeare, *Macbeth*; Chapman, *You Won't Always Be on Top* East European tour: *Macbeth*
1958	CND founded	Belgrade Theatre, Coventry, opened MacColl, *Ballad of John Axon*: first Radio Ballad (last Radio Ballad, 1964) Wesker, *Chicken Soup with Barley*, Royal Court Theatre Arts Council subsidy to Royal Court Theatre: £5,500	Delaney, *A Taste of Honey*; Behan, *The Hostage* West Ham Council increases grant to Theatre Workshop Arts Council threatens to remove subsidy; Theatre Workshop temporarily closed; reopens when subsidy is restored Theatre Workshop loses court case to Lord Chamberlain
1959	Conservatives win election		Norman, *Fings Ain't Wot They Used T'Be*; Mankowitz, *Make Me An Offer* Paris Theatre Festival: *The Hostage*

Year	Politics and society	Theatre, arts and culture	Theatre Workshop
1960	J.F. Kennedy US president Gagarin first man in space	Royal Shakespeare Company founded Arts Council subsidy to Royal Court Theatre: £8,000 'Fun Palace' first proposed	Saroyan, *Sam, the Highest Jumper of Them All*; Jonson, *Every Man in His Humour*; Lewis, *Sparrers Can't Sing*; Owen, *Progress to the Park* Paris Theatre Festival: *Every Man in His Humour* Arts Council subsidy: £2,000 *Fings Ain't Wot They Used T'Be* Evening Standard Best Musical
1961		E15 Acting School opened Centre 42 Wellingborough Festival	Joan Littlewood leaves Theatre Workshop Theatre Workshop suspended
1962	Philby flees to Moscow Macmillan sacks a third of cabinet	BBCTV: *That Was the Week That Was* BBC Radio: *The Long Long Trail* Centre 42: five festivals Peter Cheeseman appointed Director, Victoria Theatre, Stoke-on-Trent	
1963	Britain's application to join Common Market rejected Profumo scandal Great Train Robbery Macmillan resigns: Home PM Kennedy assassinated: Johnson US president	National Theatre founded MacColl, *Ours the Fruit*, Drury Lane RSC, *Wars of the Roses*, designed by John Bury	Theatre Workshop reconstituted: *Oh What a Lovely War*
1964	Labour wins election: Wilson PM Khrushchev ousted in USSR	*The Jolly Potters*, Victoria Theatre, Stoke-on-Trent: first 'Stoke documentary (last Stoke documentary, 1974) Joan Littlewood forms Fun Palace Trust	Shakespeare, *Henry IV* *Oh What a Lovely War* in New York
1965	Death penalty abolished	Tynan, 'The Royal Smut Hound' Belgrade Theatre, Coventry, forms first Theatre in Education company RSC, *Hamlet* and *The Homecoming*, both designed by John Bury	Joan Littlewood in Tunisia

Year	Politics and society	Theatre, arts and culture	Theatre Workshop
1966	Labour wins second election	Berliner Ensemble visits London	
1967	Devaluation of the pound		Farson, *The Marie Lloyd Story*
1968	'Prague Spring' crushed by USSR 'Les événements', Paris Assassinations of R.F. Kennedy and Martin Luther King R. Nixon US president	Lord Chamberlain's power to censor plays abolished MacColl, *Festival of Fools* (annual review: last Festival 1974) AgitProp Information Service established	Joan Littlewood in India
1969			
1970	Conservatives win election: Heath PM Conference on Women's Liberation		Ken Hill director of Theatre Workshop
1971		7:84 Theatre Company formed Women's Street Theatre Group formed	
1972	Miners' strike		
1973	Second miners' strike: 3-day week	Red Ladder Theatre Company formed Women's Theatre Festival McGrath, *The Cheviot, The Stag and the Black Black Oil*, 7:84 Company John Bury, head of design, National Theatre	Rankin, *So You Want to Be in Pictures* G. Raffles resigns as general manager
1974	Two elections: Labour wins: Wilson PM	Banner Theatre of Actuality formed	
1975		Monstrous Regiment Theatre formed John Bury, chairman, Society of British Theatre Designers	Death of Gerry Raffles Maxwell Shaw director of Theatre Workshop
1976	Wilson resigns: Callaghan PM		Clare Venables director of Theatre Workshop
1977			
1978			Theatre Workshop dissolved
1979	Conservatives win election: Thatcher PM		
1982		7:84 'Clydebuilt' season, includes production of *Johnny Noble*	
1988		John McGrath resigns from 7:84 Theatre Company	

PART ONE

Before Theatre Workshop, 1926–45

Politics and Performance

CHAPTER ONE

Class Against Class

The 1926 General Strike was a marvellous 'performance'. It had almost no direct political impact, but it conveyed a whiff of revolution and exposed the smooth betrayal of the workers by their political and trade union leaders. Its enactment set the political stage for the next decade or more, when politics was often best understood as performance: the Jarrow 'Crusade', the ritualised mass signing of 'Peace Pledge' cards, even Ramsay MacDonald's Palace Revolution, a sort of Shakespearean usurpation, after which, he claimed, 'every Duchess in England would want to kiss me'. During the General Strike, the participants played (and watched) cricket, went to concerts and attended theatrical performances. But the reality of capitalism remained, along with its crisis and the depression of the workers.

In the deepening slump, the working class were apparently 'extras', largely unable to influence what was happening. They were too exhausted by a home life of poverty in perhaps a two-room slum with a shared outdoor privy, and racked by disease—polio, diphtheria, tuberculosis and rickets. At work, 'rationalisation' was the vogue word: it meant processes speeded up, multiple sackings and wage cuts. The depression lent life a 'quality of fatality', made it seem an almost 'impersonal calamity'.[1]

Yet working-class life was not without its drama, as Ewan MacColl discovered. The factory where his father worked was

> An awesome, exciting place. The glare of the open furnace bathes everything in a fiery glow, the heaps of sand on the floor, the iron rails with the bogies on them and the giant ladles. And there is the noise, the scream of compressed air from the fettling room, the sustained roar of the furnaces, the clank of metal and the rattle of steel chains as the overhead gantry lowers its grab for a tub of newly tapped molten metal. Then a hooter sounds. 'Stand back there,' says my father as he pushes me against a wall, 'don't move!' And suddenly the air is filled with a swirling mass of yellow cloud. For a minute or two I am convinced that I am choking to death. As it begins to clear the moulders and their apprentices appear like devils struggling through the flames of hell. One of them pulls me to him and gives me a quick hug. His shirt smells scorched. It is my father, though he looks different here in the foundry.[2]

It was not the same kind of performance as that of politics, but it was not necessarily less dramatic. More tragic were the accidents at work, which often devastated working-class lives. The lack of any sort of National Insurance provision or employers' liability—the reason for MacColl's father's anxiety for his son—greatly intensified the suffering. When 265 miners and three rescuers were killed in a terrible pit disaster at Gresford Colliery in North Wales in 1934, those left behind had no recourse to compensation, despite a spirited performance on their behalf—and for no fee—by Sir Stafford Cripps, a left-wing barrister who put their case to the official inquiry. The truth was recorded in a grim folk ballad of the time:

> A fortnight before the explosion,
> To the shotfirer Tomlinson cried,
> 'If you fire that shot we'll be all blown to hell,'
> And no-one can say that he lied.
>
> The fireman's reports they are missing,
> The records of forty-two days;
> The colliery manager had them destroyed
> To cover his criminal ways.
>
> The Lord Mayor of London's collecting
> To help both our children and wives.
> The owners have sent some white lilies
> To pay for the poor colliers' lives.[3]

After 1926, the overwhelming majority of working-class people, when they thought of politics, probably thought of themselves as 'Labour'. But the Communist Party, which had been founded in 1920 in the wake of the Russian Revolution, seemed an increasing threat to this allegiance. The struggle between the two groupings was fierce and lasted until the Second World War. Labour tried to purge the movement of Communists, while the Communists labelled Labour members 'social fascists' and promulgated a policy of 'class against class'. When Labour won the election of 1929, the working class, and especially the poor, looked to the new government for relief. They got little. In August 1931, the prime minister, Ramsay MacDonald, discarded Labour in favour of the Conservatives and his duchesses. 'Class against class', indeed!

That September, in economic crisis, the now 'National' government cut the wages of—among others—the armed forces. Immediately, large numbers of naval ratings stationed at Invergordon, apparently organised by Communists, mutinied. They held a series of meetings and effectively went on strike. The government was forced to backtrack, there was a run on the pound, and MacDonald, perhaps panicking, called a general election. The incident was to stimulate a popular workers' drama, *The Spirit of Invergordon*, but the election results did not justify such progressive hopes. MacDonald's *soi-disant* 'National' government was returned with 551 MPs. The combined opposition totalled 57 MPs.

With Labour thus enfeebled, the 1930s seemed a decade of opportunity for the Communists. Their membership, a little over 2,000 in 1930, rose steadily to reach nearly 20,000 by 1939. To people who were idealistic and angry about the ongoing situation, Communism offered the apparently real dream of belonging to a movement that was changing the world. Many were proud of their membership of the Comintern, were inspired by Russia, and supported all the contacts with the Soviet Union that could be arranged. These were often cultural and theatrical—the Russian Ballet visited Britain, the films of Eisenstein and Pudovkin found dedicated minority followings, and when the Moscow Art Theatre visited London in 1928 even *The Times* was excited by its ensemble, commenting on the 'quality of collective understanding conveyed to the audience in a group of performances so fused in imagination that they give an impression of one performance, not of an aggregate of personal achievements'.[4] The Communist theory, propagated in the newly established *Daily Worker*, was that economic strikes would lead to political strikes, which in turn would lead to revolution. Consequently, though few in number, Communists were always to be found at the battlefront of the class war, and they added a noisy, flamboyant, even theatrical, element to the workers' struggles.

Most significantly, many Communists fought alongside the unemployed, whose numbers inexorably rose to one and a half million at the end of 1929, and then dramatically to over three and a half million by the middle of 1932. The government seemed powerless against this, and when a delegation of the unemployed visited the Ministry of Labour in 1929, they were ejected by the police. But unemployment was real enough, and terrible enough. It meant genuine hunger, a feeling of uselessness, and exclusion from the social and cultural life of the community. 'Nothing to do with time; nothing to spend; nothing to do tomorrow nor the day after; nothing to wear; can't get married. A living corpse; a unit of the spectral army of three million lost men.'[5] George Orwell calculated that two million unemployed men meant effectively over ten million persons underfed.

The Communists organised the National Unemployed Workers' Movement (NUWM), though they struggled to keep control of it: Wal Hannington, the NUWM leader, sat on the party's Central Committee for most of the 1920s and 1930s, except between 1932 and 1935. The NUWM demanded 'work or full maintenance', and by 1932 it boasted 37,000 members, paying fourpence per month in 386 branches. A prime function of NUWM was to reduce out-of-work men's personal and social alienation, and to provide mutual support for each other. They held meetings, organised educational activities and mounted demonstrations, for instance outside labour exchanges after Lord Trenchard, chief commissioner of the Metropolitan Police, banned them from meeting there. As a consequence, pitched battles between police and unemployed workers were fought across London for weeks.

They particularly protested against the cruelty and humiliation of the means test, an extraordinarily intrusive way of judging an unemployed person's circumstances, but without the results of which no 'dole' could be paid. Its potency may be judged by the case of a man named Taylor, whose body was found in December 1932 in the Birmingham canal. At the inquest,

> The widow said that her husband had been very depressed and nervous on account of being out of work. There had been a decided change in his condition since 12 November when he had to go before the means test committee in connection with his benefit. A son said his father's benefit had been reduced under the means test, from 27s 3d per week to 10s 9d. The coroner . . .. . . in recording a verdict of 'suicide whilst temporarily insane,' said, 'This man's worries following a "means test" provided the last push sufficient to make him temporarily insane and in that state he threw himself into the canal.'[6]

Situations such as this were repeated many times.

In response, the NUWM organised 'Hunger Marches', the first in 1927, but with increasing efficiency and impressiveness over the following eight years. In January 1929 they marched from Scotland to London, gathering supporters all the way. In March and April 1930, marchers converged on the capital from all over Britain. At the end of the 1932 march, over 200,000 people attended the final rally in Trafalgar Square. The marches were colourful, raucous and theatrical, especially at the rallies held along the way and at the climax of the event. There were bands, banners and a scaffold stage for the speakers bedecked with bunting, slogans and flags. The marchers sang songs, the 'Internationale', the 'Red Flag', and others such as (to the tune of 'The Youthful Guardsman'):

> From Scotland we are marching,
> From shipyard, mill and mine,
> Our scarlet banners raise on high,
> We toilers are in line.
> For victory we'll fight: we'll show the enemy our might.
> *Chorus:* We are the Hunger Marchers of the Proletariat,
> We are the Hunger Marchers of the Proletariat.[7]

These demonstrations roused the ire of their opponents, and street battles between police and the unemployed were vicious but regular occurrences across Britain. Thus, in the autumn of 1932, bloody battles were fought in Liverpool and Birkenhead, West Ham, Belfast and other places in September; in October, police, backed by Coldstream Guards, attacked over 100,000 demonstrators in Hyde Park, and there were further battles in Trafalgar Square and across London. In Glasgow, 50,000 unemployed fought with police all day on 1 October. The battle lasted till midnight, and flared again next day. In Birkenhead

> The police, without any apparent reason, made a baton charge. Unemployed and employed workers stood their ground, and one policeman was thrown through a plate-glass window. The crowd took up the offensive and the police were ultimately compelled to run; but they rallied again, and a pitched battle ensued. Workers tore up railings to defend themselves and the fighting went on until past eleven at night, thirty-seven policemen being carried to hospital. Most of the wounded among the workers were taken into the homes of their class to have their wounds dressed, in order that they should not be marked for police arrest.[8]

If it sounds like the Wars of the Roses, it was certainly as violent, and as dramatic.

CHAPTER TWO

The World of the Theatre

On the seething stew of social, political and unemployed life—part epic, part melodrama—the British theatre resolutely turned its back. The leading academic theatre historian of the time, Allardyce Nicoll, commented in 1936: 'The English theatre, lacking the spirit for experimentation, is artistically and mentally moribund'.[1] In performance it employed a form of diluted naturalism, which Joan Littlewood called 'representationalism', and it determinedly excluded intellectual or 'highbrow' plays, and perhaps especially drama from the European continent. Ibsen was much too modern and dangerous!

The Fabians, Granville Barker and Bernard Shaw, had made some attempt to raise political issues in their plays before 1914, and so had the Suffragettes, especially Elizabeth Robins, Cicely Hamilton and Githa Sowerby. But Shaw was decidedly 'safe' by 1930 and, since women had been given the vote, the awkward women playwrights had been discarded. Isolated examples of more challenging drama, such as Joe Corry's *In Time of Strife*, about the 1926 General Strike, or R.C. Sherriff's *Journey's End*, set at the front in the First World War, are still powerful, but both are wholly naturalistic in form. More unusual, perhaps, was Hubert Griffith's *Red Sunday*, telling the story of the Russian Revolution, and structured around the relationship between Lenin and Trotsky, though with scenes of the murder of Rasputin, the tsar's abdication, and so on. A collage of swift, naturalistic scenes, it opened at the Arts Theatre, a private club, in London, on 27 June 1929. Formally more daring than *In Time of Strife* or *Journey's End*, *Red Sunday* nevertheless lacks the kind of epic form its content cries out for; and its production was met by a leading article excoriating it in *The Times* and by the Lord Chamberlain with a total ban on public performances.[2]

Part of the problem was that information about the more challenging and experimental theatre of Europe was not easy to find. A few articles in often obscure magazines were published, and there were a few books about it, most notably perhaps Leon Moussinac's *The New Movement in the Theatre*, published in Britain in 1931. Proclaiming theatre 'a visual experience',

Moussinac presented a series of large photographic plates of contemporary European productions, mostly from Russia, Germany and France, with several from the USA and just three from Britain. 'We no longer ask for beauty, that dead thing', he declared, 'but for the shock-values'. His analysis of the history of theatre was startling to conventional British wisdom:

> Once the idea of a stage-property had suggested itself there was no end to the number of accessories that the actor found he required, until finally the art of acting was degraded to the practice of dressing up in real diamonds in order to be drowned—and why not really drowned? we feel obliged to ask—in hundreds of gallons of real water.

Decrying naturalism as a 'superstition' and its audiences as 'stupid and docile', he argued that the contemporary Russian theatre had destroyed these 'obsolete conventions'. He quoted 'the Communist' director, Vsevolod Meyerhold—'I construct the idea: a scaffold is enough for me'— and included photographs of his boldest Soviet productions, *The Magnanimous Cuckold* and Ostrovsky's *The Forest*, pointing out how Meyerhold's Constructivist stage was 'bare in its length and breadth, so that not an inch of its dimensions is lost to the audience'. The setting then had the function of 'a gymnastic apparatus in a circus, giving play to the performance of the actors, and placing their gestures and movements in relief. For the theatre is in its nature a realm of action.'[3]

Moussinac's book showed other productions from Russia, including by Vakhtangov and Tairov, as well as German works by Karlheinz Martin, Leopold Jessner, Erwin Piscator's *The Adventures of Gallant Private Schwejk*, *Hoppla, wir leben!* by Ernst Toller, *Rasputin*, and Brecht and Weill's *Mahagonny* (*sic*). All these suggested that naturalist characterisation had now given way to a 'new gallery of types', and Moussinac compared Communist theatre to the *commedia dell'arte*, pointing also to the way the Russian revolutionary theatre troupes performed in halls and factories, and on street corners, rather as *commedia* troupes had. The 'enthusiasm' necessary for this theatre 'is a mass phenomenon', Moussinac continued, 'and is manifested only by the masses. Only a people's theatre can achieve this intensity [. . .] The Russians are the Greeks of the modern world.'

From America, Moussinac showed the New York Theatre Guild's production of Toller's *Masses and Man*, highlighting the dynamic groupings and atmospheric lighting. But, beyond this, Britons could also read American theatre journals, such as *Theatre Arts Monthly* and *New Theatre*, as well as playscripts, which often used a far less conventional dramaturgy than anything known in the British theatre. Upton Sinclair's *Singing Jailbirds*, for example, dramatised the situation of a Communist agitator imprisoned for his convictions, and used dreams, direct address to the audience and songs, such as 'Solidarity for Ever', 'Hallelujah I'm a Bum' and

> In California's darkened dungeons
> For the O.B.U.
> Remember you're outside for us
> While we're in here for you[4]

to politically stirring effect. Other inspiring playwrights included Elmer Rice, the very ordinariness of whose characters and setting in *Street Scene* was itself a revelation. This initiative was to be developed by Thornton Wilder, who had already created the startlingly modernist *Pullman Car 'Hiawatha'*, and who was to add meta-theatricality to Rice's ordinariness in *Our Town*. Thus the play begins with the Stage Manager addressing the audience:

> This play is called *Our Town*. It was written by Thornton Wilder; produced and directed by A . . . In it you will see Miss C, Miss D, Miss E [. . .] The name of the town is Grover's Corners, New Hampshire—just across the Massachusetts line: latitude 42 degrees 40 minutes; longitude 70 degrees 37 minutes. The first act shows a day in our town. The day is 7 May 1901. The time is just before dawn. (*A rooster crows.*) The sky is beginning to show some streaks of light over in the east there, behind our mount'in . . .[5]

Part of the reason British theatre was so comparatively backward was the censorship of the Lord Chamberlain, which was absolute and arbitrary. Hubert Griffith, in an angry preface to *Red Sunday*, pointed out that his play had been banned before his lordship had even read it, and described the problem as a battle between the theatre of amusement and the theatre of ideas. It was clear which side the Lord Chamberlain was on. When Sergei Tretyakov's epic *Roar China*, translated by Barbara Nixon from the script originally staged at Meyerhold's Theatre in Moscow, was presented to him by Terence Gray of the Cambridge Festival Theatre, he banned it because Rear-Admiral G.K. Chetwode, whose advice he had specifically sought, considered it 'undesirable that young and inexperienced undergraduates should be subjected at their age' to the ideas in the play.[6]

Gray's Festival Theatre was established in 1926 deliberately to combat 'the old game of illusion and glamour and all the rest of the nineteenth century hocus pocus and bamboozle'.[7] Dispensing with the naturalist's proscenium arch, Gray created an open stage with levels, steps and a generous forestage in front of the curving, horseshoe-shaped auditorium, and installed the very latest lighting equipment. His programme included works by Kaiser, Ibsen, Elmer Rice and Ernst Toller, whose epic *Hoppla, wir leben!*—translated as *Hoppla, Such is Life!*—was heavily censored by the Lord Chamberlain. Gray responded by reading out the offending passages through a megaphone from the wings at the appropriate moments in the performance. Toller had been the best-known and most admired dramatist of the left-wing revolutionary and pacifist movements since the early 1920s and his works had been defiantly staged in small venues by the likes of Martin Browne, who presented the wildly expressionist *Masses and Man* in down-to-earth Doncaster in 1924! Toller's reputation did not save the Festival Theatre, however, and Gray wearily resigned and walked away in June 1933.

Contemporaneously, the Gate in Covent Garden, a small private club theatre aimed at giving London 'a chance of seeing the amazing experiments that were being made in the theatre all over central Europe and in America',[8] also presented Toller's work, as well as plays by the controversial Russian, Nikolai Evreinov, Pirandello, Capek, Kaiser and many more. But by 1934 its director, Peter Godfrey, had also grown tired of the struggle against censorship and for audiences, and he too left for more immediately rewarding pastures. Tyrone Guthrie and Michel Saint-Denis were others who tried to bring *avant-garde* drama to Britain, and even RADA, the establishment's actor training school, introduced Laban's movement ideas under the direction of one of his protégés, Anny Fligg.

But the most interesting and hopeful experimental company of the period was probably the Group Theatre, established in 1932 and for almost its entire existence directed by Rupert Doone. Doone trained as a dancer and in the 1920s danced with Anton Dolin, Bronislava Nijinskaya, and with the Ballets Russes. He was a putative member of Brecht's unrealised Diderot Society of 1937, and was one of the few who, being aware of European theatrical developments, hoped to create something similar in Britain. He wanted

> A simple way of acting that is flexible and easily adaptable to any play [. . .] and by improvisation to bring the actor to use his [*sic*] own powers of invention and rid him of self-consciousness. It emphasizes movement as the beginning of training and approaches it through dancing; and in the same way voice production through singing.[9]

The Group Theatre's first production was of Vanbrugh's *The Provok'd Wife*, which opened on 3 April 1932, and that summer the members held a two-week summer school in Suffolk, where they concentrated on dance and movement, singing, verse speaking and mask work, most of this taught in exacting fashion by Doone himself. Training was regarded as important and was continued sporadically throughout the Group's existence. By the end of the year their ambitions were suggesting a theatre school, as well as a co-operative to include musicians and other artists, and a programme of talks, classes and experimentation. These dreams were never realised, but the Group hired theatres and produced plays, often classical or medieval, but also some notable contemporary experimental work. In February 1934 they presented W.H. Auden's short *The Dance of Death*, directed by Rupert Doone and Tyrone Guthrie, a kind of intellectual learning play employing both overt symbolism and ballet, which in November they paired with T.S. Eliot's *Sweeney Agonistes*.

By now the Group Theatre included John Allen, Benjamin Britten, Neville Coghill, Havelock Ellis, Marius Goring, Nelson Illingworth, John Masefield, Henry Moore, Flora Robson and others among its supporters. In January 1936 they presented W.H. Auden and Christopher Isherwood's *The Dog Beneath the Skin*. This expressionist verse drama is clearly indebted to medieval miracle plays, but also perhaps to Brecht, whose *Lehrstücke* and *Dreigroschenoper* Auden and Isherwood had seen in Berlin—though Auden was later to deny any influence. We can also see shades of *Sweeney Agonistes* in the play, not to mention Thornton Wilder's *Pullman Car 'Hiawatha'*. But it was still a noteworthy achievement, an episodic epic narrative with some striking moments, such as the chorus line of Nineveh Girls, songs, meta-theatricality (the Dog tells his master: 'Funny thing that we should both be in the same play'[10]) and a stinging parody of contemporary Germany—all the Nazis are lunatics. But it has no consistent philosophical foundation. It is Germanic, perhaps, in conception, but unlike, say, Kaiser's *Morning to Midnight*, the hero Alan is in no sense discovering himself, as Kaiser's Cashier is; nor is he being driven on by war, as Brecht's Mother Courage is, or even pleasure, as are the lumberjacks in *The Rise and Fall of the City of Mahagonny*. Auden and Isherwood's fairy-tale *motif*—if Alan finds the heir he will marry the princess—gives it a silliness that undermines its power.

The play's promise remained unfulfilled. The Group Theatre itself was flagging and Auden and Isherwood's next drama, *The Ascent of F6*, marks a step backwards, being unconvincing as either political or psychological drama. Their later *On the Frontier* is also disappointing, as were other poetic plays the Group Theatre presented, Louis MacNeice's *Out of the Picture* and Stephen Spender's *Trial of a Judge*. The Group Theatre evidently believed that the way to a progressive theatre lay through poetic drama. But without a fierce need to communicate something, or perhaps a body of ideas to drive them, they were bound to fail. The history of theatre shows that significant formal advances usually depend on urgency of content.

CHAPTER THREE

Workers' Theatre

Theatre had an unexpectedly prominent place in working-class culture in the 1920s and 1930s, exemplified by the Workers' Theatre Movement. They certainly had an urgent wish to communicate. Unlike the Group Theatre and others mentioned, however, this movement's drama drew both form and ideas from working-class experience, culture and entertainment. This included traditional culture, like Easter pace-egging, crowning the May Queen, Whit Walks, and so on, most of them highly theatrical. Then there were the more common forms of popular culture, an organ grinder playing in the street for people to dance to, the band in the park, the illicit gambling groups sitting round the 'pitcher' with their look-outs posted on all sides, and the Saturday evening street markets where married couples, or those courting, wandered past performing traders and auctioneers, political speakers, a boxing booth or a roundabout. More commercial were the dance halls, pubs that provided 'entertainers', music halls and cinemas. Entertainment, even theatricality, was ubiquitous.

More politically conscious was a kind of 'proletarianism' that viewed work, usually heavy manual work, not as an instrument of enslavement, but as the means by which the working class would inevitably in the future fulfil its destiny. This viewpoint endorsed an exclusively 'proletarian' culture through organisations like the *Clarion*, a socialist weekly founded in Manchester in 1891, which by the time of the First World War had a circulation around 75,000. *Clarion* established a number of dependent enterprises that thrived in the 1920s, and beyond, even as the newspaper itself withered—it closed in 1931. A group of Clarion Singers was still active in Birmingham in the mid-1970s. Fifty years before that, across the country, there were Cinderella Clubs for children, Clarion Scouts, rambling and cycling clubs, debating societies and, more pertinently, the National Organisation of Clarion Dramatic Clubs, formed in 1911. *Clarion* even sponsored a series of annual Socialist Drama Festivals in Glasgow in the 1920s. Then there were the Plebs League, the Guild of Proletarian Art, and the Independent Labour Party's (ILP) 'Masses' Stage and Film Guild' that in 1930 presented, for instance, Sinclair's *Singing Jailbirds* and Paul

Green's *In Abraham's Bosom*, as well as Soviet films by Eisenstein, Pudovkin and others. Earlier, from 1925 to 1927, the ILP had had the use of the Strand Theatre on Sunday evenings, when they had presented lectures, recitals, dance programmes by Margaret Morris's dancers and some plays. Their own drama groups, organised in the 1920s by Miles Malleson, put on Galsworthy, Shaw and Chekhov as well as plays by Malleson, and occasional weekend summer schools. The Gateshead ILP Dramatic Club, founded in 1920, which became the Progressive Players in 1924, was not untypical.

Meanwhile in London, the Workers' Theatre Movement (WTM), after a false start in the mid-1920s, became the dominant force in working-class theatre, flourishing between about 1928 and 1935. Associated with the Communist Party's 'class against class' policy, it sought to use theatre as a weapon in the class struggle, its task 'to kindle the flame of revolt among the workers'.[1] The movement's proponents argued that all art was effectively propaganda, and therefore proletarian art should be used unashamedly to that end—to raise workers' consciousness, or highlight particular issues, or support workers in struggle. They aimed, too, to get away from what they saw as the pessimism of pro-Communist authors like Gorky, Upton Sinclair and Toller, and to provide a more positive message. Ness Edwards, later a Labour MP, wrote that proletarian drama could be a 'source of energy' for working people and could help to 'organise the feelings of society'.[2] Perhaps unknowingly echoing Hubert Griffith, others argued that the WTM could replace the theatre of illusion with the theatre of ideas. The impulse, in other words, was political, not aesthetic. When Philip Poole, secretary of the WTM and an actor with Hackney's Red Radio group, was asked decades later: *'Were [WTM] groups set up out of an impulse to produce theatre or as a political device?'* he answered unequivocally, 'Definitely political propaganda'.[3]

Hackney Red Radio troupe was in some ways typical of the Workers' Theatre Movement. Originally called the People's Players, they performed Tom Thomas's adaptation of *The Ragged Trousered Philanthropists* in working-men's clubs, to Labour Parties and for Hunger Marchers in 1927. The Lord Chamberlain had objected to the adaptation on the surely specious grounds that it included swearing—thirty-one 'bloodys', to be precise. After extraordinary negotiations, 'we finally compromised: 15 bloodys would be licensed, 16 or over not'.[4] The Hackney People's Players then wanted to affiliate to the Workers' Theatre Movement, but discovered that it no longer existed, so they appropriated the name themselves, and sought other groups to affiliate to them. They performed their satire about the Labour Party, *Malice in Plunderland*, as well as Upton Sinclair's *Singing Jailbirds* in early 1929, before rejecting conventional theatre, re-naming themselves

Red Radio, and creating the portable, politically dynamic *Strike Up!* with songs, dances, sketches and monologues devised by themselves. Other troupes were being formed all over Britain—the Sunderland Red Magnets, the Dundee Red Front Troupe, Southampton Red Dawn, Greenwich Red Blouses, Salford Red Megaphones, Acton Red Star group, Islington Red Flag and a host of others—and the Workers' Theatre Movement became their umbrella. In June 1930, Tom Thomas attended the First Congress of the International Workers' Dramatic Union in Germany. Thomas was a stockbroker's clerk, and had joined the Communist Party after the General Strike. He eagerly transmitted news from the international movement to the First National Congress of the British WTM, attended by twenty-two groups, in June 1932. A year earlier, a group had toured Scotland supporting Communist election candidates, and in November 1931 the magazine, *Red Stage*, first appeared, edited by Charles Mann, son of the well-known trade union leader, Tom Mann. Finally, in 1933, a number of British activists went to Moscow for the Olympiad of Workers' Theatres, and looked with perhaps naive wonder at Soviet life and theatre. But their performances did not impress their hosts: they were judged 'primitive', and came home considerably disheartened. In fact, from then on the movement lost impetus, and was to survive only two or three years more.

For a few years, though, it had been remarkably successful and well organised. *Red Stage* was published from November 1931 until December 1932, and provided members and groups with information and debate, discussing at length and with sympathy topics such as whether good actors who were not very politically committed should be admitted to the movement. It made scripts available, gave news of different groups' activities and published morale-boosting articles, which, however, were sometimes couched in terms such as: 'In the U.S.S.R., the theatre is the weapon of the working class. Happy proletarian faces crowd the comfortable circles . . .'.[5] *Red Stage* was succeeded briefly by the mimeographed *W.T.M. Bulletin*, which was published between 1933 and April 1934, and supplemented by magazines like the Moscow-published *International Literature*. This printed photographs of Russian plays in performance, tributes to Meyerhold on his sixtieth birthday, and reports of groups in Chicago, Korea, Europe and elsewhere. Most WTM members were Communists, and the 'proletarianism' at its base chimed with Communist Party philosophy. For individuals, 'to be Red was to embrace hope, the hope that lies in action,' as Arthur Miller explained concerning his own commitment in the USA in the 1930s.[6] In Britain, the party was happy to use the theatre groups as crowd-pullers and at cultural events, though the leadership tended to be indifferent, even hostile, to them. It might be noted, however, that Harry Pollitt, the Communist Party leader, did say that if he or other speakers could not convince the workers of the Communist case, 'then the W.T.M. could be relied upon to do the job effectively'.[7]

The groups prided themselves on being able to respond to real events fast. Though they always sought bookings from trade union branches and political parties, if there was a strike, a dispute, or an eviction, the local troupe tried to rush together a sketch and perform it on the pavement or the back of a lorry (probably with its engine running in case the police descended on them) within hours of its occurrence. This was not always applauded. In Hackney, the group was once pelted with tomatoes, and several groups were attacked physically by Fascist Blackshirt gangs. But others received more support. In Stepney, when six members of the local troupe were arrested at a performance, the spectators demanded their release, and when that was not immediately granted, they followed the police, shouting 'Down with Fascism!' and next day organised a protest meeting. Was this politics, or performance? The National Conference of 1932 urged that 'Every strike, every wage-cut, every attack on the workers' conditions must find its expression on the platform of the Workers' Theatre and no exclusive attention to general political events can be a substitute for this.'[8]

The police were a constant menace. *New Red Stage* reported in its sixth number how the police tried to stop Camberwell Red Players performing the well-known sketch, *Meerut*, about the Indian struggle for freedom from British rule, and how in Castleford workers presenting a petition to the local council had been baton-charged by police while watching the local workers' theatre group performing: 'Comrade Speight was knocked down and immediately died; other comrades were knocked senseless, and beaten up while lying on the ground. Three W.T.M. members were arrested among others—comrades Humble, Lamb and Allingham.' In its next issue, *New Red Stage* reported that the Castleford group was dividing into two: 'One section is composed mostly of comrades recently released from jail. The group arranged a good "Welcome Home" for them', and made the episode into a sketch, using verbatim press reports for dialogue, and turning it into an occasion to encourage others to demonstrate and fight.[9]

At their best, the presentations of the Workers' Theatre Movement included slogans, dialogue scenes, mime, songs, dance and mass declamations, juxtaposed unexpectedly. WTM songs varied from 'The Banker and The Boss', described as 'A Red Army March', through 'The Red Dawn', to Red Radio's 'Three Little Maids':

> Three candidates for the boss are we,
> Liberal, Labour and New Party,

> You can vote how you like for one of us three-ee,
> Candidates of the boss.
>
> Three candidates who sing in chorus,
> Well-to-do and quite decorous,
> Capitalism's the best thing for us,
> Candidates of the boss.[10]

Sketches starkly approached real life problems, as with 'Something for Nothing', published in *Red Stage* no. 5, or Tom Thomas's polemical 'Their Theatre and Ours', while 'Speed Up' addressed a common industrial problem:

> POLICEMAN: Speed-up, speed-up, move along,
> Do not idle here too long;
> Streets are free for all to tread,
> Except for unemployed and Red.

The workers protest that they are human.

> CAPITALIST: You don't like this fast routine?
> Get your pay and get out quick,
> You speak like a Bolshevik;
> Speed-up, speed-up, watch your step
> Hold on tight and show some pep.

In the end the workers speed up their call for strike action, shouting 'Strike! Strike! Strike!', very quickly down the line, and as each shouts 'Strike!' he folds his arms. There is a moment's pause, then all march quickly off the stage.[11]

This sketch gives an idea of the acting style most frequently adopted by these groups. Strength was encouraged for its own sake. Actors in *Meerut* were exhorted: 'You cannot convey the impression of rigid resistance to imperialist oppression by a weak-kneed effort, however sympathetic the actors may feel. Pretty girlish voices must be cut right out ...'.[12] Naturalism, it was urged, could only reproduce the *status quo*, so actors were encouraged to learn dance and movement. The open platform stage emphasised the performers' physicality and made the audience feel that the players were their equals, part of their community. Performers wore dungarees, perhaps decorated with a hammer and sickle, except when they wished to characterise types by costume—a top hat for a boss, a red scarf or cloth cap for a worker. These types suggested perhaps a kind of contemporary *commedia dell'arte*. As for stage props, this was 'a propertyless theatre for the propertyless class'—just as Moussinac had commended.

Jimmie Miller, who was to change his name to Ewan MacColl and become Theatre Workshop's founding father (Joan Littlewood was its mother), was typical of the young, working-class, WTM member in the early 1930s. His mother was a charwoman, his father an iron moulder whose trade union activism was intolerable to his bosses. His father was often sacked, often unemployed. He and his wife were both steeped in traditional song, immigrants from Scotland and political idealists. Salford was, of course, the place Friedrich Engels had studied for his *Condition of the Working-Classes in England in 1844*, and it was therefore perhaps an appropriate venue for the Ninth Congress of the British Communist Party, held on 8 and 9 October 1927.

Nevertheless it appears that the class struggle meant little to most people in Salford:[13] much more fury was engendered when pitch-and-toss players were arrested in August 1931, hundreds protested and there were violent clashes with the police.[14] Solidarity was as likely to be self-interested as ideological: 'The poor certainly helped the poor [...] but [...] a little generosity among the distressed now could act as a form of social insurance against the future'.[15] But in 1911 police had fought running battles with strikers in Salford.

Salfordians of the 1920s and 1930s shared a living street culture, where people sat on doorsteps gossiping, peeling potatoes, quarrelling (sometimes violently), and adolescents gathered on the street corners, while children played on the pavements. There were street festivals when women danced 'a kind of hey, remnant perhaps of some long-forgotten folk dance'.[16] But they were inconceivably poor by twenty-first-century standards, certainly poorer than the people in nearby Miles Platting, where a survey in 1933 suggested that 44 per cent of the population lived in poverty. In October 1932, Alf Purcell, secretary of the Manchester and Salford Trades Council, noted: 'Winter is upon us. Want and hunger rife in our midst. Hundreds of thousands of men, women and children in Manchester and Salford are going short of many things they need: are in desperate want: are going hungry: are suffering innumerable privations.'[17] In 1934, J.B. Priestley visited the area: 'Between Manchester and Bolton the ugliness is so complete that it is almost exhilarating [...] There used to be a grim Lancashire adage: "Where there's muck there's money." But now where there is not much money, there is still a lot of muck.'[18]

Ewan MacColl felt intense pride, as well as shame, about this background. It was 'his' community and provided him with the grounding of some of his best plays—*Johnny Noble*, for instance, and *Landscape with Chimneys*. But, as always with community, it was also his limitation. Communities can be inward-looking, back-stabbing, stultifying. Thus Salford, as well as being sociable, was also male-oriented, homophobic and fixated on the significance of heavy industry. At best communities can provide a sense of belonging, and Salford did this too, for people here had reassuringly much in common with each other, which marked them out from people not from Salford. The community is where people learn how to be 'social' and where they acquire culture, often in the form of symbols of the community. These are usually mental constructs—valued traditions, for example—but at base they are what provide people with the means to make and to express meanings. It is perhaps no accident that from inter-war Salford came not only Ewan MacColl's work, but also *Love on the Dole* by Walter Greenwood and the paintings of L.S. Lowry. Community is, in a sense, how you experience it.[19]

Manchester and Salford also had an unexpected tradition of theatre and drama, beyond that of its well-known repertory theatre. For instance, North Salford Socialist Sunday School performed *The Snow Fairy*, an 'original Socialist musical play' at Easter 1909.[20] In the second half of the 1920s there was an active ILP drama group in Salford. More pertinently, perhaps, Manchester's Unnamed Society performed Sergei Tretyakov's epic, *Roar China* privately, after Terence Gray's Festival Theatre had had it turned down by the Lord Chamberlain, and Manchester also produced in Allan Monkhouse a progressive dramatist whose plays, though scarcely noticed in London, made a strong impression in the north. *The Conquering Hero* was unusual for 1924 in its anti-war stance, and *First Blood* was a rapid and angry response to the General Strike, first performed in late 1926.

This was the community that MacColl—the young Jimmie Miller—entered when he left school on 2 February 1929, a week after his fourteenth birthday. He was already probably a member of the Young Communist League, and although he picked up odd jobs as a builder's labourer, in the Anaconda Wire Factory, and as a motor mechanic, and though he earned a few shillings writing advertising jingles and articles for trade union papers, he was more often unemployed, and soon involved with the Youth Council of the National Unemployed Workers' Movement. And he joined the Clarion Players, who rehearsed (without always presenting) *The Ragged Trousered Philanthropists*, *Singing Jailbirds* and two works by Ernst Toller, *The Machine Wreckers* and *Masses and Man*. Toller was to remain an inspiration for MacColl throughout the next decade.

Then came a projected production of *Still Talking*, a much more radical piece in form, in which Conservative, Labour and Liberal speakers were each presented in turn as cock of the midden, making a speech. Each was, essentially, the same, and after each a cock crowed. After the third cock, a Newsboy confronted the audience: 'Strike or War?' This was the cue for 'plants' in the audience to rush the stage and take over from the politicians. It polarised MacColl's Clarion Players group. Those who felt that here was a script that pointed to a more revolutionary popular political theatre with relevance and attack were set against those who felt that this was not a drama at all. The first group argued that the form took the drama back to its origins in the morality plays; the second group agreed that this was indeed returning to feudalism, and walked out. Those who remained included both employed and unemployed; the unemployed, Ewan MacColl among them, set about creating their own agit-prop group, the Red Megaphones.

This group made its debut performing parodies of popular songs of the day and a single anti-war sketch, on a coal-cart in Platt Fields, Manchester, on May Day 1931. They went on to seek venues all over Lancashire, and performed in halls, for Labour Parties and at open-air meetings, in Gorton, Moss Side, Preston, Rochdale, and elsewhere. At Rochdale they formed part of a cultural programme, the highlight of which was an address from Professor Mirsky about Stalin's Five-Year Plan. Their repertoire of sketches came to include *Meerut, Who's Who in the Berlin Zoo, The Spirit of Invergordon, Their Theatre and Ours, Rent, Interest and Profit* and more. Their aims were threefold: first, to collect food, money and clothing for strikers; second, to support and encourage them, and to explain the politics of the situation to them; and third, to create a theatre that was a weapon in the class struggle. They wore overalls—for *Rent, Interest and Profit* the three actors had labels reading 'R', 'I' and 'P' on them—and though the acting may have been crude, it had dynamism and energy. During one piece they performed a

1. The Red Megaphones perform on an impromptu stage for a working-class audience. This picture was first printed in *New Red Stage*, no. 6, June–July 1932.

kind of mechanical dance based on the movements of the textile factory machines.

MacColl drilled them relentlessly, though he 'was the same age as everyone else in the group and I really knew no more than they did'.[21] At the time, he 'really did want to tear down the world in which I found myself'—'all the time I was living on a thread of anger'[22]—and it was this anger which was behind not only the Red Megaphones, but all MacColl's later work. Though he claims equality with his colleagues, in fact already he was seeking wider and further than they. He met a 'Comrade Ludmilla' from East Europe who described agit-prop performances there, notably the use of megaphones, and he corresponded with a young German Communist, Rudy Lehmann, who sent him information on the German street theatre troupes, recordings by the Volksbuehne, and scripts by Brecht and Eisler.

MacColl ensured that the Red Megaphones were actively involved in local campaigns. They performed in support of the Communist candidate at a parliamentary by-election in Skipton, and in 1932 a widespread strike broke out in the Lancashire cotton industry over management demands for speeding up work. The Red Megaphones seized the occasion, and were to be found performing wherever there was unrest, up to four times a day outside different factories. It was 'instant theatre': they arrived at a mill in the morning, learned the specifics of the problem there during the workers' tea break, cobbled the information into a script—either altering an already-existing one or creating something completely new—and performing during the lunch break. It could be dangerous, too. In Wigan, the police tried to stop them, but the working-class audience held the police at bay and insisted they continue. On another occasion,

> 'Trouble,' says Blondie, and the next moment Jimmy Rigby stops in mid-sentence and points. For an endless moment we stare in disbelief. The horse police are charging towards us, their riot sticks held aloft like lances. The panic of the crowd is terrible to behold. They scatter in utter confusion the way ants do when their nest is disturbed. There is some resistance, but the terrain is not in our favour. There is no cover, no place to hide. In disarray, we retreat into the side streets, where a small group, mostly young unemployed, reassemble and decide to march to the houses of the councillors who are members of the unemployment tribunal. We start off, a silent group of fifteen or twenty youths. In a surprisingly short time our numbers have increased by more than 200. As we walk we hatch elaborate schemes of revenge and wonder if things will ever be the same again.[23]

The relationship between politics and performance continued problematic.

CHAPTER FOUR

The Challenge of Fascism

In January 1933 Adolf Hitler became chancellor of Germany. While the problems of the British economy were by no means solved, it seemed to be stabilising and unemployment falling, and now a new, perhaps more menacing, threat appeared for working-class, left-wing and progressive people. The nature of the new regime was soon apparent. The *Manchester Guardian*, for example, reported on Dachau concentration camp less than a year after Hitler took power:

> Amongst the prisoners who have received severe injuries are L. Buchmann, Georg Freischutz and a journalist named Ewalt Thunig. The Munich Communist, Sepp Gotz, was killed after being so beaten he could no longer stand. The student Wickelmeier was killed by a bullet. The Communist Fritz Dressel was beaten to death. Leonhard Hausmann, a municipal councillor, Lehrburger, Aron (a member of the Bamberg Reichsbanner) and Stenzel were killed . . . etc.[1]

Politics was entering a new phase. And to further underline the threat, Hitler began to expand the German armed forces: in March 1935 he introduced conscription and the following year his troops marched into the Rhineland. Perhaps emboldened by Hitler's defiance, in October of the same year Mussolini, the Fascist dictator of Italy, invaded Abyssinia, the only independent country in Africa. In spite of the British and French governments' public protestations of support for Abyssinia, the Hoare–Laval Pact merely concealed their complicity in its destruction. By May 1936, Haile Selassie was in exile and the King of Italy was proclaimed the new emperor of Abyssinia.

To find agreed ways to deal with Fascism—and especially Nazism—suddenly became desperately urgent. With capitalism apparently in continuing crisis, Hoare and many political Conservatives, bankers and captains of industry discovered attractions in it, believing it offered a way for existing interests to be protected. If not alliance, then appeasement was their preferred option. Hitler, after all, was just another Fascist, like Mussolini or Britain's own Oswald Mosley, recently a prominent Labour

MP. This strand of opinion led the 'National' government, in crisis after crisis, to hold back, temporise and hope the problem would disappear. But the country was not so easily seduced. In the election of November 1935, Labour won more votes than ever before, over 38 per cent. But still they only mustered 154 MPs to the National government's 429. Labour, too, was confused by the rapid rise of Nazism and Fascism. The leader, George Lansbury, was virtually forced to resign because of his pacifism, as the debate on the left centred around the efficacy of pacifism or the need to confront the dictators.

Early in 1933 the British Communist Party made its first tentative retreat from the 'class against class' policy and proposed a 'united front' against Fascism. In the summer of 1935, the Seventh World Congress of the Comintern, meeting in Moscow, called for a united front of all working-class organisations, and this was officially endorsed by the British Communist Party in August. There was always some confusion about what exactly was being advocated. It is, however, possible to distinguish between, on the one hand, a 'united front' that might be presented by the Communist Party, the Labour Party and the Independent Labour Party, and excluding Liberals, Radicals and others, and on the other hand, a 'popular front' that would be supported not only by the Labour movement but also by all progressive anti-Fascists. Thus, Lloyd George and even the rising star of the Tory Party, Harold Macmillan, supported a popular front, while the Communist Party at first only went as far as supporting a united front, and many in the Labour Party, remembering their betrayal by Ramsay MacDonald, were suspicious of all such alliances. In any case, many Labour and trade union leaders had not forgotten that only months earlier they had been dubbed 'Social Fascists' by the very Communists who were now urging co-operation.

Attitudes began to polarise when a British Fascist rally at Olympia in June 1934 ended in mayhem and violence. 'Hurrah for the Blackshirts!' screamed the *Daily Mail*, while many Communists took to the streets and fought running battles with Mosley's thugs. The Communists were undoubtedly the best organised and most active left-wing group on the streets at this time, and wherever the Fascists looked to advance, as in Lancashire in 1935, it was the Communists who opposed them most resolutely. The Communists also made other significant gains, such as the election of their candidate, Arthur Horner, to the Presidency of the South Wales miners in April 1936. So it was hardly surprising that when the deciding street battle occurred, in Cable Street in the East End of London, it was the Communists who organised the defence of the Jewish community, and repulsed the marauding Fascists. The battle of Cable Street has an honoured place in east end and left wing mythologies, and was brilliantly evoked in Arnold Wesker's 1958 play, *Chicken Soup with Barley*.

As the political situation shifted, so did the activities of left-wing theatres. Workers' theatre groups began to move indoors and co-operate with sympathetic professionals. Thus, the Rebel Players in east London moved to a 'curtained stage' in July 1933 to present Hubert Griffith's *The People's Court*, and that autumn they invited André van Gyseghem, the RADA-trained director of the Embassy Theatre, Swiss Cottage, to work with them. Was 'socialist realism', Stalin's perversion of naturalism, replacing agit-prop? And if so, was this to be encouraged? In April 1935, the Workers' Theatre Movement dissolved itself, and became the 'New Theatre League' (incorporating the Rebel Players, Red Radio and others) with Tom Thomas as secretary. Simultaneously, professionals with socialist convictions established a Left Theatre in 1934, including Miles Malleson, Hubert Griffith, Barbara Nixon, John Allen, André van Gyseghem and others, with Tom Thomas also on the committee. It aimed to be a socialist repertory company, taking plays to where the people were—Labour Parties, Co-op Halls and so on—as well as performing on Sunday evenings at the Phoenix Theatre in the West End. They presented, among other plays, Toller's *Draw the Fires*, Friedrich Wolf's *Sailors of Cattaro*, an adaptation of Gorky's *The Mother*, and *Stay Down Miner* by Montagu Slater, with music by Benjamin Britten, before fading out in 1936. Notably, they had been supported by the Trades Union Congress (TUC), which was, like other 'legitimate' labour organisations, beginning to see theatre as an opportunity. It was the TUC that had commissioned Miles Malleson's drama about the Tolpuddle Martyrs, *Six Men of Dorset*, for the centenary of the martyrs' transportation in 1934. Co-op drama groups, too, were increasing: by 1937 there were forty-nine of them and the following year at Wembley they staged a huge pageant of labour history, *Towards Tomorrow*, by Montagu Slater, directed by André van Gyseghem, with music by Alan Bush.

Further inspiration for left-wing theatre came from film and radio. John Grierson and the GPO and Crown Film Units made a series of documentary films, culminating in Auden and Britten's *Night Mail*, which put working-class life into a new focus, celebrating its vibrancy and strength. Some radio, too, such as the programmes of Archie Harding, highlighted working-class and left-wing concerns. From 1929 Harding had been creating dramatic documentaries, mixing dialogue scenes with facts and statistics, welded by a Narrator figure into montaged presentations like *Crisis in Spain*, broadcast in 1931, and *New Year Over Europe*, broadcast the following year. In 1933 Harding moved to Manchester, where he consolidated a style that in some ways prefigures many stage documentaries of the following decades. BBC radio also introduced Bertolt Brecht to

Britain, broadcasting Weill's *Lindbergh's Flight* and Hindemith's *Baden-Baden Lesson on Consent* in March 1930 (repeated in March 1933), and in February 1935 *The Tupenny-Ha'penny Opera*. The following year, Alan Bush and the London Labour Choral Union gave the first live musical performances of Brecht, when they presented *The Decision*, with music by Hanns Eisler.

After 1933, then, simple agit-prop was seen as too crude for the new purposes of revolutionary theatre in the time of the rise of Fascism. It was dynamic and immediate, but was unable to deal with historical processes or an increasingly complex political situation. Moreover, in the new circumstances, the potential working-class audiences were no longer on the street corners or even at the factory gates. The Red Megaphones in Salford and Manchester, still working to find theatrical means of helping to change the world, re-named themselves Theatre of Action and set about their task anew. They realised they needed to develop new skills, and to hone their technique. To this end, they found a movement teacher trained in a Margaret Morris studio who worked with them for two months. Meanwhile another member, Alf Armitt, a milling-machine operator, discovered Adolphe Appia's work on stage lighting and scenic design, and his excitement dispelled the group's doubts about working indoors. Appia's ideas had, said MacColl later, 'a profound effect on both Joan Littlewood and me, and indeed they dominated almost all our productions for the next decade'.[2]

Theatre of Action sought a theatre that depended neither on agit-prop nor conventional illusionism, but would be better than either, a 'theatre of synthesis', in which the visual ideas of Appia would be combined with actors who could dance, sing and act, and a dramaturgy which could express adequately the aspirations and needs of the working class. They identified four elements in this process, which Howard Goorney summed up as follows:

(1) An awareness of the social issues of the time, and in that sense, a political theatre;
(2) A theatrical language that working people could understand, but that was capable of reflecting, when necessary, ideas, either simple or involved, in a poetic form;
(3) An expressive and flexible form of movement, and a high standard of skill and technique in acting;
(4) A high level of technical expertise capable of integrating sound and light into the production.[3]

Their manifesto declared their ideal of touring productions exclusively to working-class areas, and listed the first items they wanted to perform: *John Bull Wants You*, an anti-war sketch; *Free Thaelmann*, a mass declamation concerning the imprisoned leader of the German Communist Party; a long poem, *The Fire Sermon*, by Sergei Funarov; and songs by Hanns Eisler 'sung by J.H. Miller'. These were later joined by, among other short pieces, excerpts from Brecht's *Round Heads and Pointed Heads* (though not, as has been claimed, *Mr Puntila and His Man Matti*, which had not been written at this time[4]).

The programme shows the influence of modernist European and American theatre, and it was just at this time that MacColl discovered Moussinac's book, which he studied with Joan Littlewood when he met her. Those who knew them later often commented on their encyclopaedic knowledge of theatre history, and this was how that knowledge began. Their first abiding influences were Appia and Stanislavsky, mixed with some ideas from Laban, Brecht and Meyerhold. The American influence came directly from the New York Workers' Laboratory Theatre, from where they obtained a copy of *Newsboy*, which was to be their first proper production, as well as Odets's *Waiting for Lefty*, which they presented without permission, the first performance of this play in Britain.

It was during the early rehearsals for *Newsboy* that Joan Littlewood had joined the company. Born in Stockwell, Brixton, she was the illegitimate daughter of a sixteen-year-old maid servant and a father she never knew. Bright, convent-educated, she won a scholarship to RADA, where she supplemented her grant with early morning office cleaning. She studied Laban's movement system under Anny Fligg, and won a speech prize presented by the radio producer, Archie Harding, who suggested she should work in radio. Unhappy at RADA, she set out to walk to Manchester to take him up on this suggestion, but broke down at Burton-upon-Trent. Here a 'very thin, very poor woman' took her in and found the means to get her to Manchester, where she found work, first with the BBC, and then at Rusholme Repertory Theatre. It was during the making of another Harding documentary, *Tunnel*, that she met Ewan MacColl, for both were in his cast. Shortly after this programme was completed, MacColl attended the Rusholme Theatre, and called at the stage door after the performance. He accompanied Littlewood home, and like Stanislavsky and Nemirovich-Danchenko at the Slavyansky Bazaar in 1897, they talked through the night:

> [We] told each other the story of our lives and discussed what we called *real* theatre. Our views, we found, coincided at almost every point. We were drunk with ideas, lightheaded with talk and lack of sleep and each of us jubilant at having discovered an ally. The morning was well advanced when Joan crept with me to the front door and I went off to the labour exchange. We continued our talking marathon right through the next two or three nights.[5]

Littlewood remembered discussing Brecht and German agit-prop; Ewan (Jimmie) sang her an Eisler song, and later asserted 'only the best is good enough for the workers', and 'agit-prop is crude in the age of Appia. Don't discount beauty.'[6] They talked politics, too, discussing the Indian struggle for independence. They were soulmates for the times, saw eye to eye about everything that energised them, and Littlewood was immediately co-opted into the creation of *Newsboy*.

Newsboy was a 'Living Newspaper', a form pioneered by the Russian revolutionaries,[7] and was staged indoors. Its focus was a newsvendor who shouted out his headlines, while around him a series of disparate scenes was played out. The Newsboy gave the action a holding spine; episodes included the wholly visual 'ballet scene':

> *As the Blind Woman comes across the stage and turns to go back, all the figures who have thus far passed in the street scene come on stage and, working on three parallel planes with the same dance movement, go through movements which bring out their individual characteristic movements. All face the audience. They combine voices with characteristic gesture, i.e. the young lady keeps repeating* 'Why don't you go away! I'll call a policeman! I'll call a policeman!' *The blind woman repeats her singsong. The 2nd Newsboy shouts* 'News Chronicle Empire. CUP FINAL DRAW. PLANS FOR ROYAL JUBILEE.'[8]

Another relied on rhythm:

> *(The characters become class workers, representing a picture of the Three Million Unemployed Men and Women. This is done through the characters facing the audience and saying the following words:* 'THREE MILLION MEN AND WOMEN' *as in rhythmic tread they form a miserable line outside the labour exchange, constantly repeating in low tones in mass:* 'THREE MILLION MEN AND WOMEN.' *The spotlight changes from amber to green.)*

1ST VOICE:	Fired from the mills.
2ND VOICE:	Fired from the docks.
3RD VOICE:	Fired from the coal mines.
4TH VOICE:	Fired from the shipyards.
ALL (*louder and louder in desperation*):	FIRED FIRED FIRED.
VOICE (*offstage*):	No jobs today. You've had yer lousy money.[9]

Newsboy represents a decisive advance from the Red Megaphones, with light, setting and dance all now playing a significant part in creating the meaning, and a new member, Gerard Davies, a near neighbour from MacColl's childhood in Salford, dancing the central role.[10]

Newsboy was often coupled with *John Bullion*, adapted by MacColl and Littlewood from a 'dreary' play called *Hammer*, though they seem to have changed it so much as to have created virtually a wholly new piece. This 'ballet with words' employed a 'constructivist' set with ramps and rostra;

moments of meta-theatre, such as the Electrician appearing on stage with a torch, claiming to have just tripped over one of the characters in the wings; and some clever staging devices, as when the clergyman, during his sermon, leans out of the pulpit to hobnob with the business tycoon in his congregation, while his 'double' behind him carries on the service. Though sometimes these shows were confusing for spectators, they were also highly imaginative, using a kind of Expressionism mingled with second hand Meyerholdisms and even odd moments of surrealism. They toured halls in Lancashire towns, including playing in the Round House, Ancoats, Manchester, and were greeted with surprising success.

New members arrived, too, including a group of Marxist Jewish traders, and perhaps because of them the group decided next to mount Clifford Odets's *Waiting for Lefty*, which attacks, among other things, anti-Semitism as a class attitude: when redundancies are to be made, the Jewish character is fired, despite his seniority in the firm. One of these new members, Les Goldman, played Fatt, the right-wing union boss, with particular verve and intelligence. The play begins with a semi-circle of exploited taxi drivers seated facing the audience. Into the semi-circle come various people who play out scenes from their life, and these stir the taxi drivers in the end, against the advice of Fatt, to strike. In the production, Alf Armitt's lights were again put to good use:

> The lights fade out and a white spot picks out the playing space within the space of seated men. The seated men are very dimly visible in the outer dark, but more prominent is Fatt smoking his cigar and often blowing the smoke in the lighted circle.[11]

The device, often associated with Brecht, of one or more characters on stage listening to and watching others in action, is a particularly effective form of endistancing, which contrasts sharply in this play with the direct involvement of the audience through the use of 'plants'. Moreover, though most of the action is constructed as emotionally intense naturalism, there is no central character, and the short scenes are montaged to lead to a conclusion: 'Not to say, "What a world!", but to say, "Change the world!"'[12] Again the production toured, having several performances in Manchester, including at the Lesser Free Trade Hall, and beyond, in Hyde, Haslingden and other venues.

After *Waiting for Lefty*, the numbers joining Theatre of Action swelled to over a hundred. Heretofore the administration and organisation of the group had been extremely informal, mostly relying on the enthusiasms of Ewan MacColl and Joan Littlewood, who chose the plays, made the bookings, and directed and acted as they chose. Now some members, ardent Communists, tried to 'improve' things, establishing committee structures and involving the party in the group's affairs. Littlewood and MacColl rebelled, but before they could address this problem, Littlewood met the exiled Ernst Toller, now in Manchester to direct a production of his play, *Draw the Fires*, at Rusholme Repertory Theatre. Set in 1917, the play depicts a group of working-class sailors rebelling against their officers, and the war itself. Cecil Davies, Toller's most knowledgeable British critic, asserts that

> Of all his plays this is the one in which virtually all Toller's deepest concerns find artistic integration: his hatred of war and experiential sympathy with the sufferings of combatants; his commitment to the German revolution at the end of World War I and his subsequent disillusion with the Weimar Republic; his lifelong stress torn between pacifism and doubt as to the effectiveness of pacifism to oppose tyranny; his passionate concern for justice, with his realisation that the injustices of Wilhelmine Germany lived on in the Weimar Republic [. . .]; his fervent belief in the inspirational effectiveness of personal sacrifice combined with his recognition that the actions inspired by it do not bring Utopia; his critical appraisal of the machinery of democracy, and his understanding of the distorting sexual consequences of forced single-sex communities such as battle-ships and prisons.[13]

Draw the Fires has a huge cast, and includes folk songs and a rating who plays a mouth organ, sailors complaining about their food (as in *Battleship Potemkin*), a sea battle and a tense scene when the central character is in prison for his political 'crime'. But the sailors' hands are calloused and hard, and Toller found the effete English actors utterly unsuitable for the parts. Joan Littlewood offered to bring in half a dozen members of the Theatre of Action—MacColl, Alf Armitt, Alec Armstrong, Gerard Davies and Bob Goldman. Also brought in were members of Left Theatre and Toynbee Players. Opening on 10 February 1935, the production ran for three successful weeks at Rusholme, and was then transferred to Oldham Grand Theatre, where two performances a day were given. It was also presented for a single Sunday performance in London on 12 May. Hanns Eisler wrote and conducted the music, and Toller, whose English was poor, worked furiously over the short two-week rehearsal period. Intense, short-tempered and demanding, he also, however, exuded 'infectious enthusiasm and dynamic energy.' The opening as he directed it was particularly striking—the men shovelling coal into the ship's engine's fire, choreographed into 'a sort of ballet'. The *Manchester Guardian* critic wrote: 'The production brought out to the full Toller's attitude towards drama, that its purpose should be not to afford an escape from life but to seize upon and interpret the great movements that for good or evil shake the civilised world to its foundations.'[14]

Meanwhile, the Communist *aparatchiks* who resented Littlewood and MacColl's pre-eminence in the Theatre of Action summoned a meeting and proposed their expulsion. There was a fierce debate, followed by a vote which split evenly, twelve for and twelve against. The chairperson's casting vote saved them. But they had had enough. They had been offered places at the Soviet Academy of Theatre and Cinema, and determined now to exchange Manchester for Moscow. The *aparatchiks* were both amazed and envious, but other members of the Theatre of Action raised the grand sum of twelve pounds as a parting gift, and the two were on their way to London to seek visas, and then the land of Stanislavsky, Meyerhold and true Communism.

CHAPTER FIVE

Slow Approach of War

Hitler had been in power less than two years, but the phantom of war was already stalking the continent, when Rev. Dick Shepherd, Canon of St Paul's and a popular voice of Christianity on BBC radio, established the Peace Pledge Union. He asked for support from all who agreed to 'renounce war, and never again, directly or indirectly, support or sanction another'. Two days later he had received postcards from over 2,000 people, and within a year 80,000 people had pledged their support,[1] often in almost ritualised mass signings. At a rally for peace in the Albert Hall on 14 July 1935 Shepherd was joined on the platform by Siegfried Sassoon, Edmund Blunden, Bertrand Russell, Aldous Huxley and others, and the following year the Peace Pledge Union's own amateur agit-prop theatre group was presenting open-air performances of *Idiot's Delight* and *The Pacifist's Progress*.[2] In June that year, *Peace News*, which became the Peace Pledge Union's mouthpiece, was first published, and the movement continued to swell even though Shepherd himself died unexpectedly in 1937. In 1938, for instance, both the *News Chronicle* and *Reynolds News* backed the United Peace Alliance, a kind of popular front for peace.

Other radical journals that largely supported the cause of peace established at this time included *Tribune*, first published on 1 January 1937, and *Picture Post*, a radical commercial magazine whose photo journalism made an enormous impact, the following year. Even more significant, perhaps, was the Left Book Club, a 'mass movement and crusade rolled into one',[3] whose membership reached nearly 60,000 by mid-1938. Organised by the brilliant entrepreneur-publisher, Victor Gollancz, and advocating a near-Communist Popular Front political position, the club soon supplied much more than simply books, diversifying into discussion groups, rambling and sports groups, groups for poetry and theatre, and more. The Left Book Club was even credited with securing the extraordinary by-election triumph of the Popular Front candidate, Vernon Bartlett, in November 1938 in Bridgwater, Somerset. In February 1937, a Left Book Club rally at the Albert Hall attracted 7,000 supporters.

The Left Book Club Theatre Guild, under the leadership of John Allen, was established in 1936. It had its own magazine, *Theatre for the People*, which published articles about European and Russian theatre and supported individuals and groups who were trying to set up their own theatre groups. It had offices in the flat of Nelson Illingworth, a former Group Theatre member who was active in left-wing and theatrical circles, and it was particularly associated with Unity Theatre, which was founded at almost the same time, and involved many of the same people.

Unity Theatre, similarly politically motivated and near-Communist, or at least anti-Fascist, emerged from the Rebel Players, who formed the New Theatre in late 1935, which became Unity in January 1936. The inaugural meeting to establish the company was held on 9 February 1936 and the first performance, of a double bill of *Waiting for Lefty* and *Private Hicks* by Albert Maltz, took place on 17 April that year. By November, Unity (the name was supposed to chime with the idea of a united front) had its own theatre at 1 Goldington Street, and had become a 'club', largely to avoid the Lord Chamberlain's censorship. Over the next few years, Unity Theatre mounted a series of successful productions, including *Where's That Bomb?*, by an ex-NUWM taxi driver, Herbert Hodge, who had been inspired by *Waiting for Lefty*, *On Guard for Spain* by Jack Lindsay, *Bury the Dead* by Irwin Shaw, at least two living newspapers, *Busmen*, supporting the striking London bus crews, and *Crisis*, written and staged within seventy-two hours of Chamberlain's Munich betrayal, and the 'political pantomime', *Babes in the Wood*, with Austria and Czechoslovakia as the babes, Hitler and Mussolini as the robber barons and Neville Chamberlain as the wicked uncle. Many of these shows were toured, both in London to Labour Parties, co-operative halls, outdoor rallies and so on, and much further afield to the Durham coalfields, Yorkshire and Nottinghamshire, South Wales and the Midlands, sometimes co-sponsored by the Left Book Club.

The Left Book Club Theatre Guild and Unity also co-sponsored a 'cultural week' in May 1938, for both aspired to be a meeting place for all the arts, and they ran film seasons, maintained a bookshop and organised training classes. These worked best, perhaps, as summer schools, such as that which the two organisations jointly mounted at Summerhill School, in Suffolk, when there were classes in dance, improvisation, mass declamation and the system of Stanislavsky. Nevertheless, Unity's standard of acting and production was not always very high and photographs of *Plant in the Sun*, for instance, show unimaginative stage groupings and actors with arms like plumb-lines, while *The Star Turns Red* has actors with rigid bodies and wooden expressions. However, by 1939, Unity had a staff of six, 300 active members and 2,000 individual subscribers. It might be unfair to categorise all these as left-leaning intellectuals who could have their opinions reinforced at Unity Theatre without much feeling of danger. But, as with the Group Theatre earlier in the decade, the real radical theatre was elsewhere.

Perhaps symbolically, it was just as the Rebel Players were transmuting into Unity Theatre, that Joan Littlewood and Ewan MacColl arrived in London on their way, as they supposed, to Moscow. But their visas had not arrived. They took lodgings with a rather grand lady who wanted someone to turn her unpublished novel into a film script, which Littlewood and MacColl began with gusto as well as amusement, meanwhile setting themselves up as theatre experts. They gave lectures where they could, and offered training to working-class would-be actors. About eight or nine people attended their classes—railway workers, a labourer, a filing clerk, an art student and others. Littlewood took movement classes, MacColl taught theatre history, and they both tried to teach voice. Besides this, they read and analysed plays, and experimented with Stanislavsky's acting system. This venture may seem arrogant—after all, they were little over twenty years old, and only one of them (Littlewood) had received any training, and that had been voluntarily curtailed. But in fact it was a superb learning period for them; it has been said before that one only really learns something when one has to teach it. They waited for their visas but these never arrived, and after about four months they ran out of money. In any case, as Littlewood said later, their enthusiasm for Moscow cooled when they saw the other people who were due to go—they 'looked such bloody bores', she said.[4] At this juncture they received an offer from the Manchester branch of the Peace Pledge Union, asking them to direct a production of Hans Chlumberg's *Miracle at Verdun* at the Lesser Free Trade Hall, and offering them a small fee. Two days later they were on the train back.

Chlumberg himself had been judicially assassinated by the Nazis, presumably in fear of this play. It now provided Littlewood and MacColl with the opportunity to try out some of the ideas consolidated in London, while simultaneously proclaiming their political position. They gathered a large company and rehearsed manically for three weeks in the Friends Meeting House, also, by the way, finding time to marry. They had previously always worked together, but now time precluded this, and after their close collaboration they were able to create a production jointly while working in different rooms. They found a kind of intensified realist style, which perhaps owed something to Toller, but which also grew out of the play's overt expressionism. *Miracle at Verdun* is set in the future—in August 1939, prophetically enough, twenty-five years after the outbreak of the First World War. The dead from that war rise from their graves and want to return, but the living panic. There are Newsboys shouting: 'Special edition!

Greatest miracle since the Creation!' in an echo of earlier MacColl–
Littlewood work, and finally the living organise a conference where the
Archbishop points out that this is not a real resurrection because it is of the
ungodly, while a scientist 'proves' it cannot happen. The dead, dejected by
this rejection, and appalled at the mess the survivors of the war have made
of the world since 1918, return to their cemetery. The play has epic
qualities and plenty of potential, which at least to some extent the
production was able to realise. Its scenes move between a cobbler and a
prime minister with multifarious characters in between, from the
graveyard, to the Arc de Triomphe, to the bar of a public house, to the
prime minister's mistress's boudoir, in varying modes and rhythms.
MacColl and Littlewood were not satisfied with what they achieved, but
the production played to full houses for two weeks, and it gave them the
springboard for a new company.

This was named Theatre Union, implying support both for trade
unionism and a united political front. With premises first above a furniture
store in the centre of Manchester and later in All Saints Church, Ardwick,
the company 'set itself the task of establishing a complete theatre unit'.[5]
Members included several from *Miracle at Verdun* as well as some from the
old Theatre of Action, and new recruits often with wider interests. Thus,
several fine artists became supporters—L.S. Lowry, Bill Sharples (soon to
be killed in the Spanish Civil War), Ernie Brooks, and his partner, Barbara
Niven, a lecturer at Manchester College of Art. New members included
two Jewish boys from the same school, Gerry Raffles and Howard
Goorney, and a university student, Rosalie Williams, all of whom would
become stalwarts of Theatre Workshop. According to Goorney, the group
'lived theatre'. They earned a living by day, true, but spent four hours or
more almost every evening, as well as long hours at weekends, with
Theatre Union. This was 'our real work'.[6] Rosalie Williams recalled the
'intensity' of this, as the group worked on breathing exercises, voice,
movement, Stanislavsky's system and more, and studied from the
'extraordinary' range of books in the group library, mostly provided by
Gerry Raffles or Ewan MacColl—Appia, Meyerhold, Greek theatre, and so
on. The kind of study embarked on is indicated by an appendix in Joan
Littlewood's *Joan's Book*. Taking the Greek theatre as its subject, the study
includes examining the ritualised beginnings of Greek theatre, tracing
elements such as the development of the chorus and the protagonist,
studying the relationship of the theatre to the people, reading many plays,
and a comprehensive list of critical and historical works, from Thucydides'
Peloponnesian War to George Thomson's Marxist interpretation, *Aeschylus
and Athens*.[7] It is a more detailed investigation than most university degrees
require in the twenty-first century, and yet is only a fraction of what the

group attempted to cover, which also included medieval theatre, Renaissance theatre, the theatre of the Spanish Golden Age, *commedia dell'arte*, Chinese theatre and so on: 'It was considered mere philandering to read latter-day classics, let alone modern plays, unless you'd acquired a thorough grounding in the ancients'.[8]

The Theatre Union manifesto proclaimed:

> The theatre must face up to the problems of its time; it cannot ignore the poverty and human suffering which increases every day. It cannot, with sincerity, close its eyes to the disasters of its time. Means Test suicides, wars, fascism and the million sordid accidents reported in the daily press. If the theatre of today would reach the heights achieved four thousand years ago in Greece [*sic*] and four hundred years ago in Elizabethan England it must face up to such problems. To those who say that such affairs are not the concern of the theatre or that the theatre should confine itself to treading the path of 'beauty' and 'dignity' we would say 'Read Shakespeare, Marlowe, Webster, Sophocles, Aeschylus, Aristophanes, Calderon, Molière, Lope-de-Vega, Schiller and the rest . . .[9]

The theatre which they sought is suggested here. All the admired past theatres, those of Aeschylus, Shakespeare, the *commedia dell' arte* and so on, had been *popular*, appealing to the lower classes, and Theatre Union saw it as its prime function to re-connect with the lower class, now industrial workers. This was thus primarily a political task. But if politics and theatre were inextricably bound up in Aeschylus, Shakespeare and Theatre Union, politics in the 1930s was a kind of theatre, too. Hitler knew this: never was there a more theatrical leader. But parliament, too, or the hustings might be seen as stages, a march or demonstration as street theatre. Better theatre practice would therefore make for stronger politics, and vice versa, and thus would the working class be challenged and encouraged.

The dramaturgy for what they called this 'synthetic theatre' included 'ordinary' heroes and plays constructed through 'contrast', in MacColl's word,[10] but which Walter Benjamin, writing at almost exactly the same time, was to call 'interruption'. Benjamin asserted that 'The interrupting of action is one of the principal concerns of epic theatre'.[11] MacColl noticed the 'contrast' between elements such as Paul Robeson's 'rich, velvety bass-baritone', a mass choir, a poem by Hugh McDiarmid, and the natural flat accent of a native Lancashire speaker.[12] But equally, in performance, these could be sees as interruptions, one of another. Significant other forms of interruption included action on stage interrupted by the use of 'plants' in the audience, or conventional stage action by direct address to the audience. The involvement of the working-class audience implied in all this was a conscious and consistent feature of the 'theatre of synthesis's' dramaturgy.

On 17 July 1936, General Franco rebelled against the elected government in Spain and sought aid from Hitler. The ensuing bloody Spanish Civil War aroused fierce passions, especially on the left, where it was strongly felt that the people's legitimate rights were being trampled on. The Communist Party immediately appealed for aid and began organising International Brigades to help support the Republic. Former Theatre of Action members, Alec Armstrong and Bob Goldman, joined, and both were killed. Unity Theatre responded to the war with Jack Lindsay's *On Guard for Spain*, performed in April 1937 and also spectacularly at a rally for Spain in Trafalgar Square in July of that year, and in the following year with a production of Brecht's *Senora Carrar's Rifles*. Theatre Union in Manchester presented *Fuente Ovejuna* by Lope de Vega, a powerful story of the revolt of Spanish peasants against the tyranny of power, but including warmly comic scenes of village life and an unusual range of attitudes to love and sex. Theatre Union's first venture into the 'classics' about which they had been so demonstrative, had true-to-life characters, swarming crowd scenes and plenty of rapid action. It also included songs, set by Ewan MacColl to contemporary popular Spanish Republican tunes, running like a thread through the whole performance, and providing a new form of dramatic structuring.

2. The young Ewan MacColl, c. 1937.

The show was extremely successful, and Theatre Union found themselves called on to provide interludes at rallies in support of Spain, the highlights of which were often the moments when the lights illuminated particular spectators, who had agreed to make personal statements in support of the Spanish people:

> We'd get Arthur X who worked as a back-tenter in a mill in Oldham, who'd say, 'My name is Arthur X, I'm 23, I earn 4 pounds 18 shillings a week, I'm married and I've got two children,' and he'd tell his story in very simple terms as part of the thing, and then we'd give a roll-call of the dead, Arthur Jenkinson, shot on the Manzares River, Alec Armstrong, decapitated on the Aragon Front, and all the local people that everybody knew, and mixed this with people making their personal statements.[13]

As MacColl says, they 'learned from' juxtaposing such direct, unsophisticated material, with the poetry of Hugh McDiarmid or the voices of a group of singers.

Every production seemed to reveal something new for the 'theatre of synthesis'. In the summer of 1938 they presented *The Good Soldier Schweik* in the Lesser Free Trade Hall, Manchester. MacColl had acquired a copy of the script made for Piscator's Berlin theatre ten years earlier by Felix Gasbarra and Bertolt Brecht, and used this (which he had not enough German to translate precisely) and the text of the novel itself to create his own version, which, by the way, he continued to work on for at least fifteen more years. Piscator had used a creaking revolve stage and cumbersome back projections in 1928, but thanks to a timely intervention by engineering research scientists from Metropolitan-Vickers, Theatre Union was able to use a thoroughly efficient projector, and the scientists also upgraded the company's lighting equipment. A smooth revolving stage, upon which were placed Ernie Brooks's black-and-white designs, was also acquired. Though the episodic structure, with comic dance and exaggerated characters, was somewhat cartoon-like, Joan Littlewood employed Stanislavsky's system rigorously in rehearsals. The whole production was another success, not least because of the fun it made of power politics and its usual concomitant, war.

Equally anti-war was the production that autumn of Aristophanes's *Lysistrata*, which MacColl also continued to work on for years. This used an architectural set with ramps in front of black drapes—the closest they had come to pure Adolphe Appia and therefore another significant step forward. Littlewood also made the old men figures of slapstick comedy and added plenty of song-and-dance routines.

But war was coming anyway, and how useful theatre, or theatrical demonstrations against it, were was debatable.

> We marched in demonstrations [. . .] to hear men like Stafford Cripps,
> Aneurin Bevan and the Communist leaders Harry Pollitt and William
> Gallacher [. . .] denounce the national government, and call for a united
> front, nationally and internationally, against fascism and war. With
> clenched fists held aloft, we chanted as we marched: 'Red front, red front,
> red united fighting front!' [. . .] It was all fine, heady stuff, and we
> returned home with our enthusiasm renewed, confident that we had that
> day significantly advanced the cause of socialism and anti-fascism.[14]

In fact the Berlin–Rome axis to concert future aggressions was already in
existence and had been joined by Japan, which invaded China in July 1937.
In March 1938 came the *Anschluss*, as Hitler swallowed Austria, and a year
later, just as Franco was victorious in Spain, Germany occupied large parts
of Czechoslovakia. The following month, Italy invaded Albania.
Meanwhile, the Moscow show-trials and even the war in Spain were
dividing sections of the left from each other, as anarchists fell out with
Communists, and Trotskyists feuded with Stalinists. The Soviet–Nazi Pact
was a desperate blow. People felt they were riding a landslide to catastrophe.

On 3 September 1939 war was declared. Theatre Union was already
creating *Last Edition*, which was to be presented in March 1940, at the
Round House, Ancoats. Its method of creation was overtly democratic—
another first—as the whole company of a dozen or so was involved in
research, the results of which were discussed before MacColl drafted the
scenes. Littlewood then sometimes adapted these during her rehearsals.
The theatre space contained two long platforms running down either side
of the auditorium, as well as a wide stage across the front, on which were
three pillars, which conveniently created discrete acting areas. This allowed
simultaneous actions to proceed, one scene intercutting another, and much
use of snapped-in follow spotlights. It encouraged interruption—or
'contrast'—as a dramaturgical device, and helped to create urgency and
forward momentum. MacColl and Littlewood themselves stood at the
corners of the front stage as Narrators, and they were able to update the
contents of the piece, as events in the political world changed. *Last Edition*
comprehensively reviewed the last six disastrous years, as the running order
indicates:

> The Home Front
> 1. The New Year, 1934
> 2. Hunger
> 3. Hunger March
> 4. Gresford Disaster
> 5. Gresford Trial
> 6. The Anglo-German Naval Agreement
> 7. Gestapo
> 8. Trinidad Strike

Spain
9. Exchange
10. Pasionaria
11. Jarama
12. Friends of National Spain
13. The Findings

Munich
14. Launcelot's Dream
15. Prague 1938
16. Who Killed Johnny the Czech?
17. Peace in Our Time
18. The Second War to End Wars
19. Research
20. Who Is the Real Enemy?[15]

This, however, gives no idea of the fast-moving excitement that characterised the performances. Stylistically, MacColl commented later, *Last Edition* was 'an anthology of everything we had ever done in the theatre',[16] and the variety of means of interruption is extraordinary. Besides the expected dialogue scenes, dances and songs, there was the use of documents in the Gresford trial scene, 'acting out'—that is, having ordinary 'characters' decide to 'act out' an event, thereby giving it a provisional quality that encourages the audience to define the issues—and theatricalising—using a theatrical *genre* to dramatise an event, as here the invasion of Czechoslovakia presented in the idiom of a gangster movie. Such techniques often simplify, but they may also help to clarify the issues, and especially to make them tendentious. The show was extremely popular, but after a number of performances it was closed by the police, and Littlewood and MacColl were fined twenty pounds each and bound over for two years.

From the start of the war, Theatre Union had lost members, partly due to its leaders' combative Communist stance, which saw the war as an extension of the class struggle by other means. Some members had joined the forces, others had left to establish a Manchester Unity Theatre, but the remainder continued to tour *Lysistrata* and new productions, an adaptation of Molière as *The Flying Doctor* and another historical piece by MacColl with input from Littlewood, *Classic Soil*, about the weavers and the Chartists of the 1840s and then, in a poetic time switch, war in the 1940s. The tour seemed to bring the goal of oneness with working-class spectators nearer. Littlewood described a performance:

> Last weekend Theatre Union was playing in a small hall to an audience of cotton workers. They just pushed back their chairs and sat around while we played to them. They were cotton workers and we were attempting to

play their lives and struggles on the stage. The barriers were down. We weren't actors, we were part of them, part of their struggle.[17]

However, once the Blitz began, and the USSR joined the war, Theatre Union dissolved itself.

Amid the disasters and traumas of war, other left-wing theatres continued. Agit-prop made a reappearance in the tube stations during bombing raids, and living newspapers were taken to the troops. Predominantly pacifist groups of actors formed themselves into touring companies, including Martin Browne's Pilgrim Players, formed in 1939 specifically to further religious drama, the Adelphi Players, who began in 1941, and the Compass Players, established in 1944.[18] Unity Theatre kept open throughout the war, and some of its branches flourished, such as Glasgow Unity, which was created out of the amalgamation of the Glasgow Workers' Theatre, the Clarion Players, the Jewish Institute Players and other groups. But as this suggests, these groups did not rely on a close-knit, single-mindedly trained, politically motivated ensemble, who had worked together for several years, as was the case with Theatre Union. Joan Littlewood and Ewan MacColl determined to continue their theatre work after the war. They gave all the members research topics in theatre history to explore, and all agreed to reassemble as soon as peace returned. Then MacColl joined the navy, and Joan Littlewood returned to the BBC.

At about this time, Joan Littlewood wrote: 'As the circumstances become more difficult, our work must become more intense.' She urged her fellows to study and master theatre history, for this would provide the guide, the spine for their work. Shakespeare's theatre drew sustenance from the 'stinkards', and so must theirs. 'Involve the audience in the action of [the] play, make them feel part of it.' Theatre Union used a mixture of informality and shock tactics, which included direct address and the use of 'plants' for this purpose. After *Last Edition*, Littlewood deplored the proscenium arch, which flattened the actors into distant pictures, and advocated something 'three-dimensional, solid, real, something for the workers to get hold of.' Lighting, too, she urged, 'can be dynamic', as their experiments with Appia's ideas had shown. She also called for 'realistic and truthful' acting, which she distinguished from 'representationalism', that kind of seeming normality which is actually arch and false, and which still today is common in the theatre. Stanislavsky already provided her with a key to such truthfulness.[19] However, she and MacColl wanted more than this, they required multi-skilled actors who could dance, sing, play a musical instrument and do acrobatics as well, for any or all these skills might be needed in the theatre they intended to forge.

They sought a different kind of play, too, one which used juxtapositioning and montage as primary tools, and one in which interruption was a crucial device. The focus constantly changed from naturalistic close-up to something more generalised—a line of unemployed workers, perhaps. Dreams mixed with reality, slogans with conversation and poetry and song, in this 'theatre of synthesis'. The functions of writer, director and even actor blurred into one another, and the final interruption occurred when reality itself interrupted fiction, and vice-versa, and theatre became meta-theatre. Left politics in the 1930s had perhaps more to do with performance than with power, and the performance of a left-wing theatre in a production like *Last Edition* or *Classic Soil*, by re-reading the history of the time, and presenting an alternative view, seemed perhaps to create a more honest political reality than other more overtly political acts achieved. Whether this could be true was a question that had to be left to the future.

PART TWO
Theatre Workshop, 1945–53
Political Theatre

CHAPTER SIX

Days of Hope

> On 26 July 1945 we were, as usual, in our top room working when David flew in with a radio. 'The whole country's falling to Labour,' he said, 'It's a landslide.' We'd been so absorbed in our great theatre that we'd forgotten all about the Election. And it was an unbelievable victory. Somebody flung open the window and began shouting the news to the street.[1]

The war that had cost the lives of 265,000 members of the armed forces, over 60,000 civilians and a further 30,000 sailors in the merchant navy, a quarter of the nation's wealth, two-thirds of the merchant fleet and a third of the national housing stock, was over, and people wanted a fresh start. The war had already got rid of the hated Means Test, and sensible planning and reforms in education had been introduced. BBC news bulletins, which had been listened to eagerly by many people, brought a new impartiality and reliability to public information, as well as a new sense of nationhood and fairness. Less easily quantified, the war had created new attitudes, such as a warmly positive feeling towards the Russians who, it was felt, had borne more than their fair share of suffering.

The Labour Party appeared to offer the best means of capitalising on the new spirit: 'I remember the enthusiasm—there has never been an election like that since—the passionate conviction; sometimes, you know, we Labour candidates, we thought we were being loved by our supporters. It was unique.'[2] People had what might seem now an almost absurd dream, that the USA would withdraw across the Atlantic and that Britain and the USSR together would build a new, peaceful, socialist Europe. When the new parliament assembled on 2 August, it contained 393 Labour MPs, as well as two Communists, Willie Gallacher and Phil Piratin, and two independent socialists, D.N. Pritt and Vernon Bartlett, and on that first day they sang—or bellowed—'The Red Flag' in a shockingly theatrical moment. In the autumn, two by-elections and countrywide local elections saw further advances for Labour. The Communist Party, strong in the trade unions if less so electorally, firmly supported the government. Apart from the dream, ordinary people wanted practical improvements—equal treatment, equal opportunities, an end to poverty, undernourishment, unemployment and ignorance. Rationing stayed in place, partly because it offered 'fair shares for all from the cradle to the grave'. Somebody said: 'This is a fairly new thing, I think—very many people have realized the previous "they" must be replaced by the post-war "we"'.[3] The class war, however, was not over. People still 'knew their place', and working-class characters in film or radio comedies were the butt of jokes because they spoke in 'funny' accents. The middle and upper classes hated life under Labour because servants were becoming impossible to obtain, and no household appliances, like vacuum cleaners or washing machines, were available. Moreover, the police, previously the ultimate weapon of the dominant class, became almost impartial, a situation which persisted until the 1980s. And some attitudes remained unchanged: homosexuality was still a criminal activity, unmarried mothers and those who indulged in sex before marriage were ostracised, and the death penalty remained. Nevertheless, Mr Attlee's government was advancing change—a comprehensive and universal National Insurance scheme, an Industrial Injuries Act, plans to nationalise major industries, most notably the coal mines, and a new National Health Service. Memories of disasters like that at the Gresford Colliery, and of pre-war poverty, disease and malnourishment drove the introduction of the so-called 'Welfare State', which received large measures of support, not least from the Communist Party. Whether it represented class warfare, a social revolution, or simply the righting of old wrongs is still debated, but it seemed for a while to justify all but the most extravagant hopes.

Foreign policy was perhaps another matter. On 6 August 1945, Hiroshima was atom-bombed. Two days later Japan was invaded by the USSR. On 9 August an atom bomb was dropped on Nagasaki. On 14 August over 1,000 American planes bombed Tokyo. The war in the east was thus settled in ominous dust clouds, which suggested that the world would not settle for a comfortable peace. From Britain's point of view, demobilising so many servicemen was a vastly complicated problem and there were mutinies, perhaps fomented by Communists, among men desperate to return to civilian life. For some, this was reminiscent of Invergordon. And in mutinies among, for instance, Indian troops, and in unrest in other parts of the empire, such as the Gold Coast (Ghana) and Malaya (Malaysia), the hand of Communism was also seen. Those brave liberators—the Red Army—meanwhile, were coming to seem less attractive as Stalin began bolting together his iron empire: Bulgaria, Hungary and Romania were all subdued, though a little leeway for local Communists was permitted in Yugoslavia and Albania. With America hardening its stance against 'Un-Americanism', Ernest Bevin, the foreign secretary and a long-time foe of Communism from his trade union days, denounced the Soviet Union. A cold war between the West and Stalin's Russia was beginning, despite pressure from British Communists, Labour MPs like Michael Foot, Konni Zilliacus and Ian Mikardo, and progressive and radical people of various stripes. The international situation seemed to be sliding into a class war on a global scale. Did the Labour government's decision in 1946 to build its own atomic bomb help world stability? It was perhaps the first sign that Communism, which had been a not unattractive ally against Nazism, was now to be confronted.

Meanwhile, the war had also stimulated cultural awareness and activity—the emergence of Theatre Workshop both embodies and signals this. But they were not the only left-wing or touring theatre group of the time. Unity Theatre established its own professional company under Ted Willis in 1946, though its tact was sometimes wanting, as when it staged an attack on the government's fuel policies in a revue called *Black Magic* just as the coal industry was—to working-class acclaim—being nationalised. In 1947, with Arts Council support, they toured South Wales with Clifford Odets's *Golden Boy*. This included sixty-five one-night stands, besides other performances. Willis wanted his actors trained in 'working-class realism', though whether he meant something like the Russian Socialist Realist version of Stanislavsky's system is not clear. According to Chambers, Willis's application of Stanislavsky was 'pedestrian'.[4] By the end of 1947 the professional company had collapsed with debts of around £2,500.

Unity's dilemma under Labour was instructive. They had been founded as a largely pro-Communist theatre in the days of the 'Popular Front', but some of their most prominent supporters, like Sir Stafford Cripps and George Strauss, then expellees from the Labour Party, were now in the Labour cabinet. Unity was perhaps inevitably confused, and it began to lose money, too. A series of somewhat predictable mainstream Labour historical dramas—about the match girls' strike, the early co-operatives, the strike for the dockers' tanner—mingled with 'old time' music halls, yet another revival of *The Ragged Trousered Philanthropists* and revues—*What's Left* (1948) and *Here Goes* (1951)—did not reduce the sense of a theatre in search of the left. Chambers comments: 'Unity's lack of innovation contrasts sharply with the work of Theatre Workshop and its playwright, Ewan MacColl'.[5]

The Glasgow branch of Unity had more success for a while. It, too, went professional in 1946, again with Arts Council support. Appalled at the lack of Scottish input into the early Edinburgh International Festivals, Glasgow Unity mounted a rival 'People's Festival' in 1947, inviting the participation of other groups, including, from 1949, Theatre Workshop. Glasgow Unity staged a number of successful original plays, too, including Ena Lamont Stewart's *Men Should Weep*, probably the first genuine working-class play to centre round a kitchen sink, and Robert McLeish's *The Gorbals Story*, which over 100,000 people saw in Glasgow, and which had a run at the Garrick Theatre, London, in 1948. Its roots may have been in Glasgow, but a number of its actors found themselves tempted by London salaries, as well as London glamour, and, instructively, the company collapsed in 1950. In 1946 Montagu Slater attempted to form a new left-wing theatre with trade union backing, and a professional group appeared at the Scala Theatre briefly, too. There were touring companies, notably the Adelphi Guild Players, founded in 1945 to take plays to places without a theatre, but they went out of business in two years. 'Times were changing', wrote their director, Richard Ward after two years touring. 'I [. . .] was conscious of being exhausted in body and spirit'.[6] The Compass Players and the Osiris Players also toured for a few years in the 1940s before giving up the struggle.

For it was a struggle, as Theatre Workshop's experience showed. In 1942, ten members of Theatre Union had agreed to the proposed training programme, and to meet after the war. Now five reassembled in Manchester: Joan Littlewood, Gerry Raffles, Jimmie Miller—who had 'gone on the trot'[7] from the navy, grown a beard and changed into a Scotsman born in Auchterarder called Ewan MacColl—Rosalie Williams, and Howard Goorney. By July 1945 they had moved to a base above the Conservative Party headquarters in Kendal, Westmoreland, where they were joined by others—Harold Bowen, who had been in *The Good Soldier Schweik*, David Scase, Pearl Turner, Gerald Wilkinson, Ruth Brandes, Nick Whitfield, Bill Davidson and the Swedish actor, Kristin Lind. Perhaps there were others. The name they decided to perform under was 'Theatre Workshop': 'Pioneer Theatres Ltd' was to be their trading name. MacColl remembered:

> The atmosphere of continuous excitement and relish which invested the meanest task with significance. The idea, the dream, the vision of a new kind of theatre, or rather of a theatre which saw itself as the heir to all the great theatres of the past, was so palpable that you felt you could use it as a hammer, a drill, a chisel, a knife with a blade for every occasion. I had dreamed of living and working like this ever since I had learned to articulate my desires.[8]

Romantic, no doubt, but potent, too, until after a few months it became clear that Kendal was not viable for the group financially. Touring local village halls brought in the merest pittance. They moved out, and locating a base remained problematic for the next eight years. At one point they were offered living and rehearsing space at Ormesby Hall, a spacious mansion near Middlesbrough, but mostly when they were not on tour the company lived in various quarters in Manchester.

The company's stated aims echoed Theatre Union's, and were very much Ewan MacColl's:

> If the theatre is to play an effective part in the life of the community it must face up to contemporary problems and at the same time revive all that is best in theatrical tradition.
>
> We believe Theatre Workshop is doing this.
>
> Theatre Workshop is an experimental theatre whose aim is to show to the widest public and particularly to that section of the public which has been starved theatrically, plays of artistic significance.
>
> By utilising all the recent technical advances in the application of light and sound, and by introducing music and dance, we believe that a dramatic form, flexible enough to reflect the constantly changing twentieth century scene, can be created.[9]

The theatre was to be widely understood, but still able to deal with complex subject matter, probably through a variety of juxtaposed styles. Politics was central to the project. Any temptations towards something more overtly artistic, or politically neutral, were firmly resisted, and members' politics were quickly obvious: David Scase was a Communist, for example, and Bill Davidson a Marxist, though not a member of the party. Joan Littlewood was something of a Communist anarchist, while MacColl thought of himself as a non-party revolutionary.

To achieve its aims, the company needed to feel itself to be a co-operative, or community. In a theatrical context, where egos, ambitions and artistic integrities are fragile but extremely pronounced, this is difficult, but here, at least for a time, it seemed to work. 'Inspiration' and skill may be necessities in artistic endeavour, but they are often perceived as threats to democracy. Inter-dependency, a sense of fraternal obligation, is a requirement for a theatre company, whether it be seen as 'generosity' or 'social insurance', and from the beginning this functioned effectively at the top. MacColl and Littlewood, though still legally married, were no longer so close personally, but they remained unusually effective as a team. This mutual respect then extended outward to the rest of the company. Kristin Lind recorded:

> Our work and life together articulated the values I had always believed in, and suddenly belonging to a group, fighting together towards the same aim, gave meaning to both theatre and life. The group solidarity is a necessity. Theatre is never one man's work.
>
> It was the togetherness that mattered. To give your best, not only inspired by Joan and Ewan with so much more experience and knowledge, but with the spirit of the Group to urge you on.[10]

Over years, Theatre Workshop members worked together and lived together, eating, sleeping and gathering socially for an evening sing-song or day's rambling in the countryside. Not everyone was a theatre historian, not everyone was a Marxist, but that basis of community, and its concomitant synergy, was certainly a strength. When Harry Greene joined the company in early 1951, he remembered that despite the agonies and hardships of one-night-stand touring, 'There was laughter, there was gaiety, there was a great sort of feeling which I was to learn was part of Theatre Workshop. There was bonhomie, a family feeling, and they made you feel good.'[11]

The sense of community was fostered partly by simply living together, but also significantly by a sense of joint endeavour, by the certainty that the work they were embarked upon was serious, worthwhile in itself and consequential to the world of politics or theatre or both. All members took the same salary, and, like the founders of the Moscow Art Theatre, vowed there would be no 'stars' among them. They had weekly 'plenary' meetings, which continued into the time the company had a permanent base at Stratford East, where matters domestic, political and artistic were raised and discussed. Was this democracy? 'It was not as democratic as it might have been', Jean Newlove recalled, partly because of their respect for Littlewood and MacColl, who were more knowledgeable and experienced than the rest of the group. 'We said our pieces, and our views were welcomed', Newlove said, but 'it was a benign dictatorship'. Especially in the early years, Ewan MacColl sometimes used the weekly meeting to make fiery, inspiring speeches to invigorate the company. Sometimes the meetings were used for critical assessments of the work in progress.

The artistic work never consisted of merely presenting productions: teaching and learning were always important, too, and the company mounted a series of weekend schools, aimed mostly at working-class would-be actors. 'We can earn our living playing and teaching locally', Joan Littlewood wrote in 1947. 'It would be self-defeating just to go on mounting shows'.[12] The schools consisted of a well-planned mixture of active classes, discussions and social events. A railwayman who attended one school wrote: 'The school was a pleasure. Joan gave us exercises to overcome our initial shyness. They were more like charades, but they broke the ice and we began to know each other. It wasn't long before we had the confidence to try everything demanded of us.'[13] The company's own training was not dissimilar, but obviously at a higher level. Littlewood argued that if musicians needed to practice and train throughout their careers, then so did actors. Training was continued when the company was on tour, and thus, over years, a shared company 'language' was developed.

Theatre Workshop's first production, which had the luxury of over two months' rehearsal, was a double bill consisting of MacColl's 'episodic play with singing', *Johnny Noble*, and his pre-war adaptation of Molière, *The*

Flying Doctor. The former needed the time to ensure the technical demands it made could be met. *Johnny Noble* exhibits MacColl's fascination with theatre technology, having complex light and sound sequences to dovetail with singing and dancing. 'Everybody had to be at the right place at the right time', he remembered, but 'we were never more than 30 seconds out on the entire show'.[14] *The Flying Doctor* was a fast-moving *commedia dell'arte* farce, with input from Chico Marx, who visited the company to discuss technique. These two productions were soon joined by Lorca's *The Love of Don Perlimplin and Belisa in the Garden*, a tribute to the most famous victim of the Spanish Civil War and produced in rich scarlet and olive-green velvet curtains as an antidote to the drabness of the times. The company received help and advice from Luis Meana of Manchester University, who had been Lorca's stage manager twenty years earlier, and who was persuaded to play maracas at some early performances. The play is part Freudian myth, part an evocation of Lope de Vega's scandalous love life and part parody of the Catholic Mass, and appears to have baffled many of Theatre Workshop's working-class audiences—silence, punctuated by a few hisses and the odd person wildly clapping seems to have been a common response. The performance also contained its own scandal. Often, as Howard Goorney's Perlimplin, a Groucho Marx-like figure, rose from his impotent embrace of Kristin Lind's Belisa, his knee became entangled in her gown, which fell to her waist, exposing her breasts for all to see. Lind seemed happy with this effect, though other actresses who played the role later did not perpetuate this piece of theatrical 'business'.

Theatre Workshop's fourth play was Ewan MacColl's documentary history of atomic science from Democritus to Einstein, *Uranium 235*, written in direct response to the dropping of the atom bomb on Hiroshima. Learning the science on the way, writing in dressing rooms and digs on tour, MacColl produced a theatrical *tour de force* that posed the same question as Brecht's *Life of Galileo*: whose science is this? What should be done with it? During some performances, Joan Littlewood became an audience 'plant', an *agent provocateuse* who shouted 'I want entertainment, not politics' to stir the audience into defining their responses. This was followed by MacColl recasting his pre-war *Lysistrata*, now named *Operation Olive Branch*, and updated with the inclusion of a group of Scottish private soldiers. The old men now became recognisable parodies of Marshal Pétain, General Patton and others, while the Magistrate was modelled on Winston Churchill. The latter's famous Fulton speech declaring the cold war became the basis for the Magistrate's arguments, and, according to MacColl,[15] audiences immediately recognised the 'cant phrases' of hypocrisy. The repertoire grew further with the addition of a lively production of Chekhov's 'vaudeville', *The Proposal*, and then, in 1948, another play by Ewan MacColl, *The Other Animals*, his most ambitious yet, examining the last hours of a political prisoner, somewhat reminiscent of Upton Sinclair's *Singing Jailbirds*.

Starting off in school and village halls, the early Theatre Workshop tours moved towards booking bigger venues—legitimate theatres, arts clubs, town halls and the like. Effectively, they were aiming at the minority audiences who normally attend theatre performances, not the working class whom they sought for their constituency. But they were blazing a hitherto untrodden trail, and whereas now theatre companies have well-documented ways of reaching particular audiences, this was not the case in the 1940s. They tried various experiments. They booked small theatres and university halls, but audiences were typically very small—eight people in a 200-seat auditorium was not unlikely. So they tried large theatres in working-class towns, such as the Theatre, Blackburn, and the Empire, Dewsbury, and found that they might now achieve twenty people, in an auditorium holding 800 or 1,000. This was no real advance. Reaching its target audience remained a problem for the company.

One well-remembered exception was in the obviously unusual conditions of a Butlin's holiday camp, at Filey, in May 1946. Theatre Workshop appeared after a 'wrestling show' in a large tent,

> to a packed house of mums and dads and their children, as typical an audience of northern, working men and women as you could find. They treated the play as they would have treated an exciting game of football. They cheered, groaned, shouted their approval, and when one of the actors tried to make a planned interruption from the auditorium they howled him down.[16]

Though the week in Filey was perhaps unique in Theatre Workshop's history, it 'confirmed our belief that there was no need to compromise or "play down" to working people.'[17]

Scientists who saw *Uranium 235* reacted unpredictably. A physics lecturer from Loughborough College insisted all his students see the production, but Nils Bohr, the atomic scientist who saw it in Sweden, disliked it intensely, perhaps because he was presented in the play as a clown. On the other hand, at least one other Swedish nuclear scientist was so impressed that she saw it four times. Another special constituency consisted of politicians. Several Labour MPs saw productions and lent their support to Theatre Workshop, including Alf Robens, Tom Driberg and Aneurin Bevan. It was also true that 'in some places', the company received a 'rapturous response',[18] even from small audiences. This, however, immediately triggered suspicions, at least in MacColl's mind, that applause might become addictive. He seems to have shared Meyerhold's attitude: 'If everyone praises your production, almost certainly it is rubbish. If everyone abuses it, then perhaps there is something in it. But if some praise and others abuse, if you can split the audience in half, then for sure it is a good production.'[19]

In February 1947, Theatre Workshop toured British army bases in western Germany under the auspices of the Combined Services Entertainment Unit. Though the British army officers were not particularly supportive, some Germans recognised affinities with their own theatre of the Weimar period. A similar recognition occurred when the following year the group visited Czechoslovakia and Sweden. Well received in both these countries, their work was compared to that of Reinhardt, Piscator and Jooss, and MacColl's plays were likened to Toller's. Such comparisons could not, of course, have been made by British spectators or critics, whose island insulation Theatre Workshop was partly founded to change. These tours provided a financial boost, as well as the novel and seductive experience of playing in good theatres to virtually full houses. The company was also able to meet other artists and theatre people on equal terms. If the ideals with which the theatre had begun in 1945 were to be further fought for, such interludes gave heart to the struggle.

CHAPTER SEVEN

Days of Disappointment

According to Hugh Dalton, Attlee's first chancellor of the exchequer, 1947 was the Labour government's 'Annus horrendus'.[1] Yet it had started encouragingly, with the coal mines coming into public ownership on 1 January. But freakishly bad weather over the next three months, as well as some inexcusable inefficiencies, reduced the new year rejoicings to chagrin. Unprecedented amounts of snow fell, and persistent freezing temperatures petrified services. The publicly owned coal, for instance, was quite unable to reach the public and stayed at the pitheads. Over two million people were temporarily thrown out of work, offices were lit by candles and newspapers reduced to four pages. People were only allowed to use electricity to cook with before 9 am, between 12 noon and 2 pm and after 4 pm. It was an ideal breeding ground for those who became known as 'spivs', who took advantage of items which 'fell off the back of lorries', supplying at steep prices items that customers in shops were unable to purchase. The black market was the only flourishing sector of the economy. The government seemed powerless. Neither John Strachey, minister for food, nor Emmanuel Shinwell, minister for fuel, seemed to know which way to turn, so that people were said to 'shiver with Shinwell and starve with Strachey'.

It was true—the country was going bankrupt. Dalton managed to negotiate a huge loan from America, but was then forced to resign for leaking details of his November budget to the press. The austere Sir Stafford Cripps took over as chancellor, and introduced tough measures of austerity (rationing became more drastic than during the war), besides devaluing the pound from $4.03 to $2.80. It was exhausting going. Barely two years later, Cripps was unable to carry on; he resigned—to be replaced by Hugh Gaitskell—and died less than two years later. And in the spring of 1951, Ernest Bevin, the foreign secretary, also gave up; he resigned in March, and died the same summer. The Labour government that had arrived so fresh and full of energy in 1945 seemed to be falling asunder, and the spirit of confidence and optimism was draining away too. Once again perhaps, Communists had a chance to take the lead with the working class.

Yet, in the general election of February 1950, Labour polled over 46 per cent of the vote, and remained in office; and in the election of October 1951, their vote rose to 48.8 per cent, almost half the votes cast, more than the Conservatives, who, however, gained most seats, and formed a new government. The working class remained loyal to Labour, whereas the Communists lost their only two MPs and saw their vote sink in each successive election. It was not for want of trying. Once Labour's 1947 decline had appeared, the Communists had ended their support, and went on the attack. In August, Harry Pollitt denounced Dalton's wage restraint policy and took advantage of the public's weariness of controls to berate the continuation of rationing. As the housing crisis continued, Communists encouraged squatters to move into empty properties, causing considerable disruption.

But Labour's Welfare State, providing pensions, child allowances and council houses (if not enough of them), ending unemployment, and virtually eliminating begging from the streets, was enormously popular, especially with working-class people. National Insurance against disasters at work, industrial injury, unemployment, sickness, maternity, retirement and death, and the free, universal National Health Service, removed much of Communism's appeal, while the public ownership of approximately 20 per cent of British industry, employing over two million workers, by 1951, removed more. A disruptive dock strike in 1949 was also blamed on Communist skulduggery, and many trade unions as well as the Labour Party proscribed Communist and Communist 'front' organisations.

There is no doubt that Theatre Workshop felt this hostility. In February 1949, Equity, the actors' union, supported a TUC resolution against Communism, and approved of the Arts Council's subsidy to Basil Dean's production of *Private Enterprise*, a play attacking trade unionism. At the same time, Joan Littlewood, affirming that Theatre Workshop was a 'revolutionary theatre', was arguing that 'Nearly half the world has emerged from the darkness of pre-history and is moving towards Communism'. The paradox, to her, was the same as that which assailed the theatre: 'Whilst T.S. Eliot dreams wistfully of a return to feudalism, young regional writers are using the language of the people to create a poetry greater than any we have ever known'.[2] She was in a very small minority. The government even banned Communists from employment in the civil service.

Events abroad also undermined Communism's appeal. In February 1948, the Communists engineered a coup in Czechoslovakia, and in 1949 the Soviet Union first tested a nuclear weapon. Then came a series of spy scandals: Klaus Fuchs was exposed in 1950, and the following year Burgess and MacLean fled to Moscow. Meanwhile, in 1950 the war against

Communist North Korea, backed by the newly revolutionised China, broke out: Communists at home, it was felt, might easily sabotage the war effort. Finally, there was the festering problem of Germany. Divided into four zones by the four victorious allies in 1945, the three western zones, controlled by Britain, France and the USA coalesced, while the fourth zone, under Soviet control, remained isolated in Communism. The three western powers wanted to reconfigure a German state, and threatened to do so without the eastern portion if the Soviets did not co-operate. The Russians responded by blockading Berlin, the old capital city, also divided into four, but sited well inside their eastern zone. To get supplies to Berlin, Bevin persuaded the Americans to join an airlift that lasted for nearly a year, from June 1948, and which effectively saved West Berlin for capitalism.

For the mass of ordinary working-class British people, Labour was 'our' party, and their traditions of solidarity worked against Communist inroads. Labour splits, from MacDonald's, through Mosley's, to the unnecessary expulsion of Cripps and Strauss in the late 1930s, had all harmed the prospects of working-class progress, and for them, Communism was little more than a split, a tiny splinter from the movement as a whole. By 1951, when Labour lost power, Communism in Britain was effectively marginalised.

For Theatre Workshop, established overtly to promote, if not the Communist Party, then certainly Communism or Marxism, to working-class audiences, the implications of this were significant. In March 1947, at the height of the food and fuel crisis, Joan Littlewood noted:

> I heard a good feature programme on Keir Hardie from Scotland—it upset me terribly—even the struggle of Socialists of his type seems magnificent and moving and *ultra-revolutionary* compared with the droolings of the 'left' of today—what on earth has happened to the revolutionary movement? Will it ever wake again—My own pre-war feelings and those of thousands of us seem prehistoric today. When I think of the songs we sang, the fierce street battles, the flame of belief in the international working class. Keir Hardie said: 'I would sooner see my son in his grave than fighting his fellow workers.' And millions of men and women all over the world believed these things. And look at today. When did you last hear the Internationale?[3]

But gradually Theatre Workshop's emphasis seems to have shifted from politics to theatre as the company struggled to continue with its touring policy. In late 1947 the company appeared in London, though few critics noticed them (apart from Robert Muller, who commented on both their politics and their theatrical methods: 'This company offers the most original, skilful and progressive productions that England has seen since the end of the War'[4]), but by January 1948 financial problems forced the company to disband temporarily. Littlewood's refusal to bend was couched in perhaps significantly non-political language: 'What we are living and going through hell for is a great theatre and such things were never born easily. Compromise is no way out.'[5] In the summer they managed a few performances of *The Other Animals* in Manchester, and toured abroad to Czechoslovakia and Sweden, with that and their very first productions, *Johnny Noble* and a reconceived *Flying Doctor*. Littlewood had been inspired to 'make something new of that old thing'.[6]

Politics continued to be less prominent through 1949. They added MacColl's new play, *Rogue's Gallery*, and Irwin Shaw's *The Gentle People* to their repertoire. Shaw was an American associated with New York's Group Theatre, where his play had had its first production in 1939. A fantasy about Fascism, it was, said Harold Clurman, 'both delicate and melodramatic'.[7] It concerns two paupers, one Jewish, the other Greek, seeking help to escape to the warm south; when a gangster attempts to hijack their cause, they take him out to sea and throw him overboard. They return, quietly pleased with their work, to continue their dream of escape. Besides these, Theatre Workshop organised tours of schools with *Twelfth Night* in the spring of 1949, and *As You Like It* in the autumn, followed by a theatre tour of Joan Littlewood's adaptation of *Alice in Wonderland*. Ewan MacColl described what happened when this show played at the Theatre Royal, Barnsley, on Boxing Day 1949:

> It was a nice show, it was a beautifully mounted show, very well directed, lovely dancing and good music [. . .] but we had abominable experiences with it. It was one of those booking disasters. We opened with it at Barnsley [. . .] and at least a third of the audience was drunk . . . (of these) a third was fighting drunk, and a third were vomiting drunk, the rest were sleeping, and they threw pennies on the stage, they threw bottles on the stage, they pissed on the stage, literally . . . That was it . . . It was not people's theatre. Let's face it, to go to a mining community, and to get blokes who've just come up the pit and to have them faced with the Red Queen and the Ugly Duchess, it's bloody ridiculous.[8]

It was the end of existing policy of touring barely political plays to large theatres, and the company disbanded again in March 1950.

In November, when they re-formed, a new policy was instigated. Productions would, wherever possible, be given single performances in village halls, old cinemas, anywhere performable in the heart of working class Britain. Consequently, in the winter of 1950–51 *Uranium 235* (before Christmas) and MacColl's new play, *Landscape with Chimneys*, (after Christmas) toured South Wales, then the coalfields of north-east England. *Johnny Noble* and *The Flying Doctor* were resurrected again for a similar tour, followed by new productions of Paul Green's *Hymn to the Rising Sun* and

Joan Littlewood and Gerry Raffles's *The Long Shift*, about a mining disaster. The policy continued into 1952, and there were schools tours of *Henry IV* and *Twelfth Night*, as well as an interlude at the Edinburgh Fringe where Ewan MacColl's next play, a political thriller *The Travellers*, was presented. But the company's problems were not solved.

'It was in touring that we began to realise just how much we'd taken on',[9] MacColl said later. Part of the problem was that Littlewood and MacColl refused to compromise on the technical side of the performance, so that the company's second-hand lorry was usually too full to carry the actors, who had either to travel by public transport, or hitch-hike. Once arrived at the venue, the equipment had to be brought in. Howard Goorney recalled carrying into halls, by hand,

> The set, lighting equipment, curtains, costumes, props, curtain rails, battens, sound equipment and speakers and sundry skips and crates, plus a large switchboard and dimmers on wheels—designed by our electrician and requiring four strong men to lift. All this had to loaded, unloaded, rigged and de-rigged. Sometimes it had to be carried up and down several flights of stairs![10]

Once inside, the hall often had to be cleaned, the stage swept, the sound and lighting equipment rigged, plotted, balanced, the props laid out and costumes ironed. After that, Joan Littlewood was quite likely to insist on a rehearsal.

Performing under such conditions placed heavy responsibilities on actors, particularly because they had to deal with unpredictable audience responses. Inevitably, this helped to bind together the ensemble and to deepen their mutual artistic trust. But the acting probably sometimes seemed the most restful thing they did. The venues themselves, for example, could take their toll. Ewan MacColl remembered cold, clammy fog drifting across one stage in Liverpool, and snow falling through a hole in the roof onto another in Blyth. No wonder members of the company became ill. After striking the set, de-rigging the electrical equipment and loading the van, company members sometimes stayed with local people— in itself often a tiring experience, though again it had its positive side, helping actors to get to know, understand and respect their target audience better. There were other jobs to be done, too, such as putting up posters, getting newsagents to sell tickets, perhaps taking tickets from door to door, selling at canteens or pitheads. In Scotland, an organisation called 'Friends of Theatre Workshop' helped with such tasks. Sometimes the takings were so low that the actors had to rely on individuals' charity to eat, at others a bag of chips with a few fish was shared among them. Forty years later, Elizabeth MacLennan, of the 7:84 Company, probably the only British theatre company that could be compared to Theatre Workshop, wrote of such experiences:

> The delights of the open road soon begin to pall—damp B and Bs with pink nylon sheets, Alsatians roaming the corridors, cold fried eggs and marble-eyed landladies, mouth-bending coffee, smoke-filled vans, breaking down, the search for cots, washing shirts at two in the morning, company meetings, greasy chips, pies and chips, pies and beans and chips, more company meetings.[11]

Even these sacrifices never really brought the reward of eager working-class audiences or auditoria without empty seats. Women and children were more likely to come than men, for whom theatre was not deemed an appropriate entertainment. But auditoria were rarely more than half full, though attendance often improved somewhat when the company appeared for the second or third time. Too often, though, working-class audiences would find the drama 'like a sermon', and only occasionally would experimental theatre win a warm welcome here. 'That was how it used to go, weeks of dreadful dates, empty halls, icy digs, then some wonderful character would open the door to a welcoming world where theatre and the arts flourished.'[12] And despite the belief in the work—the fervour, even— inevitably the group was often poisoned with petty squabbles, disillusion, tiredness and the need for money. Gerry Raffles was particularly jealous of Ewan MacColl, though MacColl and Joan Littlewood were divorced in 1950, and MacColl married Jean Newlove, the Laban-trained choreographer of the company. But gossip, rumours and resentments, personal jealousies, love affairs and the ends of love affairs become debilitating. Ideological differences also appeared, especially by 1950 when many of the original group had departed, and others had joined. Moreover, some were pleased, though more probably were saddened, that one-night-stand touring made regular actor training nearly impossible.

There were credits to set against this heavy debit account. The visit to Sweden in the spring of 1951 produced considerable acclaim and perceptive reviews that again likened Theatre Workshop to the theatres of pre-war European masters. Early in 1952, Sam Wanamaker and Michael Redgrave watched a rehearsal of *Uranium 235*, and were so impressed they booked the Embassy Theatre, Swiss Cottage, for a three-week run. Wanamaker called this 'The most exciting theatre I have ever seen'[13] and Redgrave, perceptively enough, noted that the company's work achieved a 'synthesis' that was 'moving and exciting'.[14] The three-week run was unexpectedly successful and notable particularly perhaps for a Saturday morning performance for 'the profession'. *The Times* called Theatre Workshop 'a model of what a theatre company should be'.[15] But when it went on to the Comedy Theatre in the West End, any hopes of a financial success were soon discarded. Finally there was the Edinburgh Peoples' Festival, forerunner of the Fringe, where the company appeared in 1949, 1951 and 1952. They often played to capacity audiences—an unfamiliar but rewarding experience—and members enjoyed not touring, eating better, sleeping in the same bed for weeks at a time. *The Travellers* in 1952 was especially successful (though the *Spectator* dismissed it as 'propaganda'), with the stage representing a railway station and the train in which most of the action happened thrust right through the centre of the auditorium to the back, with audience on either side.

This was followed by another schools tour of *Twelfth Night* in the Glasgow area that autumn, but even MacColl admitted that 'by early November the position had become desperate. We were once again penniless and homeless.'[16] Could touring continue? As early as March 1947 when the company was nearly ejected from Ormesby Hall after some 'theatrical' behaviour by some members, Joan Littlewood was thinking: 'perhaps we can get a theatre and live near it'. It was essential, she told Gerry Raffles, 'that we work with Laban, and for that we must go to Manchester'.[17] In January 1948, they proposed a 'theatre centre' for Liverpool, incorporating a school and an experimental theatre company. Setting their centre against the London domination of theatre and culture generally, they claimed support from George Bernard Shaw, Tyrone Guthrie, Michel Saint-Denis, Frederick Valk, Hugh McDiarmid, Rudolf Laban, Sybil Thorndike, Friedrich Wolf, James Bridie, Margaret Morris and Leon Underwood. Laban would direct the movement training, Nelson Illingworth the vocal work and Littlewood and MacColl the acting and production training. The proposed centre could open in March 1948; according to Gerry Raffles's document, all it needed was the 'active support and goodwill' of potential trustees. This, however, was not forthcoming.[18] In 1949, settling in Manchester was again mooted, and later Ewan MacColl thought Glasgow would be suitable, so that his work could be joined with the current Scottish cultural renaissance associated with McDiarmid, Norman MacCaig, Hamish Henderson and others. Henderson even identified a possible base in East Kilbride, though nothing came of this, either.

But then Gerry Raffles discovered the possibility of leasing the Theatre Royal, Stratford-atte-Bow in the East End of London, and Theatre Workshop moved there at the start of 1953.

CHAPTER EIGHT

The Plays of Ewan MacColl

'I think the only style that was ever unique about Theatre Workshop was given to it by Ewan's writing.'[1] However that may be, Ewan MacColl's plays certainly gave the first eight years of Theatre Workshop's existence much of their unique *timbre*. From his very earliest memory of a friend of his parents doing somersaults, through the 'handsome yellow tissue paper robes' he wore as a boy in the local May Queen ceremony, to the numerous street entertainers he watched as a youth—singers, escapologists, clog-dancers, Punch and Judy shows and much more[2]—Ewan MacColl had responded fulsomely to theatre in its broadest sense, and later, at school, he devoured *A Midsummer Night's Dream* and Maeterlinck's *The Bluebird*, and, in the public library, plays such as those of Eugene O'Neill.

But these glimpses only seemed to deepen his anger at his own exclusion from a world where such things were accessible. 'I really wanted to tear down the world', he recalled.[3] The anger contributed to the placing of politics in the centre of his life, but the excitement about the theatre fed his passion to communicate. Almost instinctively he seems to have realised that his mission was to articulate the aspirations of his class, to help to delineate and even shape working-class identity and working-class understanding. His anger, and the political dimension he was able to fit it to, gave Ewan MacColl the motivation to be a playwright. In other words, he was not interested in becoming a playwright as such; he wanted to communicate the working-class experience of life, and contribute with his skills, such as he felt them to be, to changing the world order which held them in poverty, or subjection.

Politics, as the character Pavilek in *The Good Soldier Schweik* is to discover, are unavoidable. Even though Pavilek refuses to speak about the assassination in Sarajevo, he is still taken to gaol. For MacColl, politics, perhaps inevitably, meant Marxism ('When a guy starts talking about politics, you can bet your life he's a Red', says Stevens in *The Travellers*[4]). Marxism, as MacColl understood it, gives the human being the decisive role in shaping human destiny. You can (or you can help to) change the world. It gives you a specific place—and indeed a specific responsibility—

for the way history develops, and in the 1920s and 1930s, when MacColl
grew up, many believed that history was more significant than, say,
psychology in the shaping of individual lives. The plays interrogate this
materialist philosophy, and its political implications, as this excerpt from
Uranium 235 suggests:

YOUTH:	And these atoms—what exactly are they?
DEMOCRITUS:	They are the elements out of which everything is made.
YOUTH:	Everything?
DEMOCRITUS:	Everything. The soil and the seed in it. The sun which warms it and the rain which moistens it. The rocks and mountains, the seas, the birds in the air and the blind worm. All are made of the same elements.
YOUTH:	And man?
DEMOCRITUS:	Yes, man too. All men, the senator, the merchant, the soldier, the slave.
1ST BUSINESSMAN:	What's that you say?
DEMOCRITUS:	We were discussing philosophy.
1ST BUSINESSMAN:	Philosophy? It sounded like treason.
SILK MERCHANT:	Did somebody say 'treason'?
DEMOCRITUS:	I assure you, sir, you are mistaken. I am Democritus, a philosopher and no politician.
1ST BUSINESSMAN:	I distinctly heard you say that the slave is equal to the senator.
DEMOCRITUS:	I merely said that, in my opinion, all men—indeed all things—shared a common origin.
WOMAN:	Does that include women?
DEMOCRITUS :	Everything that is.
2ND BUSINESSMAN:	Is this slave my equal then?
DEMOCRITUS:	In the eyes of nature, yes.[5]

The distortion of capitalism was to divide people into two classes—'In this
world there are two kinds of people; people who give orders and people
who take orders,' says Chick in *Rogue's Gallery*[6]—and class becomes the site
of conflict in MacColl's plays. Good and bad are mapped onto the class
system by MacColl. Good is associated with the working class's near
future, as here in *The Travellers*:

> How wonderful it was to feel
> One's fingers on the pulse of history;
> To know that we were the surgeons
> Who, when the time came, would cut
> The cancer out of an ailing world.[7]

And bad belongs to the old bourgeois world, which is dying, as its desperate representative, Graubard, discovers in the last scene in *The Other Animals*:

(The trumpet sounds again.)

GRAUBARD:	There it is again.
HANAU:	The second summons.
GRAUBARD:	Some cock with a full crop Impatient for the tread.
ROBERT:	It stands on the roof of night.
HANAU:	It sees the dawn.
CHORUS OF THE DEAD:	Tick-tock, tick-tock.
ROBERT:	The minutes fall like dead leaves.
CHORUS OF THE DEAD:	Tick-tock, tick-tock.
HANAU:	The world dies in a bed of mould.
CHORUS OF THE DEAD:	Tick-tock tick-tock, tick-tock tick-tock.
GRAUBARD:	My ears are practising an imposture Upon my reason. There's no clock here, no voices, Only the dry scampering of rat's feet.
ROBERT:	And the heart tolling its own funeral.[8]

MacColl is heir to that tradition of British radicalism and Marxism that stresses the historical significance of working-class men toiling in heavy industry—miners, railwaymen, steel workers, and the like. The revolution, in this tradition, is entirely a male affair, and heavy industry is the springboard to the future. Thus, Adamson, in *Hell Is What You Make It*, doubts his right to a place in Paradise because he has not helped to make it. But he promises that his labour will help to transform hell into a paradise: the industrial worker is figured as the new Prometheus. And interestingly, Paradise as described is a kind of half-remembered rural idyll, where the industrial worker lived before the factories of the Industrial Revolution sucked him (and her, perhaps) into the hellish slums of the industrial city. MacKenna, the Durham miner, tells Adamson:

> There are mountains and lakes and valleys and plains; there are toons and villages. Whiles it's fine and whiles it rains. The Spring comes as it comes here, wi' its steamin' furrows and the reek of dung on the farmlands. The days lengthen into Summer and the wheat and barley drowse in a haze o' heat. In the backend the fruit hangs heavy on the trees, and the sides o' the hills are brave wi' the purple heather and the blaze o' bracken. The nichts close in and lasses lie wi' their lads in the lithe o' corn ricks. And winter comes, just as it comes here.

ADAMSON:	And the people, what are they like?
MACKENNA:	Oh, just people. Colliers and farmers; engineers, moulders and weavers; just ordinary folk.[9]

When Johnny Noble returns from the war, 'two girls' sing 'Winter is past and the leaves are green', even though it is to the dirty industrial port of Hull that he returns.[10]

It may be a romantic vision, but it helped to put the devil of capitalism into focus. The capitalists in *Hell Is What You Make It* are so ruthless, they make hell hell for Lucifer himself, who is forced to leave this warm home. Capitalism may not be a sin, but it is certainly a crime in this view. Eustace Brokenbrow, in the same play, compares 'the work that goes into a well-planned smash-and-grab raid', with all its risks of gaol and poor rewards for selling the stolen goods, with that of the capitalist, who simply lets the workers make the commodities he will sell and take the profits from. Conversely, in *Rogue's Gallery*, the ex-cat-burglar, Chick, asserts that 'crime is a business and it's run like any other business', and later declares ruefully: 'There's only one way to get rich and that's by robbing the poor. That's what the poor are there for. They're legal game for anybody's gun. That's the big advantage of being a big-time crook, the law works with you.'[11] More than this, capitalism is responsible for the commodification of potential means of salvation, such as science, in *Uranium 235*, and for the reification of people, such as servants in *Rogue's Gallery*. It is also the begetter of wars, as in *The Good Soldier Schweik*. But working-class organisation can beat it: the women in *Operation Olive Branch* organise a proto-trade union to bring the men to their senses.

Not surprisingly, Ewan MacColl was never absorbed into what Althusser called the 'ideological state apparatus', those unofficial institutions of culture—the Sunday papers, the national theatres, and the like—that control much of our lives unseen, nor was he part of what Gramsci called the 'hegemony'. Indeed, the hegemony is itself the site of many of the struggles in MacColl's plays, as he seeks to give voice to the excluded, and to offer them hope for a better future. Schweik is a hero precisely because he retains his infuriating humanity in the face of everything the hegemony can bring to bear against him.

This fight against the 'culture industry' is an important part of what Modernism seeks to do. In terms of drama, this may mean jangling dramatic rhythms, a jerky, angular structure, vivid moments awkwardly interrupted and so on. To the extent that MacColl's plays are like this, he is virtually the first British Modernist dramatist. The influence of Russian revolutionary drama is obvious—the boxing match in *You're Only Young Once*, for instance, may derive from the boxing match in Eisenstein's production of *The Mexican*—as is that of German drama of the Weimar period, especially that of Toller—the tapping of the prison pipes by the imprisoned in *Hoppla, Such Is Life!* is directly echoed in *The Other Animals*, and the wistful mouthorgan played in *Draw the Fires* is found also in *Johnny*

Noble. Toller's mixing of verse and prose, and fact and fiction, his ability to move from public politics to private life obviously taught MacColl much, and there is frequent resort to Expressionist techniques in his plays: the dreams that punctuate *The Other Animals* are one obvious example. Lorca, too, influenced him. Yet to dismiss this—as Chambers and Prior, for example, do—as 'a rather self-conscious application to the British theatre of European innovations'[12] does less than justice to these plays. Apart from anything else, MacColl owes as much to such contemporary American drama as Sinclair's *Singing Jailbirds*, Rice's *Street Scene* and *The Adding Machine*, Odets's *Waiting for Lefty* and Wilder's *Pullman Car 'Hiawatha'* and *Our Town* as he does to any European models. Moreover, we see frequent traces of Ben Jonson and John Gay, not to mention Lope da Vega's *Fuente Ovejuna* and, importantly, English traditional games and entertainments, such as in the parody of a singing game in *The Other Animals*.

> You cannot escape.
> The quest is a stage
> In the journey between
> The bars of the cage.[13]

This is an exhilarating and unique mix, and Hugh McDiarmid's assessment seems salutary: 'MacColl's work is radically different [. . .] It deals fearlessly and dynamically with the crucial problems of our own day and generation. It is forward-looking, and for its effective production demands the utilisation of all the most advanced theatrical means'. McDiarmid adds: 'It is the work of one fully aware of, and working for, l'avant garde in the theatre the world over'.[14] MacColl is part of, not the dependant of, the European *avant-garde*, and moreover one of Britain's first members of it.

For MacColl, the playwright's problem was one of 'poetics'.[15] Like Bartók, he said he wanted to create as 'the folk create'. In this analogy, the playwright speaks, as does the folk or epic singer, not so much for themselves as for the group, the community or class. 'My ideal was the anonymous author', he said,[16] though it may be doubted whether this is a workable option for the dramatist. It is true that MacColl was remarkably careless of his work, and like many of his Elizabethan predecessors, seemed not to care that few of his plays ever found their way into print. But that was partly because he believed that language's true vitality came only when it was spoken. His joy in words was essentially physical:

> And there were the words, the new words to be taken in the mouth and savoured, dissolved on the tongue, sucked or crunched between the teeth, pouched in the cheek like gob-stoppers or licked to the smooth, brown nut kernel like sugared almonds; the jewelled and shining words of poets, the blazing words of political struggle, the endlessly uncoiling words of argument.[17]

Language is at the heart of what MacColl wished to do—to bring the vernacular spoken by working people onto the stage. This, he argued, was what the Elizabethans had achieved, and it was what was needed in theatre again. His later assessment of his work is honest enough:

> I had attempted to evolve a dramatic utterance which would crystallize, or at least reflect, a certain kind of working-class speech. In each of [the plays] there are moments when the language takes off, comes alive, but they are only moments and I was always aware that I was far from having solved the problem I had set myself.[18]

Maybe this judgment is too modest.

In fact, there is probably a misunderstanding at the heart of MacColl's concern with language. He wishes to privilege what he perceives as typical working-class speech over other kinds of speech. Indeed, he sometimes seems in danger of painting morality onto speech patterns: 'Highly educated people use language for the purpose of hiding behind it, whereas non-educated people tend to use language for expressing both their feelings and their ideas at the same time'.[19] Whether this is true or not, one of the strengths of drama is in the interplay of voices, the clashes of different registers, types of jargon, means of deploying words: the dialogism of heteroglossia, as Mikhail Bakhtin might have put it. By trying—though failing—to elevate what he perceived as working-class speech above other sorts in this way, MacColl does a disservice not only to his own plays, but also, ironically, to his working-class audience, for most of them are cleverer than this attitude implies.

In any case, there was more to MacColl's dramaturgy than its language. He knew that 'if the theatre is to play an important role in the lives of the people of our time then it must develop techniques which rival in efficiency the complex machines which working people handle every day of their lives'.[20] This position—very much in the European modernist tradition—involved a rejection of naturalistic illusionism, and a knowledge of the play's 'ultimate objective'.[21] This in turn led to a consideration of the *form* of the play. MacColl began to learn this in the 1930s, and his early adaptations, *The Good Soldier Schweik* and *Operation Olive Branch* (*Lysistrata*), lead naturally to *Classic Soil* (written in collaboration with Joan Littlewood) and *Hell Is What You Make It*. His first play for Theatre Workshop—the play that was the first produced by Theatre Workshop—was *Johnny Noble*, which tells the story of a working-class lad growing up in a 1930s fishing port, Hull. He is denied the opportunity to become a fisherman because his girlfriend's family has suffered too many calamities at this trade, so he goes 'on the tramp', looking for a job. This allows MacColl an epic journey across the Britain of his youth, its blight and despair, till Johnny gets caught up, first in the Spanish Civil War, and then in the World War. When he returns home to the ever-patient Mary (the traditional working-class male's perennial dream), he knows the future lies open, but it is also challenged by the energetic Roaring Boys who wish to restore the capitalism of the past.

Johnny Noble begins by evoking a working-class community like that which MacColl knew as he grew up in the streets of Salford, and where 'you had to develop a sense of community, you had to develop loyalties, otherwise you just didn't survive, you couldn't survive'.[22] The play therefore dramatises, and in a sense, celebrates, the 'lived relationships' of individuals to their (working-class) community. The concept of community, however, as we have already seen, is peculiarly elusive. Is class a community? There seem to be communities within communities—the group of women, the gamblers, the unemployed, and so on. As Bauman has pointed out, '"Community" stands for a kind of world which is not, regrettably, available to us', adding that if 'community' is what provides us with security, it is also what denies us individual freedom.[23] Gusfield suggests that 'community' only affects the present in so far as it refers either to a never-existent past or to a dreamed-of future. In reality, it is shifting and uncatchable. Among other things, community seemed historically to endow work with meaning, and as we have noted, MacColl accepted Marx's argument that the Industrial Revolution had destroyed community, replacing it with social alienation. Model villages such as New Lanark or Saltaire were created precisely to regain community within the Industrial Revolution, for most working people during the Industrial Revolution were thrown into 'slums', overcrowded brick-built streets where community seemed impossible. Yet in terms of sociability and mutual support, these places often showed glimpses of community that were stronger than anything experienced in apparently more salubrious surroundings. Thus, though the reality of community was elusive, it still seemed an ideal worth striving for.

Drama had, of course, addressed this subject before. Lope de Vega's *Fuente Ovejuna*, which Theatre Union had produced in 1937, shows a village community standing out against their oppressor. The community in *Fuente Ovejuna* is defined by the young lovers, which suggests an orientation towards the future, for that is where young love is always headed. The lovers' determination galvanises the community, and draws in all people no matter what their age or gender. Similarly, in *Johnny Noble*, Johnny and Mary's union draws the people together at the end to confront the Roaring Boys.

Johnny Noble re-imagines the 1930s as a process of striving for the community ideal. As such, it may be regarded as the first in a series of plays by Ewan MacColl and Theatre Workshop that address this subject. In this view, *Johnny Noble* is followed by *Landscape with Chimneys* (also known as

Paradise Street), first produced by Theatre Workshop in 1951, and then by
You're Only Young Once, written for the Warsaw Youth Festival of 1953.
Landscape with Chimneys is set in the post-war present, and focuses on the
denizens of a street in a town very much like Salford. Two soldiers, Hugh
and Frank, return from the Second World War, and the play tracks their
lives, and the lives of their neighbours, through the following years as they
love, marry, work and struggle. The key communal deficit of the period is
seen as the housing shortage, which, according to Susan Cooper, 'was
desperate. Demobilization was moving quickly [. . .] and thousands were
homeless, living cramped in rented or borrowed rooms. Despair,
rootlessness, and the strain of over-crowding brought them to a state where
their patience was ready to snap'.[24] In the play, the drama stems from
precisely this. Frank's wife, Trudy, has nowhere to go with their baby while
Frank seeks his fortune as a speedway rider, while Hugh and Clare finally
decide to end their misery by squatting in a big empty house nearby. The
police arrive to evict them, but the street dwellers band together, rather like
the villagers of *Fuente Ovejuna*, to resist. They sing a stirring union song
written originally by a striking coal miner's wife from Kentucky in the
1930s, 'Which side are you on?', thereby challenging the audience, too.

You're Only Young Once takes the concern with community into the
future. As the young couples quarrel and Johnnie the would-be boxer
decides to give up his hopes, Lil the costermonger (played originally by
Joan Littlewood) asserts the strength of community in a song:

> I've known you since you was a snotty-nosed kid,
> And I can remember the strokes that you did;
> When you hung round me barrow, you thought you were fly,
> And when you pinched the odd apple I'd wink a blind eye.
>
> . . .
>
> There's your pals on the railways and them at the docks,
> The machiners and cutters in tailoring shops;
> There's the kids on the corner, they all think you're good,
> If you let 'em down, Johnnie, your name'll be mud.[25]

Such communal solidarity in itself, however, cannot resolve the problems
of lived experience. Instead, the play proposes that these troubles will be
left behind at the Warsaw Festival of Youth, and as more and more of the
characters decide to go there, the play's rhythm speeds up, the frowns drop
away, and the play ends as a sort of celebratory ceilidh with dance, song and
laughter. Even Charlie the teddy boy is persuaded:

> CARRIE: Charlie, why don't we go?
> CHARLIE: Go where?

CARRIE: To Warsaw.
CHARLIE: What could we do there?
STEVE: A million things, if you can run, dance, sing, kick a ball, swim
or just go around feeling good. If you can play table-tennis . . .
CHARLIE: Table-tennis! There's the lark. Mister, you're looking at an
expert.[26]

Warsaw is, of course, the capital of Poland, which was then a Communist
country, and the play resolves the problem of community in the utopian
dream of the future Communist world:

We'll make this festival a taste
Of what the world could be;
With the whole world walking arm in arm
Along with you and me.[27]

This may look naive in the twenty-first century, and indeed Chambers and
Prior's accusation that the earlier *Johnny Noble* is vitiated by 'a saccharine
quality' could be widened to include *Landscape with Chimneys* and *You're
Only Young Once*, too. But, as the *Manchester Guardian* critic who saw *Johnny
Noble* said, this play—these plays—give 'a magnificent impression of the
modern workers' world in peace and war'. The energy and theatricality
carry conviction in performance. The plays produce—or help to produce—
community, at least partly as *Fuente Ovejuna* does, firstly through group,
rather than individual, struggle, and then through the centrality of pairs of
young lovers—Johnny and Mary in *Johnny Noble*, Hugh and Clare, and
Frank and Trudy, but also the outsiders, Gypsy and Kathleen, in *Landscape
with Chimneys*, and Johnnie and Mary, Charlie and Carrie, Steve and Nancy
and Dan and Jean in *You're Only Young Once*. Is it only coincidence that as
the sequence comes closer to its conclusion, there are more and more pairs
of lovers?

MacColl's other plays for Theatre Workshop show an impressive variety
of styles and political subject matter. *Uranium 235* was triggered by the
horror of Hiroshima, and only written after MacColl, who left a depressed
council school at the age of fourteen, had been given a crash course in
science history and quantum physics. It argues, rather as Brecht's *Galileo*
does, that science has been hijacked and must be won back for humanity,
but does it with a verve and theatricality that Brecht's work never attempts.
The Other Animals—inspired, by the way, by Mahler's 'Resurrection'
Symphony, which provides a background to much of the action—deals
with 'a problem of human identity', according to its author, 'a problem of
conscience . . . of a man attempting to live with absolute truths'.[28] Hanau is
a political prisoner, Robert (Hanau's first name) his *alter ego*, his
imagination that seeks an escape from Hanau's torture. The internal mental
struggles of the protagonist are presented in episodic form, mostly in verse

and with dance, song and scenes that make enormous demands on the actors. There is something of *Singing Jailbirds* here, set as it is wholly in the prisoner's cell, which recalls also Mr Zero in prison in Rice's *The Adding Machine* as well as the prison scene in Toller's *Draw the Fires*. But it has its own integrity, and its own power, and is perhaps the nearest MacColl approaches to tragedy. *Rogue's Gallery* is a Shavian dissection of the class system, in some ways recalling the exactly contemporary *Venus Observed* by Christopher Fry, though with none of Fry's trivialising whimsy. There is an autobiographical strand in the play's portrayal of a theatre company unable to obtain funding, with a liberating final realisation that such support is not necessary:

> ALLAN: We start rehearsing on Monday.
> JOAN: But how can we? We have no money.
> ALLAN: No, but we've got everything else. We've got ideas, and the taste for life. No theatre needs more than that.
> LOTTIE: Then we're really going to begin!
> KATE: This is not the way you talked before.
> ALLAN: We were looking for the easy way, but there is no easy way for people like us.
> DAVE: But we've got no equipment.
> ALLAN: Then we'll do without equipment. We'll rehearse in a back-room and find our audiences where we can.[29]

Finally, *The Travellers* was a kind of *drame noir*, atmospherically like the coeval film of *The Third Man*. Its metaphysical theme is only gradually revealed: the play ostensibly depicts an express train rushing towards an unknown destination, which we slowly realise is a third world war. Some passengers attempt to stop the train, others want to keep it going. Reminiscent of Wilder's *Pullman Car 'Hiawatha'* 'tearing through' the countryside,[30] *The Travellers* also has affinities with the medieval image of the Ship of Fools in their fools' paradise, and contains some of MacColl's most interesting characters. The play may be vitiated, however, by the heaviness of its politics, too often expatiated upon in long speeches and abstract—certainly not vernacular—language. Nevertheless, it should be added that it was notably successful in performance in 1952, and was revived at Stratford East in 1953.

Though Ewan MacColl left Theatre Workshop in the 1950s, he wrote a number of other plays. *Blitz Song*, also known as *The Long Winter*, is a Zola-esque piece of naturalism using the story of Agamemnon's return from Troy transposed to the return home of a soldier after the Second World War. *So Long at the Fair* is also about soldiers, this time a group who have been imprisoned for two years for refusing to obey orders. They now have to adjust to civilian life, which is imaged as a grotesque fairground. *Ours the*

Fruit was commissioned by the Co-operative Society, and is a well-structured documentary history of the co-operative movement, which was produced at Drury Lane in 1963. After a number of revues, known as *The Festival of Fools* in the late 1960s and early 1970s, MacColl's last play was *The Shipmaster*, a long historical play set in 1905, and performed in 1981. This impressive output, like that of other original British playwrights of the second half of the twentieth century, such as Arnold Wesker and Edward Bond, was often more highly regarded on the continent than in Britain, and productions—especially in Germany—particularly of *Uranium 235*, *Rogue's Gallery* and *So Long at the Fair* (which ironically probably contains MacColl's best dramatic language in English), were often notably successful.

In all these plays, MacColl is searching for a dramatic form that can adequately respond to his concerns. He rejected naturalism, the inadequacy of which John McGrath suggested:

> Naturalism is part of the middle-class theatre's armoury of suppression because naturalistic theatre *contains* arguments. It is very easy for a strong argument—because it is put into the mouth of one character—to be seen as that character's point of view, and (therefore) nullified.[31]

(This, by the way, is the problem with the otherwise excellent *The Travellers*.) MacColl preferred a kind of documentary descended from the agit-prop of the 1930s. As Derek Paget has pointed out, 'documentary theatre does not necessarily portray the real realistically'.[32] Therefore, 'What we really needed was to create a form which was infinitely flexible, which would make it possible for us to move backwards and forwards in time and space [. . .] and which could accommodate improvisations'.[33]

MacColl's drama is packed with variety. It includes long speeches, like Dalton's nineteenth-century explanation of the atmosphere in *Uranium 235*, or Shaunnessy's tall tale about his heroism in Venezuela, in *Landscape with Chimneys*; complex verse, like that in *The Other Animals*; and knockabout comedy, as with Einstein and the Puppet Master's Secretary in *Uranium 235*. In *Operation Olive Branch* the Magistrate 'quotes' Churchill's gestures, in *You're Only Young Once* Johnnie mimes a furious boxing match, in *Uranium 235* the Chorus 'collapse like wax figures' and in *Johnny Noble* the actors enact a battle between a dive bombing plane and a ship at sea virtually through movement alone. There is also the glorious 'ham' of *Operation Olive Branch's* Herald describing his favour-withholding wife:

> HERALD: She dances, too, but for me alone. Oh, Pelline, Pelline, my wife, my little fig tree, my honey-pot, my ambrosia, my diddle-pout, my puggy, my all. Oh, but she's so cruel to me!
> *(He throws himself on the Magistrate.)*

MAGISTRATE: That's enough now! That's enough! Unhand me! Let go of me, I say![34]

There is the boogie-woogie in *Johnny Noble*, the raucous dance in the pub, and also the traditional Broom dance in *You're Only Young Once*, and an Irish jig and a ballroom waltz in *Uranium 235*. As for songs, there are notable traditional tunes with new words in *Johnny Noble* and *You're Only Young Once*, as well as, in the latter, the jazzy, futuristic 'Space Girl's Song'. In *Operation Olive Branch*, there is something approaching an American croon –

> I can't sleep when the moon shines on the plain,
> Can't sleep with the red moon shining on the plain,
> 'Cos I ain't with my baby, oh honey, I'm in pain . . .[35]

– and, in *Landscape with Chimneys*, a series of songs in different idioms: a Latin-American number, 'I Met Her in Venezuela', the fierce American Union song, 'Which Side Are You On?', 'Dirty Old Town', the lazy ballad that has since become well known, and more.

These are embedded in a structure that depends on contrast, or interruption, for its effect. For instance, in *Uranium 235* Democritus' exposition is interrupted by

(The 1st Actor suddenly steps out of his role and interrupts the proceedings.)
1ST ACTOR: God! What a load of codswallop!
1ST ACTRESS: Why? What's wrong?
1ST ACTOR: The whole bloody scene's wrong.[36]

In *The Travellers*, the intense scenes are interrupted by the sound of the train's wheels accelerating:

KATHERINE: They can stop the train if they have a mind to. Goodbye, Mr MacLean.
MACLEAN: Wait . . . I'll come with you.
(They disappear along the corridor. The lights go out. The rattle of the wheels is faded up and then held behind.)

MICROPHONE
VOICE: Attention please! There is no occasion for passengers to be disturbed by the blackout. It is merely a precautionary measure in the interests of security.
(The rattle of wheels is faded up again for a moment, then held down behind second voice on changed acoustic.)

CAUTIONARY
VOICE: Everything is taken care of. Everything is planned.
The bland impersonal voice soothes nerves; the hand
Of authority erases fears.
(Brief reprise of wheels.)
Breath condenses beads of tears upon the window's eyes.

Ties speak to wheels in triple time; the whistle cries
In the muted darkness.

(*Blast of train whistle.*) Etc.[37]

In *Johnny Noble*, the beginning of the war is presented through 'a great sustained phrase of music', then by the voice of the prime minister speaking from Downing Street. The drone of a plane interrupts this, and this in turn is interrupted by the 'heavy ticking of a clock'. Then we are on a train station, with an echoey voice announcing the next trains, and couples standing in 'yellow pools of light'. The men are called to the train, the couples embrace and as there is 'a sudden, loud blast of escaping steam', the women wave their handkerchiefs. The train departs, time is lost—'And everything is left unsaid except—Goodbye'.[38] Each brief glimpse, interrupted by the next, helps to 'uncover' the truth, in Walter Benjamin's word.

We have in MacColl's work, in fact, excellent examples of montage. Montage is more than simply interruptions, however: Eisenstein referred to a 'montage of attractions', meaning more than the use of contrast or the juxtapositioning of unexpected sequences. He suggested that montage was dynamic and provocative, that the arrangement of vivid incidents ('attractions') was in itself a means of stimulating the audience into making meanings.[39] Montage may be figured as 'link' montage, which is thematic, and seen in *The Travellers* and *Landscape with Chimneys*, or a 'collision' montage, which is more like that of *Johnny Noble* or *Uranium 235*, and which fractures continuity in such a way as to shift the responsibility of making sense of the events shown onto the audience.

This process is encouraged by MacColl's use of meta-theatre, derived perhaps from Thornton Wilder, to demystify his processes. It is frequently seen in his play's openings. Thus, the pre-war *Classic Soil* begins:

ACTOR: The play has started. The lights are focused
         on the central figure of the first scene.[40]

Johnny Noble opens:

1ST NARRATOR (*singing*):   Here is a stage –
2ND NARRATOR (*speaking*):   A platform twenty-five feet by fifteen.
1ST NARRATOR (*singing*):   A microcosm of the world.
2ND NARRATOR (*speaking*):   Here the sun is an amber flood and the
                             moon a thousand-watt spot.
1ST NARRATOR (*singing*):   Here shall be space,
                             Here we shall act time.[41]

Landscape with Chimneys begins:

(The curtains rise on an unlit stage on which only the merest suggestion of a set is visible. The stage manager is discovered checking the wing openings. This done, he looks up at the lights.)

STAGE MANAGER: How are the lights?

ELECTRICIAN: Four out front and four on the set. I'll bring them up.

(The front of the house spots are faded up.)

ELECTRICIAN: I'm using them for outdoor effects.

STAGE MANAGER: They're a bit gaudy, aren't they?

ELECTRICIAN: It's meant to be sunshine.[42]

Even the late *Ours the Fruit* relies on the same aesthetic:

(Apart from black curtains and eight packing cases of various sizes, the stage is without furniture. When the auditorium lights fade, the stage is lit merely by working lights. Theatrical company enter, wearing street clothes, and look about them.)

1ST GIRL: Is this it?

PRODUCER: This is it.

1ST MAN: A bit bare, isn't it?

PRODUCER: There'll be lights and music. They'll help.

(Actor appears from offstage carrying tall hats.)

3RD MAN: Look what I've found.

2ND MAN: At least we won't be entirely naked.

PRODUCER: I don't really think that costumes are absolutely vital ... I mean, you can be a convincing villain without a special uniform.[43]

Many of these plays continue this anti-illusionism throughout. For instance, the Stage Manager's is by far the longest part in *Landscape with Chimneys*. About a third of the way through, he asks the audience: 'Don't you ever feel you're being cheated? I mean after all, you've paid your money to see a play, a drama, and so far nothing's happened.'[44] Later, he has an argument with a 'real' character about the nature of drama, box-office appeal against 'truth'. And near the end, Gypsy enters and asks the Stage Manager, 'Have you seen Hugh?' 'Not since the last scene', the Stage Manager replies. In *Uranium 235*, the Singer apologises that 'we couldn't afford to put Roman soldiers on the stage. For that kind of thing you need subsidies, which we don't have. We're not a rich company.' A little later a character rushes on, asking another to help him fix his costume. 'Where's Dalton?' he asks. 'He's got a difficult costume change', comes the reply. 'This jumping about from one character to another is bloody confusing.' And so on. Such self-conscious theatre reassures the spectator that what she or he is watching is 'only' a show, but suggests that it is 'believable' at some level because there is no attempt to fool the audience. This is, of course, the 'great theatre of life', in which 'all the world's a stage'. By demystifying the stage, the play also demystifies the world. Who holds the power here? The technician, the worker, who with a flick of a switch can transform the stage, the world. There is no magic in this, it is simple, and implies that the world, too, can be changed.

This thesis is complemented by MacColl's deliberate use of performativity. 'MC squared equals E' is a ballet. Earlier in *Uranium 235*, the second actor proposes:

> Perhaps we ought to examine those problems in our own way.
> 2ND ACTRESS: Which way's that?
> 2ND ACTOR: As actors.
> 1ST ACTRESS: Where do we begin?
> 2ND ACTOR: At the beginning, where else?[45]

In *You're Only Young Once*, the teddy boy and his girlfriend only become animated when they 'act out' the science-fiction film they have seen. And *Rogue's Gallery* includes a small acting company in its cast and is full of such 'acting out', both comic and intense. Actors even report on what has happened in earlier scenes by acting it out, during which they criticise each other, show one another how such an action was performed originally, and so on.

This theatre, a material reality, is thus a vehicle for both perceiving and representing reality, both what is meant and how it is conveyed. The plays perform class and class struggle, and thereby demystify the operation of class power. In *Johnny Noble* the people at home read about the Spanish Civil War in their newspapers. It seems a long way away, but, says the Narrator,

> it could be you . . . we'll act it.
> 1ST YOUTH: But don't I need a black shirt?
> 1ST NARRATOR: Don't worry—Fascism doesn't always wear a black shirt.
> MICROPHONE VOICE: It is early morning. The city is still asleep. You have lain awake all night waiting for this moment, the moment when time stops . . .[46]

The actors seem to go to sleep, while the execution is 'danced' in a kind of slow motion parody of itself. When the lights come up, everyone is discovered still sleeping. The Narrator wakes them up, and a letter comes from Johnny to Mary. 'Oh, Johnny, I wish you were here', she says, and immediately he is. And he explains how, before he was involved in the Spanish Civil War, he used to feel 'there was no place in the world' for him, now he knows he has a place and he is important.

> I've discovered that everything that's worth looking at in all the towns and cities of the world was built by people like us. I don't feel lonely any more because I know there's a man in Madrid just like me and at this moment

he's fighting a German tank with a bottle of petrol [. . .] I know who I am now and I know why I'm here.[47]

This play dialogues with political reality, demonstrates an argument, suggests alternative narratives, and hence alternative possibilities, through its hybrid form—a dance, a song, an 'acting out'. MacColl's drama is thus able to suggest that nothing is permanent, nothing is as it seems. In 'Dirty Old Town', probably MacColl's best-known song, from *Landscape with Chimneys*, Ginger sings: 'I found my love *by the gasworks croft*'. This is clearly an impossible place to find love, yet the fact is stark. 'Dreamed a dream *by the old canal*.'[48] People who inhabit places 'by an old canal' are not usually permitted to dream. But here, the possibilities suddenly extend, and they can be realised.

It is important, too, that the stage itself is a public platform, not a mystical altar. From the days of the Red Megaphones, MacColl's drama aims to focus his chosen audience's attention on ideas and events, rather than on the characters' individuality. This non-subjectivity implies empowerment rather than introspection. Furthermore, the presentational mode implicates the audience, and thereby invites them to adopt an attitude.

PUPPET MASTER:	Let us pause here.
SECRETARY:	But the audience . . .!
PUPPET MASTER:	The audience?
SECRETARY:	Is it wise to let them see so much of you?
PUPPET MASTER:	They will have forgotten me by the morning.
SECRETARY:	Are you sure?
PUPPET MASTER:	I know my audience. In a few minutes they will leave this building imagining that a man can walk out of his own life. They don't realize that they are the main protagonists in the play.[49]

It is a challenge few audiences can resist. The black drapes at the back of the *Johnny Noble* stage—what are they?

> Following the performance of *Johnny Noble* on a 'bare' stage in Glasgow, a hundred or so schoolchildren were asked to write an essay on what they had seen. Almost without exception, they described, in great detail, the streets in which they themselves lived. A similar response was made by children in South Wales and County Durham.[50]

After the legendary performance of *Uranium 235* at Butlin's holiday camp, Filey, in May 1946, Howard Goorney commented:

> *Uranium* was not an easy show—it was telling an involved story through many different theatrical styles—but the audience were thoroughly absorbed. So much so that when the time came for me to 'interrupt' from

the auditorium as part of the action, I was man-handled by a large, outraged lady, and told to 'get out if you don't want to listen.' The warm response of the Butlin holidaymakers to *Uranium 235* was a confirmation of what we had always believed—that there was no necessity to play down or compromise when faced with a working-class audience.[51]

Sean O'Casey called *Uranium 235* 'a fine documentary play dealing fearlessly and poetically with the crucial problems of our day', adding that 'Marlowe is in the wings'.[52] Perhaps if more attention had been paid to Ewan MacColl's plays before 1956, the amazement at the plays of Bertolt Brecht would not have been so great. MacColl is not Brecht, though perhaps for British theatregoers he was a kind of Marlowe to Brecht's Shakespeare, for his best plays have an epic quality not dissimilar to Brecht's. MacColl no less than Brecht disproves Karl Marx's contention that epic is not a possible form today, an irony he would have enjoyed. And as the old manual, industrial working class fades into British history, it is right that we should understand it. Ewan MacColl's is virtually the only drama in English that puts the twentieth-century British working-class's experience at its centre.

CHAPTER NINE

Actor Training

Perhaps Theatre Workshop's most original feature was its practice of training for all company members. Initially the motivation came from Ewan MacColl's desire to project his message with maximum impact. 'It was necessary to train from the very beginning and look at the concept of theatre in a completely new way'.[1] Her unfinished training at RADA had told Joan Littlewood that a training method was needed that not only helped theatre to be relevant to the world, but also one which would produce the kind of versatile actor she and MacColl both sought. Moreover, the Workers' Theatre Movement's desire for 'strong' movement, and its strictures on 'girlish' voices were well remembered.

From the 1930s, training was almost relentless. In 1938, Rosalie Williams joined Theatre Union and was 'overwhelmed':

> The range and intensity of the training programme that Joan and Ewan had worked out, and the combination of their unique talents seemed quite extraordinary [. . .] Each night at seven o'clock we reported to a huge empty room over a furniture store in Deansgate, Manchester, and also on Sunday afternoons and evenings. We started each evening with relaxation exercises, lying on the floor. Then voice production, Stanislavsky, ballet, movement and mime.[2]

The training programme had probably begun seriously with the production of *Newsboy* in 1934 when dance had first been employed, but what Williams experienced here was a largely self-created syllabus worked out by MacColl and Littlewood without reference to existing curricula, largely by trial and error. It related in part to particular productions they were working on, and much was learned from practitioners such as Toller, but it also derived from ideas learned and deduced from books such as Moussinac's *The New Movement in the Theatre*.

After the war, with Theatre Workshop, the intensity, but also the sophistication, of these classes increased. Even during periods when the company was disbanded, they met together to continue training. Thus, during the 1947 tour of Germany, when Littlewood and MacColl remained in England, Gerry Raffles wrote that he would have liked to have returned to an art gallery that the company had visited, 'but that would mean a day off, and Howard insists on training and exercises daily.' Joan Littlewood wrote to Howard Goorney: 'You seem to be organising the training excellently. You are right, we must raise our standards. I don't want production to have to cover up weaknesses. It is important that results are assessed and criticisms made by the whole team, at your weekly production meetings.'[3] This level and intensity of training continued until the mid-1950s, by which time not only the original members of the company, but probably many of the 'second generation', had actually left. With the emphasis in the work changed to new plays after 1956, training perhaps inevitably declined, though Murray Melvin remembered that at least up until 1960, most days' rehearsals began with an hour's work on the movement techniques of Rudolf Laban, often taken by Jean Newlove, the company's Laban specialist, though sometimes by Joan Littlewood herself, and that these 'warm ups' fed directly and often imperceptibly into the rehearsal proper.[4]

A typical timetable for Theatre Union's training programme before the war consisted of:

Monday	Voice Production	6.30–7.45		
	Drill	7.45–8.20		
	Sonnets	8.30–10.0		
Tuesday	Stanislavsky: Units and Objectives			
	Mime to music—'Little Town Gal'			
Wednesday	2 chapters of *Catherine de Medici*			
	R & J	Act II Sc IV	Units and Objectives	
		Act II Sc V	” ” ”	
Thursday	*Agamemnon*—Aeschylus			
	R & J	Balcony scene—Clare, Howard		
		Act III Sc V		

A note added to this piece of paper for Thursday adds: 'have units and obs worked out'.[5] 'Drill' here refers to what might now be called 'movement', and 'Sonnets' refers to a voice exercise that will be further discussed below. Two weeks later the music for mime was 'Edie was a Lady'. It is not clear what the *Catherine de Medici* book was, but a later class programme refers to 'two chapters of the Commedia dell'Arte'. Another class included 'Looking at Breughel'. The main emphasis, however, is the exploration of Stanislavsky's basic technique, something no other theatre in Britain was even interested in at this time. It seems pairs or groups of students were given specific scenes to prepare and then present.

A later timetable was drawn up during June 1947, while the company
was on tour in Felixstowe:

Wednesday	10-30–11.0	Movement (Rosalie)
	11.15–11.45	Voice (in pairs)
	11.45	Stanislavsky (Ewan)
Thursday	9.30–11.30	rehearse scene (*Blood Wedding*)
	10.0–11.10	Movement (Rosalie)
	11.45–1.0	Singing
Friday	9.30–11.30	rehearse scene
	10.0–11.0	Movement (Rosalie)
	11.45–1.0	rehearse scene
	11.15–12.15	Voice (in pairs)[6]

Here what is most noticeable is that those members of the company who
were not rehearsing were training. No-one, in other words, wasted their
mornings. It appears, by the way, that the production of *Blood Wedding* never
took place, because the copyright was unavailable.

The Theatre Workshop syllabus, like that of the earlier Theatre Union,
began with studying, both theatre—history and theory—and politics. From
the period of *Last Edition* before the Second World War, when members of
the company researched the various subjects that were to be incorporated
before Ewan MacColl actually created the script, at least until the time the
company settled at Stratford East, the politics was paramount, especially
because of MacColl's commitment, though it should be remembered that
Littlewood, at that time at least, considered herself a Marxist. A note
written by MacColl for Theatre Union members asserts:

> Some people in Theatre Union don't yet realize how much they must be
> involved in the life and struggle of those around them. People still talk of
> *education* and divorce it from the experiences of the working class—there is
> no longer any education worth the name except that which is assimilated
> during our participation in the class struggle. Ideas about theatre or politics
> or literature or anything else mean nothing unless they are translated into
> action.[7]

The study of theatre history and theory included the Greeks, the
Elizabethans, Molière and other past theatres, as well as contemporary
European theatre. So, when Mordecai Gorelik's *New Theatres for Old* was
published in 1947, it was ransacked for useful, or useable, information.
Joan Littlewood's notes on this book, which may be for her own
consumption, or may be the basis for further research, perhaps by other
members of the company, highlights various of Gorelik's points. First, she
points to Gorelik's description of how Belasco embraced Zola's naturalism

as an act of rebellion against America's theatre establishment. Beside a number of page references for Meyerhold, she has written 'Biography Analysis'. Gorelik calls Meyerhold 'the Theatricalist director *par excellence*', refers to his work on Molière, notes how for him, 'the audience was the focus of dramatic art, and that 'by the outbreak of the Soviet revolution he had introduced gymnastic training for actors, resurrected the pantomime tradition of the Commedia dell'Arte [and] tried out improvisation in performance.' And he was 'on the Communist side of the revolution'.[8] Littlewood's notes also point to the description of Toller's *Masses and Man*, to the revolutionary Russian theatre of Eisenstein, Vakhtangov and Okhlopkov, to Piscator's epic theatre of the 1920s and Brecht's *The Threepenny Opera*, and then to the American workers' theatre. Finally, there are a number of references to Gorelik's interpretation of epic theatre, including to lighting and stage design for epic. It is a revealing response to this stimulating book.[9]

The physical training session usually began with relaxation. Again, it is worth reproducing a typical sequence of exercises, exactly as the notes have preserved them, to understand how this was developed:

> Head – arms – shoulders hands trunk – legs – feet
> Lying down – standing – half standing – (muscles)
> Relax – now as a group – lie down and get up –
> Breathe rhythmically
> Now give that group movement meaning –
> Refugees from bombing
> Relax setting –
> Free Trade Hall (as men and women of the Chartist period)
> Crouching – relax –
> Crouching under a cart when rambling – it's raining
> Put your arms up in the air. Relax, letting them down.

Another sequence is entitled 'Relaxation in walking':

> Walking as a group – slowly – using each other's bodies
> Running relaxed
> Swinging along quickly as on a ramble
> Lunging forward with arm movement – and then arm circling movement
>   for contrast[10]

These are, in fact, quite complex and difficult relaxation exercises, and indicate perhaps both the advanced level of many of the Theatre Workshop members, and also the absolute lack of any guidance for those devising the exercises. Relaxation in movement is extremely difficult to achieve, and it is from studying this kind of raw document that one comes to appreciate the level of work of the Theatre Workshop actor. From internal evidence, such as the references to rambling, it is likely that Ewan MacColl was also involved in the creation of these exercises.

Initially, movement exercises were also worked out piecemeal. By the time Theatre Workshop was established they were usually led by Rosalie Williams, herself a graceful if dainty dancer, who had the actors jumping, twirling, gliding and so on to the beat of her tambourine. The work was based largely on a mixture of *commedia dell'arte* (as Littlewood and MacColl understood it) and Jacques-Dalcroze's Eurhythmics, though Littlewood was also extremely keen on Rudolf Laban's movement work. Even in the earliest Theatre Workshop years the movement work was thoroughly impressive. For instance, actors performed the old *commedia* fencing lunges, with precise foot and hand movements; then half lunges; then with the arm up, dropping it as the lunge returned. They used Callot's well-known engravings as a basis for grotesque movement, and the development of dramatic types based on movement.

Littlewood used Eurhythmics to devise a number of 'weight transference' exercises, such as putting the left foot forward to kneel on the right knee, put the head on the knee, fold the arms, transfer the weight to the left knee and stretch the arms upwards. A series of exercises centred round frog movements, leaping round the room in a squatting position, then jumping like a frog onto the partner's back. This could be followed by holding the partner in a wrestling hold, struggling, till one (pre-agreed) partner jumps on the other's back. This exercise is interestingly reminiscent of some of Meyerhold's Biomechanical *études*. The same could be said for the exercise of miming scrubbing the floor, first 'truthfully' and then gradually making the essential movements rhythmical, abstract. The same exercise was performed for other working actions, such as two actors miming work with a long-handled mallet, and a third holding a stave. Here is the programme for a whole training class, lasting probably an hour or more, aimed at developing rhythm in action:

I. Basic simple action   Walking   1. Normally – slowly
                                    2. Backwards – tiptoeing
                                    3. Swift walk
                                    4. Run – swift run
                          Skipping 1. Simple
                                    2. Skipping with arms flinging sideways
                                       – alternate – add head turning
                                    3. Skipping with one arm stretched up
                                       – opposite foot curled under –
                                    4. Skipping with head thrown back and
                                       legs kicking out backwards
                                    5. Skipping with hands on thighs –
                                       trunk bent forward and knees up

3. A page from Joan Littlewood's notebooks: weight transference.

Try 1 2 3 4 5 as walking exercises.

II. Work with partner

1. Circling – as wrestlers for a place
   To a 1–2–3 rhythm. Then complete
   circle.
2. Just walking in circle
   Then pursuing in 3 and retreating in
   3
3. Holding hands and hopping round –
   then hopping round the room
4. 2 people holding hands running
   round room
5. One skipping the other walking
6. Two people meeting on the street – 4
   beats.[11]

Some of these notes are obviously elliptical, but the drift of the session is clear, and its progression from simple walking through to the improvisation of a meeting on the street, to a pre-determined rhythm, is extremely impressive. Joan Littlewood herself describes these classes as 'Eurhythmics and the beginnings of Biomechanics', though very little was known of Meyerhold's system of Biomechanics at that time. Another exercise—two people running round the room, one going backwards and pulling, the other being pulled and going forwards, is similarly Biomechanical. Equally significant were movement exercises that led towards Stanislavsky's system: one set of notes begin: 'Sitting up straight, half sitting, standing, half standing, kneeling, crouching', and are annotated: 'Now enhance each pose with some imaginative idea. Enhance it with given circumstances [. . .] Swat a fly in one of these poses. <u>Give everything a living purpose</u>—a live objective and real action.'[12]

The movement work at Theatre Workshop became genuinely advanced after Joan Littlewood made contact with Rudolf Laban in 1946. She had had classes from Anny Fligg, a former student of Laban, at RADA, perhaps the only class there which she had appreciated, and at Theatre Union in the 1930s she began to develop her own system, derived from Laban's, 'however patchily'.[13]

Rudolf Laban was born in 1879. He taught Mary Wigman before the First World War, and Kurt Jooss after it. 'He sought ways to free dance from the restrictions of music, believing that the natural rhythms of the body were more inherent than metric rhythms.'[14] He was asked to choreograph the opening of the 1936 Olympic Games in Berlin, but when Goebbels saw a rehearsal, it was banned. Laban left Nazi Germany soon afterwards, and came to England, first to Dartington Hall in Devonshire, then moving to Manchester where he worked with industry to help to maximise the efficiency of workers' movements. His ideas also became increasingly

4. A page from Joan Littlewood's notebooks: eurhythmics.

influential in education, largely through the efforts of his collaborator, Lisa Ullman. In 1946 some members of Theatre Workshop were invited to participate in an open day at Laban's Manchester studio. Laban was impressed with them, while for Littlewood and MacColl, it was a revelation. 'After a session with Laban, you began to look at the world with different eyes', Joan Littlewood wrote.[15] She asked Laban for assistance with Theatre Workshop's weekend courses, and Laban responded by asking his 'dancing star', Jean Newlove, to help. For four months, Newlove worked with the company at weekends. Then she brought Laban and Ullman to a performance of *Johnny Noble*, after which, with Laban's encouragement, she joined the company as choreographer, movement teacher and performer. Laban himself came not only to performances, but to Newlove's rehearsals, and his comments informed, but did not determine, her work and that of the company.

According to Howard Goorney, Jean Newlove, though, 'young and enthusiastic' when she arrived at Theatre Workshop,[16] had had plenty of experience. At the age of seven she had been offered a scholarship to study with Eduardo Espinosa in London, and in 1940 had been offered a place as a student dancer with Kurt Jooss. She had auditioned for Laban at Dartington, and then had assisted him by lecturing, demonstrating and working in industry, as well as by using his work to further the war effort before 1945. After her full-time career with Theatre Workshop was over, she won prizes for dance and choreography in Moscow and Warsaw, choreographed for the Royal Shakespeare Company, and continued as one of the world's leading experts on Laban's movement theory and practice. Her influence on the development of Joan Littlewood's and Theatre Workshop's style and achievement was immense, and has been largely overlooked.

As Newlove herself says, 'Everybody moves, but not everybody moves well'.[17] What Laban was able to do was to tabulate the principles of movement, and thus analyse them with fundamental effects for the actor:

> Once we know WHERE we are going in space, we must observe and analyse HOW we are going and WHAT KIND OF MOVEMENT ENERGY we use. Our choice of the type of muscular energy, or [. . .] EFFORT, which determines how we carry out an action, is the result of previously experienced inner impulses. Coupled with our chosen spatial direction it produces a definitive expressive movement quality.[18]

Laban's work frees actors from their natural efforts and enables them to use the space all round them. Murray Melvin pointed out how rarely Littlewood's actors touched each other in performance, as each retained his or her own space around them. Littlewood herself supervised the building of a life-size icosohedron, a 'crystal' with twenty surfaces. The edges were

5. Jean Newlove in *Uranium 235*.

made of wooden slats, but there was space between them so that the actor could enter and explore the maximum angles and spatial dimensions through which the limbs may move: up and down, back and forward, and from side to side.

6. The icosohedron.

Equally important was Laban's work on the 'Eight Basic Efforts'. By analysing movement through time and space, and by its weight and flow, he defined eight efforts, according to their direction (direct or indirect), weight (heavy or light) and speed (fast and slow). Thus, a direct, heavy and fast movement was a punch; an indirect, heavy and fast movement was a slash; and so on, through the press, the wring, the dab, the flick, the glide and the float. These could be varied in intensity according to the situation, and they thereby revealed the effect of feelings on movement. As Peter Bridgmont, a Theatre Workshop-trained actor, has observed: 'Psychologically, if the weight is not behind the movement then the intention behind any action is weak and does not give strength or purpose to it.'[19] The affinity with Stanislavsky's system is already apparent here.

Jean Newlove was able to use Laban's principles to create specific character through movement for Theatre Workshop actors in particular plays. Knowledge of and continual practice with, Laban's work helped the actors enormously to increase their range, and incidentally also to cope with some of the more complicated stage settings devised for Joan Littlewood's productions by John Bury. Theatre Workshop were the only company in Britain who consistently trained in movement, and as Jean Newlove explained, they were able to reach an advanced level, including leaps and entrechats—unheard of for most actors. 'We were very adventurous', Newlove remembered. 'We'd try all sorts of things', improvising in movement, working with space and time and weight, exploring different combinations of these, exploring direct walks with the feet but perhaps indirect body movements, or varying speeds, so that a naturally quick person was slowed down, or a slow one speeded up, and so on. Actors thus learned technique, which, in Newlove's opinion, was 'the half way stage':

> Their bodies were technically able to implement, complement their character. What they wanted to do in the character—their bodies were able to sustain it. They were able to extend their movement range. It liberated them to play different roles, and let them think in the role.[20]

In addition, Newlove led the actors in 'limbering up' before each performance, and was able to revise specific efforts and movement characteristics of the actors before each performance began. Her work probably reached its apogee in *Uranium 235*, for which Howard Goorney quotes her description:

> In *Uranium 235* we had to split the atom, and because our actors were trained as modern dancers, it wasn't much trouble to get them to understand that they had to actually present the atom in a ballet. The bodies were intertwined and twisted, leaning over in the most difficult, extraordinary positions, legs up in the air. An actor from the ordinary theatre, asked to do this, would probably walk out, saying it was ridiculous, but of course it wasn't. We wanted to show the splitting of an atom, not simply describe it in words.

And she recalled that Sigurd Leeder had said that 'These actors move as some of the best dancers I've ever seen'.[21] Ewan MacColl concurred. He wrote that Jean Newlove: 'was a dancer, [and] a magnificent teacher who fired us all with the desire to encompass space. It was because of her efforts that Theatre Workshop [. . .] achieved a standard of movement which would not have disgraced a company of dancers.'[22]

As with movement, so with voice. Joan Littlewood and Ewan MacColl proceeded at first by trial and error, centring initially, and correctly, on breathing. MacColl worked out a series of exercises that involved breathing while exercising—with arms circling, while touching the toes, while lifting, while 'bicycling' with feet in the air, and while rising onto the toes and returning to the ground. Some exercises, probably devised by Littlewood, derived from Jacques-Dalcroze's Eurhythmics. One note reads:

Costal   high
Central   breathing
Abdominal   low

Breathe and walk – together – but walk relaxed
    Loosen the teeth
Stand and breathe, rolling the head
Add arm movements
    leg movements

Expand in – 1 2 3(breathe in)
Hold – 1 2 3
Contract – 1 2 3(breathe out)
Hold – 1 2 3

then on to 4
But go easy – don't strain
Nothing does the nose so much good as breathing through it[23]

This work was complemented by plenty of exercises involving specific sounds. Littlewood's notebooks are full of lists such as: '*Oo, Oh, Aw*, O, *Ah*, U, Er, A, E, *Ay*, *I*, *Ea*', and 'Boo boh baw bah bay bee'. Then there are phrases, such as two words which run specific consonants together: 'fit time', 'trite truths', 'verve vixen', 'sock sold', 'huge general', 'dumb mouths' and many more.[24] There are also poems to be spoken, such as work by John Donne, Hugh McDiarmid, Browning's 'The Pied Piper' (a particular favourite) and sonnets, to be spoken with music, such as one of Bach's Brandenburg concertos. Littlewood writes: 'Listen. Say your sonnet in your head to the music. Leave pauses between the thoughts, and let the music take over. Use pauses for breathing, mark your sonnet for breaths. Try it first very softly to yourself. Then aloud, as strong as the music.'[25]

In 1946 or 1947, however, Nelson Illingworth, an Australian who had worked with singers from the New York Metropolitan Opera House, as well as, reputedly, Fyodor Chaliapin, saw a performance by Theatre Workshop, and invited himself to help them. A Communist and member of the 1930s Group Theatre under Rupert Doone, he had tried to establish his own theatre school and production company in the 1930s, to be called Labour Stage, a kind of English version of the American Group Theatre. His supporters had included John Allen, Herbert Marshall, Alan Bush, Jocelyn Herbert and Margaret Leona, but the project foundered, perhaps because of his operatic rather than theatrical background. His voice was deep, rich and resonant, and reminded Kirsten Lind, a member of Theatre Workshop, of a Russian folk singer.

Now he began with the basics for the Theatre Workshop actors. First, they were to breathe in, to fill the whole body with air, and then breathe out evenly, vocalising the 'Ahhh' sound as they did it. Then they counted to fifty slowly, evenly, with the smallest intake of breath at twenty-five. Illingworth taught the *bel canto* method. For this, breathing was the foundation of the voice's work. The actors had to sit as if thinking, elbows on knees, the abdomen kept up and in to give greater support. They breathed in and held the lung expansion for as long as possible. They breathed out from the bottom of the lungs, the breath coming straight up from the diaphragm without compression, as if breathing onto the hands to warm them. All the muscles of the throat and the tongue were completely relaxed in this exercise. He also suggested thinking of the breath as a column stretching from the diaphragm to the throat, which travelled along the tongue as it was expelled.

In Illingworth's system, vocalisation was to happen *on* the breath, not *in* it, very much a singer's conception, and the vowels were to be thought of as a stream or river, with the consonants mere sticks thrown onto its flow. The consonants, he argued, would come naturally once the flow of vowels was established. Speech was thus to derive from the diaphragm, or even the solar plexus, as if the sound was following a straight line drawn from the small of the back to the bridge of the nose. In other words, it was produced by the whole body, not simply the larynx. Indeed, resonance in the head was positively discouraged, as Illingworth taught that this produced a dead, colourless tone, and made the voice 'sing' sharp. The body was to be set as if it had settled down into the diaphragm, but was ready to spring up, as in diving, rather than be braced, as a soldier's on parade. The company sang and chanted endlessly, as unexpected vocal resources were discovered, and the Workers' Theatre Movement's objections to 'girlish voices' were finally met.

Undoubtedly Nelson Illingworth was a strong influence for the good on Theatre Workshop actors, but there was a sense that his emphasis on the full voice sometimes apparently excluded articulation of meaning, and created something that was externally produced. After one performance, Joan Littlewood complained that Illingworth would have appreciated a performance by Ewan MacColl as Don Perlimplin, but that this external quality produced acting which was, to her, 'dishonest'.[26]

It was in fact only when the full voice that Illingworth taught was allied to the Laban system of efforts that the voice problems were properly solved. For it is possible to 'punch' a line of dialogue, or to 'flick' it, to produce a very different effect. Indeed, this technique was still consistently employed by Ewan MacColl long after he had left Theatre Workshop and had become a concert folk singer. As Jean Newlove noted, at Theatre Workshop 'voice was always considered as an extension of movement',[27] and Peter Bridgmont expanded this with reference to a particular exercise: 'The phrasing and dynamic shape of the sentences [. . .] can become apparent if the actor moves to the lines while they are read by someone else. This may be a slow and gentle process at first, but gradually the "dance" quality of the speech becomes more obvious.'[28]

Joan Littlewood and Ewan MacColl were also the first in Britain to attempt seriously and consistently to apply Stanislavsky's system to their work. *An Actor Prepares* was first published in 1937, and in 1938 Patience Collier remembered first working with Theatre Union in *The Good Soldier Schweik*:

> It was my introduction to Stanislavski [*sic*], and it was a revelation and such a change from the mechanical approach to work I had been used to. We took exercises from his book, *An Actor Prepares*, and applied them to the parts we were playing—things like units and objectives, imagination, concentration and so on.[29]

MacColl invented exercises for the actors, such as coming home, closing the curtains, taking off the shoes, putting a record on the gramophone, resting in a chair, looking at a book, taking the record off, and so on. How many units are there? If the main objective is going to bed, how does each objective, each unit, relate to that? Plays, too, were split into units and an objective found for each character in each unit. And the units were properly related to the 'Through Line of Action', Littlewood urging actors to form 'an unbroken series of images, moving pictures', so strong that they would provide a stimulus for action, exactly as Stanislavsky did.

Other exercises developed by MacColl or Littlewood included many for the imagination, related to Stanislavsky's concepts of the 'Given Circumstances' and the 'Magic If'. These began with the actor being asked, first, simply to close the door, then, to close it imagining that the police were coming. What if that session was not being held in Manchester but in a Lake District Youth Hostel on a sunny summer morning? Or in a London night school on a November evening with thick yellow fog outside? Members were to sit on a chair, but to imagine it was a stalls seat at a theatre in Moscow, or that it was an electric chair, or that they were waiting for the result of their child's operation, and so on. The emotion memory was useful for, as MacColl explained in the 1960s, it could be used to draw upon 'Emotions that have moved you profoundly, and they may be somewhat removed from the artistic experience that you're about to undergo but they have to imbue that experience on the stage. They inform it with truth, invest it with reality.'[30]

The focus on 'truth', so central to Stanislavsky's system, was also central to MacColl and Littlewood. They both continued throughout their careers to contrast 'representational art', that is, performance dependent upon remembered rehearsal, with 'living the part'.[31] Ewan MacColl, in his autobiography, discusses how he used the system to decide how to sing particular songs, ending with the key explanation: 'This is not a blueprint for the singing of 'Lamkin' but a rough guide to the way I, Ewan MacColl, sing 'Lamkin'.[32] It was 'his version' of the song, in other words, a concept that was always crucial to Theatre Workshop. Written in the 1980s, this account of folk singing carries the same urgent need for 'truth' as his comments to Theatre Union actors in the late 1930s: 'To be attentive and to appear to be attentive are two different things'.[33] Joan Littlewood, too, can be seen seeking the same truth: the day before her death in 2002, she granted permission for Theatre Clwyd to perform *Oh What a Lovely War* with the injunction that 'there be "no bloody acting"'.[34] 'Acting' was 'representationalism', the opposite of truth.

Most importantly, this work enabled the crucial link between Stanislavsky's system and Laban's 'mastery of movement' to be made by Theatre Workshop. As Stanislavsky structures the actor's work around a sequence of objectives, divided into units, so Laban is concerned above all with the motivation of movement. Newlove quotes Laban's observation: 'Man moves in order to satisfy a need,' and goes on to pinpoint the significance of this for the theatre audience: 'By observing and analysing movements [. . .] it is possible to recognise the need of the mover and to become aware of his inner attitude which precedes the action'.[35] It is the emphasis on what precedes action which unites Stanislavsky and Laban.

Theatre Workshop actors trained in all the elements of performance— relaxation, movement, voice, Stanislavsky's system, and more—but they also practised integrating these elements. This was done largely through games and improvisations, perhaps beginning with 'identity games'. Each actor steps through an imaginary door and says who they are. Afterwards, can the others remember each? This gives way to Blind Man's Buff. Other games had other uses. When actors in rehearsal have lost inspiration, and the work is becoming dull, Littlewood suggests an apparently irrelevant game, such as pretending to be a shoal of fish swimming through dangerous waters.[36] It is diverting, and tests the actors' sense of movement, alertness and awareness of each other. Games, which are now quite widely used, were a revelation then.

There were also specific improvisation exercises, more clearly 'set pieces' in Theatre Workshop's early period, such as the story that involved the daughter of poor parents leaving home. While the parents sit by the fire, the daughter gets up, 'goes to the mirror, fluffs her hair'. Later, she 'gets up again, goes out to the garden, dreams, dances'. Here we see the need to integrate acting and dance, which is even clearer as the improvisation continues. She leaves home, and seeks a job, asking 'over and over again', a kind of Expressionist dance action, which becomes even more demanding on the actor as she goes 'through huge streets with towering skyscrapers, forlorn, terrified'.[37] How does the actor convey this in her improvisation? Other suggestions for improvisation include: a thin man and a fat man meeting; an Indian coolie and a white man; two old gossiping women telling scandal about a woman in the street and a 'Yank'; a Red Army liberator and a father in a Belsen-like camp. Crowd scenes for improvisation included the Brecht-like 'Food's gone up to pay for the war' and a street scene in Salford, perhaps directly relating to work on *Landscape with Chimneys* or perhaps *Johnny Noble*. They also devoted time to 'Stagecraft', learning to feel the stage, spatial relationships and so on, and finding the way, blindfolded, across an obstacle-littered stage, perhaps trying to avoid knocking anything over. Finally there were full-blown 'Production' classes, which sought to integrate physical work with the history and theory work, when members were given simple stories to improvise in specific styles, such as Naturalism, melodrama, slapstick, 'sentimental romantic' and tragic realism.

The work was carefully considered, and extensive feedback was given to the actors, and then discussed by the whole group. A flavour of this feedback may be obtained from some excerpts from Joan Littlewood's comments on the 'sentimental romantic' improvisation:

> [The actors] made a fundamental mistake—How do we know this? The given circumstances which were invented were static, picture postcard ideas, the idea of the idyllic farm labourer and beauteous girl wife setting was static when put into this plot. Or can we perhaps say that they did not succeed in welding the given circumstances to the plot? They were extraneous to each other [. . .] I think you'll find that such circumstances need some dynamic action to make them useable. In romantic comedy this does not exist [. . .] Another thing—don't miss the wood for the trees—don't lose yourself in extraneous and small details before you have solved the most important question—*How shall you do this?* In any job of creative work go straight to the fundamental problem—simplify.[38]

Littlewood then goes on to recommend French, Spanish and Italian Romantic writers, and continues the analysis by referring to the problems of a modern working-class housewife, whose struggles should provide the actors with inspiration.

Discussing Howard Goorney's exercise in slapstick, she says:

> it is a mistake to be supercilious towards this form. As you know, it had a prominent place in Greek and Italian comedy. If they could use it to good effect, we can. You have seen what tremendous satirical point it can have in the Marx Bros films—*Duck Soup* being one of the best examples and also

the most political. The Russian theatre has also made tremendous use of slapstick. Is there a more complete way of destroying false dignity, hypocrisy and vulgarity than by staging them and then by throwing things at them, cutting their top hats in two, producing eggs out of their mouths, performing acrobatics over a bourgeois beauty or showering eggs on a dignified politician. Slapstick can be tremendously useful but it must be fast-moving, well-timed, clear—your effort needs more ideas, and some production, Howard.[39]

These comments illustrate perfectly what Kenneth Tynan meant when, years later, he described Joan Littlewood's 'pursuit of a dream of theatre as a place of communal celebration, a Left wing shrine of Dionysus dedicated to whipping the Puritan frown from off the popular image of Socialist art'.[40]

More importantly, Littlewood also provided each actor with a critique of their work during the course of particular tours. Again some of these are worth quoting, partly because of the unsparing honesty and endless patience with each member of the company they demonstrate, but also because they show clearly the seriousness with which Joan Littlewood approached her art. Of Ben Ellis, at about the time the company stopped touring (unfortunately the notes are not dated) she wrote:

> Bennie has several valuable natural gifts which are crying out to be used and developed but as yet he is not bold enough to use them. It seems to me that he is afraid of himself and afraid of making a fool of himself in his work. He diffuses his emotions to some extent and seems to have avoided losing himself in a completely self-absorbing creative task [. . .] the first performance (of Malvolio) lacked bold flights of imagination which are always present in great work [. . .] he seemed to be working against himself, trying for moods and character which were stillborn because the fundamental through-line was not sufficiently clear and positive in his imagination. There are no negatives in the theatre, even a negative mood must be worked out in action, inner and outer action [. . .]

In another such report, she comments:

> *Benny*—Your voice is good. By that I mean that the timbre is fairly rich and strikes pleasingly on the ear. It carries well and rarely becomes thin or metallic. There is a tendency to over-modulate into low registers which results in loss of breath and consequent swallowing of voice.
>   *Bad habits*—Habit of throwing back the head in moments of emotional stress which results in strangling the voice. Tendency to elocute passages, i.e. to speak them for their sound rather than their sense. Artificial decoration of words by *imposition* of inflexion. Elongation of vowels. Tendency to reduce accent by consistent use of legato phrasing, even on single words such as 'Yes' and 'No'.

And of John Blanshard, she wrote:

> It seemed to me that during the first year's work John had to overcome a possibly unconscious resistance to a new physical approach to acting (Chubakov, *The Proposal*; Gorgibus; Swingler) [. . .] perhaps John's work is altogether too sound and logical [. . .] John must learn that acting like life is not always logical. He should give room to a more uninhibited range of imagination, explore the deeper reaches of his character . . .

And later, of the same actor:

> *Tendencies*—There are two main tendencies. These are, to use a consistent pressing effort and to place the voice always in the same spot. The first of these tendencies results in heaviness and the second motivates against light and shade. The flattened Yorkshire vowels tend to emphasise the basic suggestion of tonal flatness while robbing speech of much of its crispness. A fault which you share with most people in the group is the tendency to limit the tonal range of the voice.[41]

Significantly, it was not only Joan Littlewood who made these reports. Here, for instance, is Jean Newlove's assessment of John Blanshard, which complements the above:

> *General comments*—Your movement is fairly flexible but occasionally becomes very flat and heavy which can make it uninteresting.
> *Tendencies*—The main tendency is of course this reluctance (or laziness) to use any great effort when moving even when such movements require efforts such as slash, thrust, etc. Another tendency is to do everything in slow time which probably is a result of taking a purely literary approach to the study of movement. Primarily one should attempt all work through a body-understanding; an actual experiencing of the infinite qualities, plastic shapes and space patterns whilst moving. It is afterwards, when such movements are analysed, that we apply the reasoning process.
> *Rate of progress*—Has been steady technically for some considerable time until recently. But owing to this 'reasoning' attitude, the dynamic or eukinetic quality is never present. Rather one feels that an exercise or study has been sincerely worked on and the result is a fairly competent performance. But in movement and dance one lives passionately what one expresses through one's body. At the moment, it is like watching two people: one coldly reasoning out the form whilst the other attempts, mostly quite competently, to perform the task. Be more concerned with content and you will develop greater expressiveness.[42]

These judicious comments, with their detailed care and passionate concern for improvement, by both Littlewood and Newlove, show more vividly than anything else perhaps how significant the training of the performers in Theatre Workshop was, and—at least partly—why the company were original and unique in Britain, not only in their time, but perhaps in the whole of the twentieth century.

PART THREE

Theatre Workshop, 1953–56

Repertory Theatre

CHAPTER TEN

New Elizabethans

In the 1951 general election, the Labour Party polled the most votes in its history. But the Conservatives won more seats, and Winston Churchill returned to Downing Street to usher in what some saw as a new era in Britain.

Churchill's Conservative government presented a face far different to that of the Conservatives of the 1920s and 1930s. They supported full employment and funded the Welfare State. They boasted they were 'setting the people free' with income tax cuts and an end to rationing, but in reality their policies were cautious and conciliatory, and depended heavily on consensus. The *Economist* magazine coined the term 'Butskellism' to indicate the similarity between the old policies of Labour's Hugh Gaitskell and the new policies of the Conservative chancellor of the exchequer, R.A. Butler. The consensus muffled 'extremism' and, by pandering to materialism and philistinism, was able to marginalise virtually all forms of rebellious idealism or individuality. As Harold Pinter put it: 'You had to conform, there was a great, great deal of conformity about'.[1] Thus in the theatre, bland bourgeois values were re-affirmed by the pre-eminence of T.S. Eliot and Christopher Fry, the acceptable face of the intelligentsia. Nor was the consensus disturbed by the leaders of the Labour Party, who while retaining the support of the overwhelming majority of working-class people, spent years bickering with each other. The working class Bevan opposed the patricians, Dalton, Gaitskell and their successors, over public ownership, German rearmament and imperialism in general while it may be that some disillusioned Communists infiltrated—or joined—the Labour Party, and voted a group of left-wing rebels onto the party's all-powerful National Executive Committee. If not impotent, Labour was at least hobbled.

One area of policy in which the Communists had apparently made ground on Labour was housing: by encouraging squatters, they had shown quick sympathy that exposed the limitations of moderation. Now the Conservatives, having promised to build 300,000 new houses per year, neutralised this. Harold Macmillan was appointed housing minister, and soon outstripped his promise. In 1953, 327,000 houses were built. In 1954, the figure was 354,000. Most were council houses, but many were built for sale, too. Squatting became less a necessity for newly-weds anxious for independence than a spectacular rarity performed mostly by attention-seekers. The stifling conformism of the Tory decade was nowhere more apparent than in the endless rows of brick-built houses with tiny gardens that lined the suburban roads of British cities.

In April 1955, Churchill suddenly resigned the premiership, and the glamorous foreign secretary, Anthony Eden, took over. It was the last piece of the jigsaw that saw the New Elizabethan Age cemented into the popular imagination. In February 1952, King George VI had died, and he was succeeded by his young and attractive daughter, Elizabeth II. She embodied new hope, though Churchill's presence in Downing Street meant the hope was tempered with something less unpredictable: Britain had perhaps the best of both young and old worlds. That year the Comet became the first jet airliner to go into service with BOAC. In October, Britain exploded her own atom bomb in the Monte Bello islands. Abroad, too, things seemed to be changing. In America, Dwight Eisenhower became the first Republican president since 1933, while the following year, Stalin died, and a ceasefire was brokered in Korea. 1953 was the year of the sumptuously brilliant coronation, preceded by the conquest of Everest by a British team. The fact that neither the New Zealander Edmund Hillary nor the Nepalese Tensing Norgay—the climbers who made the summit—were actually British was somehow overlooked in London. The New Elizabethan Age did not wish to consider truths of this kind. If the hopes of 1945 had been misplaced, then here surely was a new beginning of British greatness. As if to prove it, Roger Bannister ran a mile in four minutes, and England regained the cricket Ashes under their new captain, Len Hutton (soon to be Sir Leonard). Perhaps the most extraordinary triumph that year was the award of a Nobel Prize to Winston Churchill for—of all things—Literature!

The truth, well concealed under the gloss, was that Churchill was frequently drunk, and indeed that he had had a stroke barely three months after taking office. Serious questions as to his fitness for office, however, were never asked. The New Elizabethans, unlike their predecessors, the first Elizabethans, had no time for protesting 'stinkards' or disrespectful groundlings. Indeed, the mid-twentieth-century counterparts of these plebeians, workers in heavy industry, found that their jobs and way of life were disappearing as lighter manufacturing—electronics, synthetic fibres, motor vehicle making—took their place. The old working class, the site of Karl Marx's revolutionary destiny, was being diluted, and diminishing in numbers and potency. But their concerns went unexpressed, and the state provided for them not only bread—rising incomes, and alternative, apparently dehumanised, employment—but also circuses. It found the perfect vehicle to stifle dissent—television. Churchill suspected—with no real evidence—that the BBC was in the grip of Communists (a delusion among right-wing people that long outlasted that prime minister), and in 1954—not necessarily as a direct result—the government passed the Television Act, which introduced commercial television to Britain. Within a year, four and a half million homes had television. Three years later, the figure had nearly doubled, the BBC had gone 'down market' and, perhaps, consensus was assured.

How was it possible to make a 'great theatre'—Joan Littlewood's avowed aim—in the light of these depressing and continuing social and political circumstances? The question was vital to the future of Theatre Workshop. Was the touring policy—one-night stands in tiny and often isolated working-class communities, like mining villages—viable any longer? It had been tested, and seemed to have failed. Besides, many in the company were exhausted, and eager to settle down. A national Theatre Conference in 1948, attended by, among others, Sir Stafford Cripps and Aneurin Bevan, had promised local authority financial support for the arts, including theatre, through the rates. If the company settled in a sympathetic working-class area, such support could be highly significant.

The arguments that raged in the company from 1952 into 1953 concerning whether to stop touring and settle in the East End of London are important for an understanding of Theatre Workshop. They are not unrelated to the arguments within the Clarion Players in the late 1920s as to whether to perform traditional plays, or to move towards agit-prop. They remind us also of the Workers' Theatre Movement's debates over outdoor performance as against the curtained stage. And the debate was not unique to Theatre Workshop. When the Adelphi Players stopped touring in 1947, it was only after a not dissimilar internal debate: 'The majority wanted to get closer (with important reservations) to the established theatre, while the minority [. . .] felt it had begun to break new theatrical ground, and wanted to experiment—with plays, audiences, methods of acting and production and staging'.[2] Is the raw energy of political commitment sufficient to compensate for crude theatricality? Is it possible to make working-class spectators feel at home in a red plush auditorium intended for conventional theatre-going people? Part of the problem, faced by all theatres with a mission such as Theatre Workshop's—7:84 Company decades later faced it, too—was, in the words of Jean Newlove, that 'the poor didn't want to know' great theatre.[3]

Ewan MacColl wrote that by the end of 1952 'it was plain that we had reached the point where we would either have to disband or find another way of working'.[4] Some members of the company by now had small children, and though there were devoted people around the country prepared to help them, such as Norman and Janey Buchan in Scotland, the company was not earning enough to pay its members anything like a living wage. And touring was gruelling. Besides, most actors, like other artists, need some form of response to their work, not necessarily from newspaper critics, but something of more value than the transient applause of a few inexperienced spectators. A critical moment in the company's history had arrived.

MacColl, who vehemently opposed the move to Stratford East, suggested that in the days of touring, they had asked: 'What are we doing wrong that mill workers in Haslingdon only come in small numbers? . . . that we do a play about miners, and take it to Kirkcaldy, and the miners won't come?' These were, he suggested, 'perfectly valid questions, and by trying to answer them, we could formulate some kind of rationale. But now', he suggested, if the company moved to Stratford East, the question would become: 'How are we going to get Harold Hobson [theatre critic of *The Sunday Times*]? What's he going to think of this?'[5] For MacColl, these were self-defeating questions. But Hobson's reply to them is not without force. Theatre Workshop at Stratford East, in his view, 'revolutionised British theatre', and he argued that bringing 'left wing theatre into the heart of London's boulevards possibly produced new strengths'. In the end, Hobson asked, should a company like Theatre Workshop 'play to a hostile audience [in the West End] which doesn't know the ideas, or search out people [in working-class communities] who are inclined to agree' with the viewpoint presented?[6] This argument, though valid in some respects, misinterprets one feature of the move to Stratford East: it was nowhere near 'the heart of London's boulevards'; yet it was not 'the provinces', either. This proximity that was not regional was to remain an unsolved problem.

Jean Newlove maintained that the company before the move to Stratford and the company afterwards were like 'chalk and cheese'.[7] Many of the original group, such as Rosalie Williams and Bill Davidson, had already left. And those who supported MacColl's resistance to the move to Stratford felt

> that just by coming to London, and getting swallowed by the metropolitan theatre scene, the whole of the ten years or more before were going for a burton. But we came to London, and we said, We will build up a working class audience in London the way we've done in Barnsley and Tonypandy and Newcastle-on-Tyne and Manchester. But in actual fact we didn't, of course. We put on some of the shows from the basic repertoire, like *Johnny Noble* and we did *The Other Animals*, and we did Marlowe's *Edward II*, a beautiful production of that, and audiences weren't coming, Stratford people certainly weren't coming. We were back to the point almost where

we'd started, when we started touring, when we were playing to twelve and twenty-five people. We were getting twelve and twenty-five people at the Theatre Royal.[8]

Consequently, Ewan MacColl, co-founder and most urgent driving force in Theatre Workshop, drifted away over the following years.

MacColl went on to become better known as a leader of the 'folk revival' of the following decades, and the maker of the Radio Ballads. Jean Newlove felt that he could have continued to sing 'in his spare time' as he already did, but acknowledged that he felt the company's integrity was inevitably lost in London, in competition with the West End and for the approval of critics whom he did not respect. 'But maybe he was *too* intransigent', she added wistfully.[9] It seems clear that Joan Littlewood's deepest beliefs chimed with MacColl's. Perhaps the most moving passage in her whole autobiography describes MacColl's departure:

One day, Ewan MacColl, James H.Miller, Jimmie, call him what you will, prime mover, inspiration, Daddy o't, walked out, quit, buggered off—and, not to put too fine a point on it, resigned. Theatre Workshop had been his life, his pride and joy, the vehicle for all his plays. Whether improvised in the back of the lorry or on some God-forsaken railway station, Jimmie's songs had always lifted our spirits: 'I've a little baby, he's the apple of my eye' when his son Hamish was born; 'I'm a rambler from Manchester way' when we were all squatting on Edale Station waiting for the train that never came. Or, in the early days:

> To the old place down at Deansgate
> Where Theatre Workshop dwells
> With Les Preger, Patience Collier and the rest . . .

Where was he going?

To join the 'Hootenannys', one of the many groups of folk artists who'd become fashionable. Folk-songs and singers were in demand at this time and the Hootenannys offered real money. He'd never earned money with his plays in England and all the hopes and dreams of his youth had faded, but abandoning Theatre Workshop to sing in London pubs—what a waste![10]

Later she said: 'I wish we'd never gone to Stratford East'. When asked why the company had gone, she replied: 'Because it was the only place we could get for twenty quid a week'.[11]

CHAPTER ELEVEN

Stratford East

Touring had been posited on the belief that the working class through the United Kingdom formed a viable community, into whose collective consciousness Theatre Workshop could tap. But place gives particularity to community, and Stratford-atte-Bow, whose prosperity was built on the Eastern Counties Railway Depot and the second-largest fruit and vegetable market in England, had a tradition of political radicalism, as well as a variegated theatrical history, which made it seem attractive to several members of the company.

In the 1760s, it was the Thames watermen, the weavers of Spitalfields and the coal-heavers of the East End who demonstrated in favour of 'Wilkes and Liberty', when John Wilkes was repeatedly expelled from parliament for attacking the king's speech and publishing an 'obscene libel'. The first genuine working-class Labour candidate for parliament was William Newton, who stood for the constituency including Stratford in 1852, again in 1868, and for a third time in 1875. In 1867, with tens of thousands of East Enders out of work and nearly starving, there were considerable bread riots. By the 1880s, both H.M. Hyndman's Social Democratic Federation, and William Morris's Socialist League were active and supported here. In June 1888, Annie Besant published an article about the 'white slavery' at Bryant and May's match factory in Bow, and a few days later the 'match girls' went on strike—an unprecedented action for low paid female workers. With support from George Bernard Shaw, Sidney Webb and others, two weeks later the strikers won their argument and the management capitulated. The following year, the labourers in the docks, perhaps learning from their sisters, struck for 'the dockers' tanner', and they too secured victory.

In the twentieth century, East End radicalism was notorious. Sylvia Pankhurst split from the mainstream Suffragette movement in 1912, and founded her own radical and socialist East London Federation of Suffragettes here. Her open-air meetings became legendary, protected by her 'People's Army' of seven hundred men and women, and in early 1914 she launched her newspaper, the *Women's Dreadnought*, here. The East End was also the stamping-ground early in the century for two Labour leaders, George Lansbury and Clement Attlee, and in 1926 the Stratford Labour Party was compulsorily disaffiliated from the national party because it refused to expel its Communist members.

Against this, the first branch of Oswald Mosley's British Union of Fascists in the East End of London was established in Bow in 1934. Mosley particularly targeted the East End because of its Jewish population. As 'outsiders', they—like asylum seekers in most ages—were vulnerable, apparently defenceless and therefore easy prey for bullies. The Fascists were opposed by the Communists, based in the Tenants' Defence League and led by Phil Piratin. In autumn 1936 the Fascists announced their intention to march through the East End. Despite the offence and mayhem this was likely to cause, which was pointed out by many—not least Clement Attlee, leader of the Labour Party, who led a delegation to the Home Secretary to ask for the march to be banned—the National government insisted it should continue. On the day, 4 October 1936, the police tried desperately to enable the march, but they were thwarted by barricades and huge numbers of opponents, who barred the way at Cable Street and defeated Mosley's—and the government's—intent. The rise of his party was checked, but British Union of Fascists candidates continued to gain votes in local elections; in 1937 one of their candidates was William Joyce, later notorious as 'Lord Haw-Haw', the British Nazi traitor. It may be added that Fascists were still active in the area including Stratford in the 1950s in Theatre Workshop's time.

War came in 1939. Twenty-eight minutes after its declaration, the first air-raid siren sounded across London's East End, and before the war was over, the sirens had whined no fewer than 1,223 times, once for every forty hours of the war. In the first days the evacuation of children was organised, but in the 'phoney' war the fear of bombing receded, and by the following spring many children were home again. It was only in the autumn of 1940 that the Blitz began, targeted on the docks of east London. Every night for nearly nine weeks, hundreds of aeroplanes droned overhead, dropping bombs that flattened homes and killed or maimed people indiscriminately. On 10 September, 400 people were killed by a single bomb. In response, and in defiance of authority, people took to the underground for shelter during raids—the East Enders were the first to camp in the stations. Still the air-raid shelters were inadequate, and Phil Piratin led a shabby group of working-class Londoners into the exclusive Savoy Hotel to escape the bombs, an action which finally did bestir the authorities to furbish new shelters for the East Enders. In the underground, some people stayed put for weeks at a time, and all those who took refuge there were provided with entertainment—concerts, theatre shows and so on—and a resilient community spirit was forged. In the next years,

> LCC [London County Council] sponsorship of 'Stay at home and Play at
> home' holidays led to a growth of open-air theatre in the parks. There
> were swimming galas, fetes, Punch-and-Judy shows and, for those who
> were slightly older, fun dancing [...] and carefree singsongs [...] But
> here, too, cultural frontiers were sometimes unexpectedly crossed. Thus
> for a week in August 1942, and again eleven months later, the Sadler's
> Wells Ballet performed in Victoria Park; in the warm evenings an
> appreciative audience could see Fonteyn and Helpmann dance—for
> sixpence.[1]

The East End suffered its last tragedy on 27 March 1945 when a V2 rocket
landed on a block of flats, destroying sixty homes and killing 134 people.
No wonder that when peace came there was dancing in the street, open-air
parties, bonfires and plenty of heavy drinking.

Perhaps not surprisingly, Phil Piratin was elected to Parliament in 1945,
one of two Communist MPs in the House of Commons. But the process
of rebuilding was slow, notably in the field of housing, and there were
Communist-inspired squats in upper-class apartments in Bloomsbury and
Kensington, as well as Communist-organised strikes in the docks, notably
in 1948 and 1949, when Attlee threatened to bring in troops to smash the
strikes. By 1953, Stratford-atte-Bow was a community in transition. Phil
Piratin had lost his seat in parliament to Labour, and new estates were
offering homes to those bombed out in the war. While many were
apparently left behind in the old 'two-up-and-two-down' pre-war houses,
others moved to suburbia further east. Familiar family structures were
broken up. New light industry began to move to the area, providing better
working conditions and wages. But so too did the gangsters: serious crime
focussed on east London in the 1950s became a particular menace.

The theatrical tradition of the East End was one of illegitimacy and
bravado. In 1740, Henry Giffard opened a theatre at Goodman's Fields
without securing the necessary patent from the licensing authorities. But
he employed the young David Garrick, who made his first London
appearance here as Richard III on 19 October 1741, and soon caused such a
sensation by his acting that this illegal theatre threatened to oust the major
patent theatres in Drury Lane and Covent Garden from their primacy. But
the following year Garrick was inveigled to join Drury Lane, and the threat
receded. Later theatres in the East End were similarly illegitimate, if less
salubrious. In 1838 James Grant reported on the unlicensed Penny
Theatres, or 'Gaffs', in his *Sketches in London*. Mostly patronised by young
people, he found that 'At the east end of the town, they literally swarm as to
numbers. Ratcliffe-highway, the Commercial-road, Mile-end-road, and
other places in that direction, are thickly studded with Penny Theatres.'[2]
Some of these held hundreds of spectators, others mere tens. Some were
splendidly housed with a pit, gallery and even boxes, others were little

more than a derelict shop or warehouse. But the programmes in all these 'penny gaffs' were similar, usually lasting for less than an hour, and repeated up to nine times in a single afternoon and evening. Shakespeare was a favourite author, *Hamlet, Macbeth* or *Richard III* being performed in a matter of twenty minutes. A soot-smeared Othello was most popular of all. The rest of the programme mingled even shorter works—frightful melodramas, excruciating farces, old-fashioned pantomimes, punctuated by comic songs, clog dances and the like. With an influx of Jews into the area in the late nineteenth and early twentieth centuries, this fare was somewhat improved by a number of distinctive Yiddish theatres. But it was the Theatre Royal, which opened its doors on 17 December 1884, that came to dominate live entertainment in the area.

The theatre, converted from a wheelwright's shop, was described in *The Era* as being 'ugly in the extreme' outside, 'but the interior presents a very pretty and attractive appearance'.[3] The originator of the project, Charles Dillon, chose for his first production Bulwer Lytton's *Richelieu*, made popular earlier in the century by William Charles Macready, and revived by Henry Irving. But although comparatively well received by the press, and followed by a typical series of popular Victorian dramas—*East Lynne, The Lady of Lyons, The Shaughraun* and several Shakespeare productions—the theatre found it hard to fill its seats, and Dillon's management soon gave way to that of Albert O'Leary Fredericks. He managed to stabilise the finances, while offering a programme for which the following is perhaps not untypical:

July 27 1891 for a week
The New and Original Sensational Drama, in a
Prologue and Four Acts (re-written), entitled –
HUMANITY
Or, A Passage in the Life of Grace Darling
Written by Hugh Marston and Leonard Rae. New scenery by Locket,
Hillyard and R. Browne. Produced under the Direction of
Mr John Lawson.

John Lawson plays Hasson Cleopatra, alias Parker, in disguise as a Persian Jew
And later—Jacob Silvani, in his original conception of the 19th century Jew.
Other characters—Joshua Langley, an Outcast,
Jacob Cuthbert, a Demon
Pious Pat and Nugget Ned, miners
Binks, a travelling photographer
And Grace Barton, the lighthouse keeper's daughter,
(played by Miss Ada Burkinshaw)

The theatre presented a new play each week. The programme for spring 1891 included *East Lynne, Dangers of London, Little Lord Fauntleroy* and *The*

New Mazeppa. That summer the fare included the opera *Pepita*, Irish melodramas like *The Fenian* and *Leaves of Shamrock*, as well as expected dramas such as *Jane Shore*, *Lights o' London* and, that autumn, *Romany Rye*. Meanwhile, Albert Fredericks was elected to the local council as a Labour member, and later elevated to alderman. When he died in 1901, the theatre passed to his daughter, Caroline, who spent over £5,000 refurbishing it, including installing electricity, and by the First World War the theatre was thriving.

In 1919 Caroline Fredericks died, and two years later the building was badly damaged by fire. It struggled to re-open, presenting now old-fashioned melodramas like *Sweeney Todd, the Demon Barber*, but even so, by 1926 it was forced to close. Its continuance became precarious, and in 1932 the Fredericks family lost control. In 1935 there was a 'grand re-opening' when Ivy Maurice and her 'unique' repertory company—'the only company that gives three performances in one—Drama, variety, farce'—took over, performing twice nightly a programme which changed every two days. Thus, a typical week's programme consisted of: Monday and Tuesday—*The Soldier's Rosary*; Wednesday and Thursday—*Smilin' Through*; Friday and Saturday (for adults only)—*Should a Wife Refuse?* On Saturday afternoon the company presented a 'Grand children's performance'—*Uncle Tom's Cabin*. Admission prices were threepence for the gallery, sixpence for the Pit, ninepence for the upper circle and one shilling for stalls and dress circle.

After the war, the actor David Horne secured a twenty-year lease on the theatre and ran a middle-of-the-road but not unambitious three-weekly repertoire. His 'scenic director' was Richard Southern, later an influential theatre historian and theorist. He charged prices ranging from a shilling for an unreserved seat in the gallery, three shillings and sixpence in the upper circle, seven and sixpence in the dress circle and stalls, to one guinea for a box. The programme in Horne's first year included *The Second Mrs Tanqueray*, *Pygmalion* and, at Christmas, Anstey's *Vice Versa* followed by a traditional Harlequinade. Later seasons continued this kind of fare. In 1947, it contained *Mrs Warren's Profession*, Priestley's *I Have Been Here Before*, and Horne's own *Demaris*, in a review of which J.C. Trewin noted that 'the fervour of the company and the responsiveness of its audience showed that Stratford-atte-Bow is both fortunate in its repertory players and well pleased with them',[4] though *The Times* opined that *Demaris* did not 'reach the usual standard at this theatre'.[5] This kind of repertoire, however, was unsustainable in Stratford. Horne estimated that the theatre needed to sell 4,500 tickets each week to remain solvent, but he was unable to achieve this, at a time when an average of over 60,000 people per week attended the local dirt track speedway races.

In 1949, weekly repertory was instituted, but in April 1950 the theatre became a 'try out' venue for new musicals, including *Lili Marlene*, *Cowboy Casanova* and *Bob's Your Uncle*, none of which reached the West End. Later that year it was presenting *Box and Cox* and *Lady Audley's Secret*, and its last show before Theatre Workshop took over was *Jane Comes to Town*, an adaptation of a *Daily Mirror* cartoon strip. The theatre before 1953, therefore, had a history of struggling to achieve an interesting repertoire in the face of a depressing apathy in the local population, and consequently unending financial struggle. Not much would change quickly when Theatre Workshop assumed the tenancy.

The condition of the building when Theatre Workshop entered it was somewhere between poor and appalling, but at least the rent was low. The theatre was situated within a maze of two-up two-down houses, and was damp, smelly and cold. The antique, anthracite-fired boiler barely functioned. The carpets and seats were torn or worn out, the paintwork was peeling where it was not rubbed away, the roof leaked and there was no hot water. The stage itself was high, wide and echoey. Nevertheless, the company set about cleaning it, and creating somewhere not only to perform but also, at least in these early days, to sleep, for there was no money for the actors to rent accommodation. But the place obviously exerted some sort of fascination, for after its initial booking of six weeks the company stayed, and in 1955 raised enough money to purchase the building.

There was no income except from the box office, and some Sunday evening concerts, often 'Ballads and Blues' from the now semi-detached Ewan MacColl. Audiences in the first few years were usually as small as they often had been on tour, and though there was nothing new about empty seats in Theatre Workshop's auditoria, here particular efforts had to be made to build up the numbers. Often the actors met spectators after the performance to thank them for coming, and sometimes to hold out a bucket for any contributions. The programme changed, at least initially, every two weeks, though this soon became three weeks, but the local people largely remained indifferent. When audience numbers began to improve two or three years later, it was mostly non-local and non-working-class people who came. Was it possible to create a new kind of audience for theatre, however good? Would it ever be possible?

The new situation also demanded a new management structure. Though Ewan MacColl's name remained on the headed notepaper for a couple more years, a new triumvirate led the company now: Joan Littlewood, Gerry Raffles and the designer, John Bury, who was certainly less fervent about politics, and perhaps less committed to Theatre Workshop, than Ewan MacColl had been. Gerry Raffles became 'our General Manager and our only hope', in Joan Littlewood's words,[6] and his success may be gauged from Murray Melvin's comment that 'Gerry enabled Joan to do what she wanted, which was plays. That's all she did—he took care of the admin, finances and the rest of it.'[7] John Bury pointed out that Raffles's was 'the worst job of all. Joan was having a ball—it used to drive her mad, but she was having a ball.'[8] Littlewood and Bury, in fact, planned what they wanted, and Raffles attempted to finance it. He quarrelled with Littlewood frequently about the size of a cast, how long a production could run for, and inevitably the budget, but neither she nor Bury ever accepted his stipulations smoothly. 'Nobody else could have done Gerry's job', Bury commented wryly.[9]

Theatre Workshop remained nominally a democracy, but in practice democracy was diminishing. According to Clive Barker: 'The contradictions culminated in a company meeting which voted to remove Gerry Raffles as Manager. This was never acted on, and at that point certain things became clear: Joan led the company but Gerry held the power.'[10] Perhaps this was inevitable as some actors became interested in working in other theatres, and new actors replaced them. The earlier political fire burned lower, though plenty of the old sense of artistic mission remained.

Of the first plays put on in the spring of 1953, Alan Strachan noted the 'pared-down, rigorous truth' of *Twelfth Night*, the subtle Edwardian naturalist comedy, *Hindle Wakes*, and Sean O'Casey's *Juno and the Paycock*, as well as a 'coruscating' *Alchemist* that autumn.[11] In January 1954, Joan Littlewood presented *Richard II*, which to many was the highest point of her first year's work at Stratford. George Cooper played Bolingbroke and Harry H. Corbett Richard, in a production that examined the play anew, and sought to find how its ideas might resonate with the times. It is difficult today to believe how original this was in 1954. The climax came on John Bury's gloomy, dimly-lit prison set, when the king was seen wearing sackcloth and tethered to a stake, limping in a slow circle round it, and startling the spectators with 'I wasted time and now doth time waste me'. The production was revived the following year, coinciding thereby with the Old Vic's production of the same play with the elegant and elegiac John Neville in the title role giving a perfect example of what Littlewood called 'representationalism'. For Tom Milne,

> Joan Littlewood's production had rough edges in the minor roles and costumes, but the core of the play was thrust forward with passionate conviction, and it was impossible to fail to be excited, to think about the play and what it meant. By contrast [the Old Vic] production, elegantly dressed and spoken, remained quite dead.[12]

Harold Hobson, the fearsome critic of the *Sunday Times*, wrote:

From the start Mr Corbett's Richard is more than half-mad. His high, treacherous, sing-song voice, his glazed eyes, his up-tilted chin, his fancifully managed hands, his swift, light, stooping, little runs and leaps are all marks of a man who has only a distorted grasp of reality, and is living in an interior world of his own that touches objective existence only with disastrous obliqueness.[13]

This was a wholly new way of approaching Shakespeare.

Joan Littlewood presented two further plays from the Elizabethan period in 1954: Marston's *The Dutch Courtesan*, and the anonymous *Arden of Faversham*, which went on to be one of 'the biggest, the most unexpected, the most extraordinary successes that a British company has known in France'[14] when it was presented at the Paris International Theatre Festival in 1955. In May 1954 Theatre Workshop produced Ibsen's *An Enemy of the People*. There was a local scandal in West Ham about the water supply not unlike that in the play, and the gallery was packed for the first night. Littlewood staged the scene of the public meeting with Dr Stockmann on stage, and his family in one of the boxes. His audience was played by the real theatre audience, and, as he harangued them, they cheered, clapped and shouted out their approbation. In March 1955, *Volpone*, updated to a louche contemporary setting, was largely ignored by the British critics, but when it too was presented at the Paris International Festival that summer, it was greeted with stunned admiration. One French critic wrote:

> We do not possess a single company in France comparable to this one. Nothing which resembles its ardour, its generosity, and, to say all, its youth [. . .] You have set the Festival of Paris alight in its first week. We salute you with joy as being the purest, the simplest, and the greatest artists.[15]

Theatre Workshop had been invited to represent Britain at the Paris Festival, and though discouraged by the British establishment, they had made the visit unsupported, carrying the stage sets as hand luggage to save expense. After this, they returned to Paris in 1956 with *The Good Soldier Schweik*, in 1959 with *The Hostage* by Brendan Behan and in 1960 with another Jonson play, *Every Man in His Humour*. Each time the British establishment fumed, and each time the company were praised and admired.

Later in 1955 came Joan Littlewood's only serious encounter with Bertolt Brecht, and it was one of the few occasions when she disappointed. Perhaps she was too radical theatrically for Brecht—for she was more daring, more unorthodox than he ever was—or perhaps her innate anarchism tangled with his more overt Marxism. It seems also true, however, that she was unable to do justice to Mother Courage at the same time as directing the play. Oral tradition has it that Brecht had insisted that, for the British premiere of this play, the central part must be taken either by

7. Volpone (George Cooper) and Mosca (Maxwell Shaw) as spivs in Ben
Jonson's comedy, Stratford East, 1955.

Joan Littlewood or by Gracie Fields. Since Gracie Fields was otherwise
engaged, Littlewood took it herself. In fact, Oscar Lewenstein negotiated
the production with Brecht, who, when he heard that Littlewood was *not* to
play Courage, threatened to withdraw performance permission. Littlewood
hastily took over the part late in the rehearsal process, and did not impress.
She cut Courage's most famous song, tried to get by with too few actors,
added music where none was asked for and had the scenes changed too
obtrusively by the actors themselves. As for her own performance,
London's two most influential critics were for once unanimous: Kenneth
Tynan of the *Observer* called her 'over-parted and under-rehearsed'[16] and
Harold Hobson of the *Sunday Times* called her 'colourless, indecisive and
often inaudible.'[17]

Though in 1955 Littlewood lost her two most compelling actors, Harry
H. Corbett and George Cooper, her Elizabethan bow was not yet shot. She
presented notable productions of the tragedies, *Edward II* in 1956, and *The
Duchess of Malfi* and *Macbeth* in 1957. *Edward II* was played on a vast stylised
map of England and depicted not simply the downfall of a king, but the
puzzlement and struggles of a human being in a production that made
unprecedented contact with the audience's humanity. There was no false
'beauty' about this, and certainly no statuesque sorrowing in the
conventional manner of English star performances: rather it was a steadily
focused drive to death. As for *Macbeth*, Littlewood's approach to the play
was original and its execution incisive. It was set in the 1930s, and initially
offended because it appeared to criticise not only the modern army, but also
the royal family, a piece of genuine bravado in the sycophantic New
Elizabethan Age. This Macbeth was like Franco, an army general who
became a dictator. At the outset he was facing the firing squad: the events of
the play became a series of flashbacks as he confronted death. This required
some reordering of the scenes, and some cutting, but the result was
certainly startling. Littlewood justified her procedures in the face of
criticism:

> We try to wipe away the dust of three hundred years, to strip off the
> 'poetical' interpretation which the nineteenth-century sentimentalists put
> on these plays and which are still current today. The poetry of
> Shakespeare's day was a muscular, active, forward-moving poetry, in that it
> was like the people to whom it belonged. If Shakespeare has any
> significance today, a production of his work must not be regarded as a
> historical reconstruction, but as an instrument still sharp enough to
> provoke thought, to extend man's [*sic*] awareness of his problems, and to
> strengthen his belief in his kind.[18]

The originality of this conception may be hard to comprehend today.

Probably this sequence of productions did not intentionally amount to a
co-ordinated map of Britain under Elizabeth and Churchill, but effectively
this is what Theatre Workshop and Joan Littlewood achieved between 1953
and about 1956 or 1957. Less overtly political than Theatre Workshop's
earlier incarnation as a touring theatre, less specifically Communist in
times less sympathetic to such apparent extremism, Joan Littlewood's
pageant was nonetheless shockingly different from the pageant presented
by the political hegemony of early 1950s Britain, or that of the conventional
theatre of Stratford-upon-Avon or the Old Vic. As Dominic Shellard has
pointed out, 'What is perhaps most noticeable about the London stage
between 1952 and 1954 is how completely indifferent it was to
contemporary events'.[19] Instead of the sham grandeur of the Elizabethan
coronation, the performed gravitas of an almost senile prime minister, the

deft claiming of a mountaineering triumph which rightly belonged to younger, different nations, on Theatre Workshop's stage was performed a more truthful and a more interesting Britain. This had space for Schweik's cheerful proletarian subversiveness in an age of absurd military conscription; for the warmth and truth of a Dutch courtesan whom her 'betters' deemed a tart; the agony and madness of trying to rule this realm of Britain; the terror and pity of the pitiless dictator facing the firing squad; the petty-minded money-grubbing of Jonsonian spivs, symbol of the materialistic philistinism of the age. This was a swirling, knife-sharp kaleidoscope of contemporary humanity and its pitiable, risible, fretful comedy. Not many critics—or even spectators—were looking, but Littlewood exposed a face of the age which the age probably did not much care to see. It was too smug, too complacent, too dull to wonder if indeed that which it deemed immutable—royalty, hierarchy, respect and so forth—was in fact fragile, in flux, only a constructed illusion. Theatre Workshop's was a brave examination through a series of productions of classic drama, of the shadows behind the shiny gloss of the New Elizabethan Age.

To make the received repertoire of classic plays into such a coherent critique of contemporary society was an intensely original project, probably unique in British theatre history. That it was achieved on a shoestring, without subsidy, is staggering. This fact alone should make some later artistic directors of more prestigious national companies blush.

CHAPTER TWELVE

Matters Financial

Artists have always needed patrons to subsidise their work; but for that work to be valuable, they have also needed freedom, a lack of restraint. The licensed jester is a symbol of the artist. Theatre Workshop never solved this conundrum, failing to receive the levels of subsidy lavished on other, lesser theatres, and at the same time falling foul of the theatrical censor.

The history of state subsidy for the arts in Britain effectively begins during the Second World War, when the Treasury made a grant to the Pilgrim Trust for concerts in villages and small towns. To cater for any further such requests, the Board of Education set up a Council for the Encouragement of Music and the Arts (CEMA) in April 1940, with John Maynard Keynes as its chairman. Its first grant was of £150 to the Pilgrim Players, a religious touring company run by Martin Browne, and in the next five years it added to them an unexpectedly diverse list: the Adelphi Players and Adelphi Dance Company, Salisbury Repertory Theatre, Birmingham Repertory Theatre, the Birmingham-based Travelling Repertory Company, Sadler's Wells opera and ballet, Ballet Jooss and Ballet Rambert, Norman Marshall Theatre Company, Donald Wolfit's lunch-time Shakespeare recitals at the Strand Theatre, and more. In 1942 CEMA set up regional panels with assessors, including experienced professionals like Lewis Casson, to assess applicants, and the same year it effectively rescued the eighteenth-century Theatre Royal, Bristol, which became the Bristol Old Vic. In August 1946, CEMA mutated into the Arts Council, with Keynes still in the chair. However, instead of pursuing CEMA's original remit of taking music and the arts to areas without artistic facilities, the Arts Council's policy soon became one that largely sponsored building-based companies, though—inconsistently enough—they guaranteed Unity's professional company against loss for their tour of Odets's *Golden Boy* to South Wales mining districts in 1946, and they continued to fund the Midlands-based Travelling Repertory Company for several years.

After the first week's performances in Kendal in August 1945, Theatre Workshop had amassed sixty-seven pounds, five shillings and ninepence. Immediately, on 20 August 1945, Joan Littlewood wrote to CEMA enquiring about the possibility of a subvention. The reply came in the form of a criticism of the company's organisation and budgeting. According to Joan Littlewood, the official they dealt with stated: 'Your business organisation appears to be weak. A group earning an average of eighty pounds a week is hardly a financial proposition.'[1] Her word-for-word recall may be doubted, but the drift of the Arts Council argument is only too believable. Help is given to theatre companies not on the basis of their artistic or social ambition or excellence, but on the soundness of their business plans. This position still largely holds. According to Ewan MacColl, 'from then on for the next four or five years, [Theatre Workshop] was constantly moving from one financial crisis to another'.[2] In 1946, following a further rebuff from the Arts Council, company members all wrote begging letters to plausible benefactors, but the advice they received in replies suggested only applying to the Arts Council. The Arts Council, however, would not consider a company that was continuously losing money. It was a vicious circle. Some advisers told the Council that the work of Theatre Workshop was excellent, others said it was poor, opinions perhaps formulated more according to political than aesthetic criteria. It was the company's 'attitude'—a euphemism for politics, surely—that was wrong.

Effectively, for years the members subsidised the company by accepting low—sometimes almost invisible—wages, by performing all sorts of chores actors are not normally asked to perform, and by working hours so long they almost defy belief. Occasionally they received a contribution from Gerry Raffles's supportive and moneyed father. In February 1948, the Theatre Conference chaired by J.B. Priestley and attended by, among others, the chancellor of the exchequer, Sir Stafford Cripps, criticised the Arts Council for the inadequacy of its policies with regard to funding. Cripps, probably at least partly in response, cut Entertainment Tax, and later that year the government's Local Government Act empowered local authorities to raise a rate of up to sixpence in the pound for expenditure on the arts. Few local authorities actually did so, and the Arts Council's policy remained frozen where it had been, at least as far as Theatre Workshop were concerned. That year, a quarter of its total budget was given to Covent Garden Theatre. In October, Joan Littlewood noted: 'Our debts are ghastly pressing. Three "legal actions" if we don't cough up this week'.[3] There were further appeals for help but the Arts Council failed even to answer their letters, and the company went into abeyance, having just returned from Sweden. When Tom Driberg, a supportive Labour MP, tried to obtain help from the government, it was clear that Llewellyn Rees of the Arts Council was working assiduously to undermine the company.[4] In the end, even Ewan MacColl had to admit: 'Our aims could not be achieved by touring, at least not unless we were subsidised'.[5]

For Theatre Workshop, this was another reason to find a settled base. But when the newly arrived company appealed for help from local councils, they were offered merely help with their publicity, always provided that any help given would not cost the councils anything. In 1954, the Arts Council gave Theatre Workshop £150, though at the end of the year they wrote that they wished to be sure of Theatre Workshop's 'financial stability' before they could offer anything more. Perhaps on cue, the company was sued a few months later, and when the bank refused further support, bankruptcy was the only option. This happened immediately after the triumphant appearance at the Paris International Festival, for which no financial support had been forthcoming, and in fact the French hosts had had to lend them money to return to Britain. In the light of the Paris success, however, the Arts Council offered a further tiny subvention to the company. The subsidy for that year therefore finally reached the meagre total of £500, and the same amount was awarded in 1956.

In November 1957 this amount was raised to £1,000 in view of the fact that West Ham Council had raised their contribution, but in the early part of the next financial year, the Arts Council proposed to end their subsidy, apparently because Theatre Workshop had failed to build a local audience. Once again the company went out of business. In consequence, the novelist Graham Greene wrote to *The Times*, offering to give Theatre Workshop £100 if nine other benefactors could be found to do likewise to make up the £1,000. M.J. McRobert, deputy secretary of the Arts Council, responded with partly spurious reasons for the cut, whereupon Joan Littlewood herself replied, setting out her case. Meanwhile, West Ham Council declared its opposition to the Arts Council's policy, in the light of which the Arts Council once again reversed their position, and in October the theatre opened again.[6]

The first production was Brendan Behan's *The Hostage*, for which no 'New Writing' grant had been awarded because the script had not been submitted two months in advance of the first performance. This was not surprising, since the script was still being made then, a concept of creativity that the Arts Council seemed incapable of understanding. *A Taste of Honey* by Shelagh Delaney was concurrently being acclaimed, and the Arts Council's treatment of this play demonstrated another, but equally obfuscatory, facet of their approach, at least to Theatre Workshop. In June 1958 an equivocal report by the Arts Council reader meant that this production of a new play was only grudgingly awarded a minimal grant of £150 against loss. In return, the Arts Council was to be guaranteed 10 per cent of any profits it made. By January 1959, when the play's success was evident, the Council was sniffing suspiciously at the actors' contracts and trying to find out about the financial arrangements of the possible forthcoming film of the play. They were obviously worried that they would not receive their 10 per cent, or that it might be reduced by the actors' receipt of reasonable wages. By May 1960, they were still seeking every penny of the 10 per cent profits, despite Theatre Workshop's bank overdraft. Gerry Raffles calculated that *A Taste of Honey* made the theatre more money in less than a year than the Arts Council had granted it since its inception. But still the Arts Council wanted its bond. Matters were further complicated when local councillors, seeing plays like *The Hostage* and *A Taste of Honey* transferring to the West End, also thought to withdraw their grant. '"You can't tell me," expostulated a councillor to a theatre administrator in the bar, "that those two (that is, Joan Littlewood and Gerry Raffles) aren't making a fortune out of the borough"'.[7] In fact, their wages were approximately three pounds per week.

The battles continued for as long as Joan Littlewood was associated with Theatre Workshop, and indeed beyond then. A brief comparison with the grants awarded by the Arts Council to the decidedly more respectable Royal Court Theatre, whose Angry Young Men were usually neither Communists nor working class, is instructive. The Royal Court's first grant was for £5,500 in the 1958–59 season, when Theatre Workshop's was stuck on £1,000. In 1960–61, Theatre Workshop, whose running costs were nearly £20,000, received £2,000 and the Royal Court £8,000. Two years later, Theatre Workshop's grant rose to £3,000, by which time the Royal Court's grant was £20,000.

'Over the years, no rich heiress was ever courted so assiduously as we courted the Arts Council', Ewan MacColl remarked,[8] and in 1988 Joan Littlewood wrote:

> I passed my working life in the U.K. to the accompaniment of noises from a long line of Arts Council directors telling me my work wouldn't do for them. The truth being that they would have liked to see Theatre Workshop in hell since it challenged all the standards they held high.[9]

Should oppositional theatre be funded by the state? The question has been debated for decades. On the one hand, the state has an obligation to the taxpayer to use all moneys it receives through taxation responsibly; on the other hand, if democracy is to mean anything, those who pay taxes have a right to expect their viewpoint to be heard in drama or any other medium. There were plenty of explanations as to why Theatre Workshop was treated so shabbily for so long by the Arts Council, ranging from simple political expediency through to Joan Littlewood's refusal to work with a small company of actors. It has been pointed out also that a decade or two later, her subsidy would surely have been much larger. But this is to ignore the pioneering trail that she blazed. Perhaps the plays Theatre Workshop presented were too subversive. Perhaps Stratford East was in the 'wrong' place so that it could never attract the 'right' audiences. Joan Littlewood's creative methods were never understood, any more than the company's managerial procedures were approved. The Arts Council had less money then, of course, and the whole business of state subsidy for the arts was less accepted than it has become. But one feels the truth is that Littlewood was never respectful enough of the Council, its officers or its policies, for there ever to be anything but hostility between them. Since they held the purse strings, Littlewood suffered the loss.

The final irony is that when, many years later, Howard Goorney came to write *The Theatre Workshop Story*, the Arts Council, which had in a sense virtually starved him as an actor with Theatre Workshop, now handed him a munificent grant to write about it.

CHAPTER THIRTEEN

The Theatre Workshop Actor

If any particular years can be isolated from the development of a constantly evolving enterprise such as Theatre Workshop, the years 1953 to 1956 could be distinguished as those when the actors came into their own. The years of uncompromising training bore undeniable fruit, and the continuation of a stable ensemble, even though the membership inevitably changed slowly over the years, made an enviable difference, as an assessment a few years later made clear:

> One of the most exciting features of the Theatre Workshop seasons of 1954 and 1955 was the extraordinary development of Harry H. Corbett and Maxwell Shaw, within a permanent company, in varied and often unexpected roles in such plays as *The Long Voyage Home*, *Arden of Faversham*, *Volpone*, *Mother Courage*, *Androcles and the Lion* and *The Good Soldier Schweik*. There was no question of engaging a 'suitable' actor for certain roles. The permanent company had to meet the challenge and the results were stimulating, often exciting. This challenge in being invited to play roles apparently rather outside his existing scope is the only way in which an actor can really develop.[1]

While this is part—and an important part—of the reason why Theatre Workshop's actors were so impressive at the Theatre Royal, Stratford East, it takes no account of the extraordinary and intense relationship these actors developed with their director, Joan Littlewood, and this must be explored before a final account can be taken.

Forty years later, Victor Spinetti, an actor largely associated with the last phase of Theatre Workshop's life, made an attempt to convey this:

> Joan was their mother superior and dean of discipline who made them read books and rehearse through the night; thunderous Joan with her woolly cap pulled down menacingly over her forehead when they put on a sloppy performance. Or Joan flinging that same hat high in the air and skipping when they triumphed. Which they often did.[2]

Spinetti also said: 'Joan held us extremely tightly, but inside you felt completely free'.[3] That support, from which the actor can soar, was crucial.

Littlewood herself said that actors should feel 'as necessary as bread and wine and libraries'[4] and that in her theatre (as in Meyerhold's) 'everything should come from the actor, since only the actor appears on the stage'.[5]

First, Littlewood paid attention to every performer on the stage: 'As far as Joan was concerned there were no "spear-carriers", and she gave all the attention that was needed to any problem that affected the smallest or largest role'.[6] Even when the company was on tour and exhausted, the art of acting was always taken extremely seriously, and Littlewood discussed the performances with actors, both in the group and individually, late into the night. There was reason for James Booth's remark that 'You never felt that you were working for her. You were always working with her.'[7] Ewan MacColl recorded that Littlewood 'had an inexhaustible store of patience and the ability to coax performances out of actors which were far in excess of their normal level of achievement'.[8] Each actor was an individual within the ensemble, and Joan Littlewood's understanding of so many difficult egos is illustrated by her dealings with the young Barbara Windsor. On the one hand, she had the ability to disconcert Windsor: 'On the first day of rehearsals we all turned up word perfect, and the first thing she [Joan Littlewood] did was pick the script up and say, "Well, this is a load of fucking rubbish, isn't it?" And tore it up'.[9] On the other hand, she defended her when she might have felt threatened. While making the film of *Sparrers Can't Sing*, Windsor recalled: 'A cameraman told me I was doing too much with my face in the close-ups. He said, "This is a movie, not theatre." But Joan said to him, "Fuck off. Don't tell my little actress what to do"'.[10] During a rehearsal of *Fings Ain't Wot They Used T'Be*, Littlewood had Windsor and Toni Palmer improvise as horses, and after this had continued for a certain time, Windsor told Littlewood, 'We're fed up with this, Joan, we're going up the market to do our shopping'. Littlewood apparently turned to the other actors and commented, 'They're the only ones with any sense'. This was a relationship of mutual respect, partly at least as a result of Barbara Windsor's determination to stand up for herself. On one of Joan Littlewood's director's notes to her actor, Windsor scrawled, 'Don't fucking aggravate me, Joan. I've got enough problems.' Littlewood found this both extremely funny and thoroughly admirable.[11] As Toni Palmer commented, Joan Littlewood 'was an extremely clever woman who wanted to get something out of people in very different ways from anyone else. Everybody else had Barbara Windsor bouncing her tits, but Joan saw in her a real ability.'[12]

Littlewood undoubtedly gave many actors self-belief, so that, as James Booth explained, they found they could achieve levels of performance they never knew they were capable of.[13] She pushed Victor Spinetti to go 'out front' as the audience for the first night of *Oh What a Lovely War* were entering the theatre, and talk to them informally, chat, ask them how they were, and so on. 'For the very first time, he was free, confident, easy.'[14] She made a nervous Patience Collier overcome her self-doubt over singing in *The Hostage*, so that Collier later remembered 'singing this song every night in a gentle, pretty voice to marvellous applause, and it was Joan's doing. It really was quite magic, it was all in my head, but Joan had put it there, and I became so happy on the stage, and so relaxed.'[15]

However, Joan Littlewood did not simply understand her actors. She identified their problems and refused to allow them to ignore them. Thus Victor Spinetti found placing his feet problematic, and Littlewood sent him a note: 'Your performance is wonderful, but your feet are waiting for a bus'.[16] More seriously, she compelled the actor who played Marlowe's Edward II to confront his own latent homosexuality, which in 1956 was no easy task.[17] And some said that Littlewood liked confrontation for confrontation's sake, and would deliberately create situations where equanimity was impossible. 'She could be dangerously and woundingly outspoken', Ewan MacColl remembered.[18] Certainly she was frequently abrasive, and often notably foul-mouthed, larding her speech with large numbers of the most scarlet swear words she knew. She was renowned also for testing an actor's resilience and commitment. Brian Murphy recalled: 'Joan stripped you down. All your inhibitions were exercised so you knew what they were, then if you could stick it—it was a mental and physical assault course—she built you up again with an assuredness that your place was there on the stage.' 'That was her genius', he added laconically.[19] According to Sheila Hancock, 'she could be an absolute cow', but she also 'gave you courage to take risks and be outrageous'.[20] Larry Dann, who appeared in *Oh What a Lovely War*, illustrated something of her technique in detail:

> She did her famous 'destroy and build up' on me during *Oh What a Lovely War*. While we were on tour in America we picked up these four American actors. I was twenty-three and unbearably conceited, and she began taking parts away from me until I only had four entrances and for all of them I would get reams of her colour-coded notes [. . .] The notes basically said: 'last night's show was very slack, what the fuck's going on?' or that I was 'no bloody good', had no 'pzazz'. I was so depressed. Then the night we opened in New York, Joan came up and said: 'These Americans aren't very good, take all your parts back.' I floated through that show.[21]

Women seemed to suffer from Joan Littlewood's harshness more than men, and there are plenty of anecdotes about actresses in tears at Stratford East. It was those who stood up to her, like Barbara Windsor, who were able to do their best work there.

If this could be excused it was because it was part of Littlewood's policy to use whatever tactics seemed to her necessary to push each actor to the limit of his or her capability. 'She wouldn't allow self-indulgence', said Toni Palmer,[22] but this was so that the actor could 'find' the truth of the part for her or himself. Murray Melvin explained this when describing his acting in *A Taste of Honey*: 'Not once in rehearsals was it mentioned that the boy I was playing was gay [. . .] I had to find the person'.[23] In Littlewood's theatre, the actor had to 'find' the character, yet retain enough of themselves so that the audience knew it was an artistic creation. In the theatre, we 'believe' what we are seeing, yet simultaneously we know it is a fiction, that we are watching, not 'real people', but actors. It is *their version* of reality. This is the exact opposite of what was—and is—usually seen on British stages, that pretence which Littlewood called 'representationalism'. Toni Palmer articulated this as well as anyone: 'Being Joan's kind of actor means portraying your version of somebody else', she said.[24] This is an extremely sophisticated notion. Peter Bridgmont made the distinction from his days as an actor in the company: 'I remember [. . .] Joan Littlewood commenting that the audience always knew when a performance was a complete creation of the actor or when it relied on the actor's personality. In the first instance the audience will join you, but in the second they will somehow be disappointed'.[25] The distinction is between, on the one hand, an actor who 'finds' the character—his version of the person—and on the other, one who relies on other extraneous factors, such as 'personality', or 'tricks of the trade', or pre-existing conceptions. The actor must be 'inside' their version of the character throughout. Littlewood criticised Louis Jouvet's performance in Molière's *Ecole des Femmes*, for 'representing, not being'.[26]

To achieve this kind of artistic truth, actors had to explore the play as a whole, the world to which their version of the character would belong. They were expected to research the historical and social background of the action, its political implications, other works by or about the author, and so on. Then, actors might be asked in rehearsal to change parts in order to understand better the other characters, and the nature of their relationships. Littlewood's rehearsals were demanding, and required intense concentration, which the actors trained for. According to Victor Spinetti, she 'created the kind of concentration in actors that you had as a child, making something out of Plasticine'.[27] A timetable given to actors for a week in 1948, when *The Flying Doctor* (*F.D.*) and *Johnny Noble* were being performed, *Don Perlimplin* and *The Other Animals* were in rehearsal, and general training was also being fitted in, gives some idea of the demands on Theatre Workshop's actors:

Mon aft   2.30–6.30   Mary & Johnny (4–5.30 Jean with Doreen)
" *evening*   7.30–9.30   Movement in 1st scene – *Perlimplin*

Tues   9.30–10.30 Movement. Guards and Hanau
           10.0–10.30 Voice production (Led by Bennie)
           10.30–11.0 Exercises/Marg/Jean with Doreen (L.Girl)
           11.0–1.0   Unemployed sequence
           2.30–6.0   "   "
           7.30–9.30 Movement in 2nd scene – *Perlimplin*
           9.30–10.30 March of Dead

Wed   10.0–10.30 Voice exercises (Led by John)
           10.30–11.0 Exercises/Denis/Jean with Julie
           11.0–1.0   Boxing sequence with Jean
           2.30–4.30 Evening street – Eddie, Mary, Neighbour, Youth
                      Narrator, Girls
           7.30   F.D. at Boggart Hole Clough

Thurs   9.30–10.30 Girl in white, green
           10.0–10.30 Voice exercises (Led by Julie)
           10.30–11.0 Exercises/Howard/Jean with girls and David
           11.0–1.0   Letter scene
           2.30–6.0   Gestapo scene
           7.30–9.30 3rd scene – *Perlimplin* (Parrot House)
           7.30–9.30 Jean on lunatics entrance with Hamlets [*sic*]

Friday   9.30–10.30 Lunatic scene movement
           10.30–11.0 Voice work – Ewan
           11.0–1.0   The coming of war
           2.30   Station scene
           4.0   Gun laying scene
           7.30   Last scene

Saturday 10.0–12.30 Last scene. F.D. 2 perfs

Sunday will have to be worked too in preparation for a run through with costumes on Sunday evening.[28]

Such a heavy schedule was quite unique in British theatre in the 1940s and 1950s, as was Littlewood's approach to performance through the physical. Truth on the stage is concrete, physical, rooted in what Stanislavsky called 'action'. 'Actions' were what Littlewood's actors had to find, a task made easier by the training they had received in the techniques of Rudolf Laban. Thus, a scene from a play by Molière was first approached through mime, walking it through to the accompaniment of music by Couperin. Only after 'we'd caught the gist of the story' were the actors allowed to 'throw in one or two phrases'.[29] Howard Goorney as John of Gaunt was encouraged to clown his way through his most famous speech, to speak the lines in gibberish, and to find the physical efforts, in Laban's sense, implicit in the speech.[30] Dominic Shellard has pointed out how backward British acting was then, compared with Europe and America: Jean-Louis Barrault and the Comédie Française's technique was rooted in the physical, in contrast to the fixation on the voice and the beautifully spoken, which seemed to dominate British classical acting. Brecht's concept of the *Gestus*, also a physical notion, was undreamed of in Britain, while the American 'Method', developed by Lee Strasberg and Elia Kazan, was an equally foreign approach, with nothing remotely like it practised in Britain. Even 'the brash, glittering, technically perfect American musicals, symbolised by Rodgers and Hammerstein's smash hit, *Oklahoma!*',[31] left complacent English producers rubbing their eyes. Littlewood reacted differently. When she saw the New York-based dance company of Katherine Dunham perform in a Manchester music hall in 1949, for example, she was at first enthusiastic: 'Colours flashed and rippled as barefoot dancers leapt into the light—citron, lemon, bronze. Eyes accustomed to a northern winter's light were dazzled with viridian, purple, saffron—and flower patterns of cerise. Improvised mouth music accompanied some of the dancing'—and then she wanted to understand, and perhaps adapt what she had seen. Noting that Dunham was an anthropologist as well as a choreographer, and that her company was 'really a social experiment', she went on to pinpoint what was significant for her in Dunham's performance: 'The training of the company and the choreography', and these, she asserted, were 'the work of a highly cultivated mind'.[32] Dunham, Laban-trained, exposed one more example of what the British theatre was failing to do.

Joan Littlewood and the Theatre Workshop company led the breakout from the suffocating insularity of British theatre around 1950. According to Brendan Behan, compared to the famous Abbey Theatre, spectators at Theatre Workshop felt they were 'watching a jet-propelled bomber'.[33] When a new actress arrived at a rehearsal of *Johnny Noble*:

> It was a gloomy afternoon and we were vainly trying to capture the mood of a dockside street on a warm summer evening. She watched, listened to David's tape of sirens, kicked off her shoes and walked right into the imagined street and, with imaginary chalk, marked a hopscotch oblong on the floor. One after another, the others began watching as she hopped around and wobbled on one leg as she bent to pick up her imaginary chalk.[34]

Instinctively, this actress had found how Theatre Workshop approached scenes. Jean Newlove insisted that Theatre Workshop actors 'were encouraged to approach their characters through an exploration of their movement habits and relationships',[35] a thoroughly un-British, continental approach. The dynamic application of Laban's system, for example, enabled their bodies to lead their minds in the creation of exceptionally clear dramatic portrayals. Thus, in *Arden of Faversham*, the murderers, Shakebag and Black Will, stalk their prey over rough, tufty ground, through bog and over rocks, in dense fog. They trip, lose one another, find each other again. The movement was worked on without any reference to the words, because the movement derives from the situation. The fog is dense, the characters must stop to listen. Perhaps they touch one another to reassure themselves their companion is still there. Jean Newlove had the actors rehearsing with closed eyes. What were the movements? Not as light as a dab nor as heavy as a thrust; consequently she invented the 'dab-thrust'. Only when the physical actions were telling the truth did the actors begin to consider the scripted lines. In *The Flying Doctor*, Gorgibus, a lumbering old fool, fears he has lost his daughter, so that his movements speed up: he remains 'heavy' but now becomes unexpectedly fast, too. Marinette, meanwhile (played sometimes by Joan Littlewood, by the way) was also heavy, 'a very grounded character', according to Newlove; when she attacked Gorgibus with her feather duster, her energy increased, but her movements never became light. In *A Christmas Carol* the actors learned to pirouette and turn to give the illusion of skating, while as miners in *The Long Shift* they learned to hew coal by the use of their bodies. This was not conventional mime, but the practical application of Laban's dynamic system.

This use of movement as the basis for a performance was complemented by one of Joan Littlewood's best-known techniques, the use of 'reality' for actors. This was applied to Brendan Behan's *The Quare Fellow*:

> For the first week of rehearsals of *The Quare Fellow* we had no scripts. None of us had even read the play. We knew it was about prison life in Dublin, and that was enough for Joan. None of us had ever been in prison, and although we could all half-imagine what it was like, Joan set out to tell us more—the narrow world of steel and stone, high windows and clanging doors, the love-hate between warder and prisoner, the gossip, the jealousy and the tragedy—all the things that make up the fascination of dreariness. She took us onto the roof of the Theatre Royal. All the grimy slate and stone made it easy to believe we were in a prison yard. We formed up in a circle, and imagined we were prisoners out on exercise. Round and round we trudged for what seemed like hours—breaking now and then for a quick smoke and furtive conversation. Although it was just a kind of game, the boredom and meanness of it all was brought home. Next, the 'game' was extended—the whole dreary routine of washing out your cell, standing to attention, sucking up to the screws, trading tobacco, was improvised and developed. It began to seem less and less like a game, and more like real. By degrees the plot and script were introduced, although some of us never knew which parts we were playing until halfway through

the rehearsals. The interesting thing was that when she gave us the scripts we found that many of the situations we had improvised actually occurred in the play. All we had to do was learn the author's words.[36]

The actors had to *know* the reality, not be content with imagining it. Before commencing work on the first scene of *A Taste of Honey*, when Helen and Jo arrive exhausted, Avis Bunnage and Frances Cuka spent time dragging suitcases about the stage. In an extension of this use of 'reality', Joan Littlewood had the cast of Henry Chapman's *You Won't Always Be on Top*, which concerns a group of builders at work, actually learn bricklaying from a professional. And those who were playing soldiers in *Oh What a Lovely War* were put through long sessions of drill with a serving sergeant-major. All this was an extension, perhaps, of the original Theatre Workshop aim of 1945: 'In our theatre [. . .], an actor will be able to walk into a steel foundry and pass as a puddler, our actresses will be able to stand at a loom and look like any other Lancashire mill-girl'.[37] This work certainly produced an unusual level of honesty. 'She taught me truth',[38] Nigel Hawthorne wrote of his time with Joan Littlewood, and the 'stark authenticity' of the playing was often noticed.[39] 'What is a good actor?' she was asked in 1947. 'Part priest, part poet, part clown', she replied.[40] But it is notable that neither priests, poets nor clowns are permitted self-indulgence, and this vice, which Littlewood noticed in other theatres, was anathema to her. Thus, in *Volpone*, 'the Shakespearean voice' was nowhere given rein, and the actors, 'deprived of tights, ruffs and declamation [. . .] have to act'.[41] Harry H. Corbett 'found' Andrew Aguecheek in *Twelfth Night* by forgetting the conventional 'funny' character, and simply playing the action in the part. He himself was amazed, and 'never looked back'.[42] Moreover, nothing was to be taken for granted, or generalised. Joan Littlewood wrote: 'The smallest contact between characters in a remote corner of the stage must become objectively true and relevant. The actor must be freed from the necessity of making [. . .] generalisations.'[43] For this reason, she urged her actors to go to the parks and pubs and onto the streets to observe real people in real life. For they had to give audiences their version of the person they were portraying, and this involved respect for the truth of life as well as the actor's artistic truth. The problems were never-ending, but some of the solutions claimed on the way were unforgettable.

Theatre Workshop could not have achieved what it did without the permanent ensemble of actors—Littlewood's 'priests, poets and clowns'—which perhaps reached its most impressive in Theatre Workshop's 'middle period', the years immediately after the company settled at Stratford East. A brief selection from among the parts played in those years by the leading members of the company indicates the range and complexity that they were asked to encompass, unparalleled then in the British theatre. Harry H.

Corbett, for instance, during this period, played, besides other lesser parts, Joxer in *Juno and the Paycock*, Shakespeare's Richard II, Chris Hawthorne in *Hindle Wakes*, Bob Cratchit in *A Christmas Carol*, Khlestakov in *The Government Inspector*, Dick Dudgeon in Shaw's *The Devil's Disciple*, Peter Stockmann, the mayor, in Ibsen's *An Enemy of the People*, Mosbie in *Arden of Faversham*, Robert in *The Other Animals* and Sir Politick Would-be in *Volpone*. Howard Goorney's parts included Corbaccio in *Volpone*, Thomas Stockmann in *An Enemy of the People*, John of Gaunt in *Richard II*, the Mayor in *The Government Inspector*, Scrooge in *A Christmas Carol* and Lomov in *The Proposal*. John Blanshard's parts included Argan in *The Imaginary Invalid*, Nat Jeffcote in *Hindle Wakes*, the Magistrate in *Operation Olive Branch* and Corvino in *Volpone*. George Cooper, besides playing the title roles in *The Good Soldier Schweik*, *Jupiter's Night Out* (an adaptation of Giraudoux's *Amphitryon 38*) and *Volpone*, also appeared as the Captain in *Juno and the Paycock*, Black Will in *Arden of Faversham*, Cockledemoy in *The Dutch Courtesan*, and Alan Jeffcote in *Hindle Wakes*. Maxwell Shaw was Arden in *Arden of Faversham* and Mosca in *Volpone*. Among the women, Avis Bunnage played the name role in *The Dutch Courtesan*, Toinette in *The Imaginary Invalid*, Juno in *Juno and the Paycock*, Mrs Jeffcote in *Hindle Wakes*, Petra Stockmann in *An Enemy of the People* and Mrs Forster in *Landscape with Chimneys*. Julia Jones was Fanny in *Hindle Wakes* and Mrs Stockmann in *An Enemy of the People*. Leila Greenwood was Viola in *Twelfth Night*, Lysistrata in *Operation Olive Branch* and Beatrice in *Hindle Wakes*. It must be remembered, too, that these actors, when not playing leading parts, were still cast in smaller roles: Harry H. Corbett, for instance, had several small parts in *The Good Soldier Schweik*.

The productions were always controversial, aimed at facing contemporary Britain with an unblinking and radical stare. That despite this, so many of these actors should so often be praised by a press doubtful about Theatre Workshop as an enterprise (why couldn't they be based in the West End?) and more than doubtful about its political stance, is an extraordinary tribute to their work. A flavour of the performances can be gleaned from some contemporary reviews. Avis Bunnage, for instance, was admired for her sustained intensity: in *The Devil's Disciple*, she gave 'a fine portrayal of a bitter and disillusioned widow', while as Franceschina in *The Dutch Courtesan* she played with 'vixenish, jealous feeling' in a 'portrayal of anguished passion'.[44] Equally compelling, but utterly different were the performances of Leila Greenwood, whose Lysistrata was, according to one reviewer 'radiant', while another suggested she endowed the part with 'a gentle charm. There is nothing volatile in her work, but rather a performance so accomplished and delightful that in a company of such talent she remains always the focal point.'[45]

These performances have a good deal of the seductive power of good naturalistic acting, and there are many reports of the actors' near-naturalism. Rosalie Williams gave a 'charmingly natural performance' in *Jupiter's Night Out*, while John Blanshard's clergyman in *The Devil's Disciple* was marked for its 'stern realism'.[46] Howard Goorney and Julia Jones were commended for their performances in Fenn's *The Fire Eaters* in terms perhaps less acceptable today than they were then. W.A. Darlington, in *The Daily Telegraph*, noting that 'this continues to be the most successful season that the old Theatre Royal has had for years', added that 'Howard Goorney, as the resistance leader, and Julia Jones, as a nurse, worked their way into the yellow skins of their parts', in an apparently successful piece of naturalism.[47] But that this was not quite naturalism was evident from other performances by Goorney. In *An Enemy of the People*, for example, his 'spiteful intensity' was 'hovering on the verge of caricature',[48] a comment clearly suggesting that Goorney was presenting his 'version' of Stockmann, rather than that he was 'being' Stockmann. The same may be observed of notices of Maxwell Shaw's Mosca, in *Volpone*, that he was 'a fly fellow' and 'a sly, spear-collared gigolo', in a performance that was 'by far the most convincing Mosca' that the *Observer's* reviewer had ever seen.[49]

As for the range of parts that these actors created, Howard Goorney, for example, could produce an extraordinarily energetic Sganarelle in *The Flying Doctor*, as he 'leapt and turned with puppet-like agility',[50] but also be the utterly different Corbaccio in *Volpone*, 'walnut-wrinkled in beret and wheelchair', a performance, by the way, that this critic opined 'could not be bettered'.[51] Similarly, Barbara Brown was able to move from her performance in September 1954 as Alice in *Arden of Faversham* which the *Daily Mail* described as 'an acute psychological study', *The Times* praised as a 'country Clytemnestra', and Kenneth Tynan said that her 'rampant *Bovarysme* [. . .] could hardly be bettered',[52] to her performance three months later in *The Prince and the Pauper*, in which she was 'more likeably human than many of the glittering principal boys of pantomime'. All these players were capable of moving with extraordinary facility between intense individual 'realism' to other, more theatrical modes such as the vigorous clowning in *The Dutch Courtesan*: 'There is some exquisite buffoonery between that remarkable elastic-faced actor, George Cooper, as an extraordinary character named Cockledemoy, with a vintner named Mulligrub, handled so competently by Joby Blanshard'.[53]

George Cooper was one of the outstanding actors of the company at this time. His performance as Jupiter, in *Jupiter's Night Out*, had 'many vivid and neat strokes of acting and an arty beard to augment the few leaves [which comprised his costume]' and played the part with 'compelling roguery'.[54] His particular triumph, however, was as Schweik, which he played with a

Lancashire accent that reminded some spectators of Marriott Edgar's *Albert, 'Arold and Others*. Maurice Wiltshire suggested that 'anyone who lives within reasonable distance of Bow Bells and delights to laugh at the deflation of pompous authority can do no better than take the Tube to London's Theatre Workshop and enjoy the spectacle of Jaroslav Hasek's immortal hero in the flesh'. Cooper's performance, he said, was marked by 'an angelic imbecility that hides the shrewdest of common sense.'[55] The *Evening Standard* was even more fulsome:

> In Mr George Cooper, the Theatre Royal, Stratford, have found a remarkable clown, who convinces us that he may well have been Schweik himself. At least a Lancashire version of Schweik [. . .] Mr Cooper, with his North Country accent and his beaming face, constantly shifting from bewilderment to resignation, manages to make it a hilarious fate [. . .] In the last analysis, it is upon Mr Cooper that the success of *The Good Soldier Schweik* depends. And he never lets us down. There has not been a much funnier performance in London this year.[56]

This reviewer may have been convinced that this was 'Schweik himself', but the fact that he was also a 'clown' with a 'North Country' accent gives this assertion the lie. This was clearly George Cooper's *version* of the good soldier Schweik.

In the same production of *The Good Soldier Schweik*, Harry H. Corbett was hailed by the *Observer* as 'an actor of genius': 'Whether scratching and mumbling as a punch-drunk malingerer or cavorting, bewhiskered and brandy-sodden, as a romantic policeman, Mr Corbett shows greater command and composure than any young character-actor in my memory'.[57] Corbett's work for Theatre Workshop was indeed consistently applauded, never more so than in his appearances in Elizabethan drama. Joan Littlewood herself said, 'You should have seen him in my Shakespeare. He was a beautiful clown'.[58] Though this may have done him less than justice in one sense, it catches part at least of his approach to creating his versions of so many Elizabethan characters. His Mosbie, in *Arden of Faversham*, was unusual enough for *The Times* critic to 'wonder what he would do with Shakespeare's Crookback', while Kenneth Tynan in the *Observer* described his 'dark, cringing bravura' in this part. Richard II was probably his most extraordinary performance, one that certainly helped to change perceptions and performances of Shakespeare for ever. The critic of *The Times* was extremely disturbed by his performance: 'Can [this] possibly be Shakespeare's play at all? Is it not that lost play about Richard which some editors have postulated, and on which they suppose that Shakespeare based his own pathetic symphony?' The last phrase gives this writer away. The idea of Shakespeare writing a 'pathetic symphony' keeps him safely, cosily comprehensible—and, perhaps, irrelevant. Yet there was something in Corbett's performance that the critic, despite his preconceptions, could only admire:

> Mr Harry Corbett's king is not merely effeminate, and cruelly capricious, his sudden fluctuations from arrogant self-assertion to cringing submissiveness are from the outset symptoms of insanity. In his downfall a latent streak of religious mania grows into a monstrous obsession. For the deposition scene he shambles on in a coarse and ragged robe and gives away his crown with a crazy cunning. In the dungeon at Pomfret he is tethered by a chain round his ankle like the dangerous lunatic he evidently is. For the first time the lines that strike us as sounding the key-note of the character are his Queen's at their tragic parting:
>
> > What, is my Richard both in shape and mind
> > Transform'd and weak'ned? Hath Bolingbroke depos'd
> > Thine intellect?[59]

8. Harry H. Corbett as an effeminate King Richard II, facing rebellion, Stratford East, 1955.

Another critic captured the brilliance of the performer's ability to relate the internal truth to the external, while simultaneously making Elizabethan history relevant to 1950s Britain:

> Harry Corbett in the part of Richard displayed deep understanding of the character and with great artistic ability interpreted it with a variety which never ran counter to the inner consistency of the part of a ruler mentally unbalanced from the beginning of the play. Mr Corbett was properly theatrical in externalising the mind of a real man and it was noteworthy how exactly Shakespeare's words express a condition of mind which is so grave a problem with us today. The actor interpreted the character through the malady, making it sadly familiar to our understanding whilst keeping it in period.[60]

This was a performance that gave back to the age both its own pretensions and its own pitifulness. Corbett's achievement, which is more broadly true of the Theatre Workshop company of actors as a whole, was to set British acting on a new, more truthful, course.

PART FOUR

Theatre Workshop, 1956–63

Popular Theatre

CHAPTER FOURTEEN

Never Had it so Good?

The old world in which Theatre Workshop had been forged, with its poverty, its struggles against unemployment, and its fierce battles with Fascism, a world in which Communism shone like a torch to the future, seemed by 1956 in Britain to have passed beyond recall. When the Soviet Communist leaders, Nikolai Bulganin and Nikita Khrushchev, visited the country in April that year, it was more like a comic courtesy call than an embassy from a better world. For Britons, hope and happiness lay in the new washing machine, the television set and the dream of a Morris 1000 car of your own.

The political skirmishes of the late 1950s lacked the urgency and giganticism of those earlier decades. Perhaps the most pressing of the new concerns revolved round the atomic bomb, upon which the country's entire defensive capability seemed to depend. For those opposed to nuclear holocausts, there was the Campaign for Nuclear Disarmament (CND). 'The bomb was at the centre of our consciousness', Harold Pinter remembered.[1] At Easter 1956 (fully ten years after Theatre Workshop's production of *Uranium 235*), the first march for nuclear disarmament took place. Debate about the nation's morals centred on the chancellor of the exchequer, Harold Macmillan's introduction of a form of state lottery, Premium Bonds. True, the House of Commons also voted to abolish hanging for murderers, when a Labour MP, Sidney Silverman, introduced a Private Member's Bill, which passed by nineteen votes, after members had agonised over cases such as that of Timothy Evans, hanged for a murder he certainly did not commit in 1951, and Ruth Ellis, a woman whose crime of passion had brought her to the gallows in 1955. But the Commons's will was for the time being thwarted when the House of Lords, with clear government connivance, voted the Bill down. Passions ran high on this subject, and the government was forced the following year to bring in a new Homicide Act, which greatly restricted capital punishment.

As for the theatre, 1956 seemed to be the year it made a breakthrough into relevance. On 8 May, John Osborne's *Look Back in Anger* received its premiere at the Royal Court Theatre, just over two weeks before Theatre

Workshop presented *The Quare Fellow* by Brendan Behan. Osborne's white-hot rhetoric might have protested that there were no more brave causes to champion, but Behan's play gave that the lie, for his was a passionate assault on capital punishment. Nevertheless, both productions brought unexpected excitement: as Kenneth Tynan noted: 'For too long British culture had languished in a freezing-unit of understatement and "good taste"'.[2] Overstatement and bad taste were not exactly what Theatre Workshop and, perhaps, Unity Theatre, had been promulgating unnoticed by theatre critics (and, consequently, the theatre-going public) since the mid-1940s, but something of their political and social commitment suddenly became fashionable.

1956 was to be marked more significantly, however, by the Suez crisis, which changed social, intellectual and political life from the flummery of early 1950s Toryism into quite distinct new configurations. In July, Egypt's President Nasser nationalised the Suez Canal. Fearing a loss of contact with the empire—or commonwealth—east of Suez, and knowing how much of the western world's oil came through the canal, the prime minister, Anthony Eden, supported initially at least by the Labour Party, protested energetically, but apparently to no avail. After considerable ructions, Eden made a secret deal with France and Israel which gave the latter *carte blanche* to attack Egypt. Britain and France would then give both sides an ultimatum, to which Egypt as the attacked victim could not possibly accede, whereupon French and British troops would enter the conflict on the side of Israel. By the end of the month British bombs were falling on Cairo, and on 5 November Egypt was invaded. The rest of the world, and many in Britian, especially those on the political left, were outraged. There were marches, demonstrations and meetings, and on 7 November the United Nations demanded a ceasefire. The USA had refused to support Britain and France, and now there was a run on sterling. Eden was forced to retreat in confusion and humiliation. In a clear lie, he denied to parliament that there was any plot, and retired to Jamaica, sick in body and at heart. In January 1957, he resigned.

The Suez debacle drew attention away from the other major international tragedy of the year, the Soviet invasion of Hungary, which also took place in the first week of November. On 4 November, Soviet troops ordered the Hungarian government to surrender or be bombed. The Hungarians had no choice, though illegal radio stations could be heard in desperate defiance:

> Civilised people of the world. On the watch tower of a 1,000 year old Hungary the last flames begin to go out. Soviet tanks and guns are roaring over Hungarian soil [. . .] Save our souls. This word may be the last from

the last Hungarian freedom station. Help us—not with advice, not with words, but with action, with soldiers and arms.[3]

To no avail. Communism as practised was revealed for what it had become.

Khrushchev's denunciation of Stalin and his 'personality cult' had already been a heavy blow to those western progressives and socialists who still wanted to see the USSR as a beacon of hope. As more revelations leaked out in the following years, such a position became increasingly untenable. Unrepentant intellectuals who remained members of the British Communist Party, such as Alan Bush and Ivor Montagu, lost influence, while the non-Communist 'New Left', and intellectuals like Bertrand Russell and George Orwell, became more significant oppositional figures. Where before there was a call to wage the class struggle, now Socialism in Britain seemed to be more an ethical stance, one that could repudiate such chicanery as the vote-rigging scandal by Communists in the Electricians Trade Union in 1956. The 'space race' seemed to further exacerbate hostility. In October 1957 the Soviet Union launched its Sputnik, sent the dog Laika into space the following year, in 1961 launched Yuri Gagarin, the first man, into space, and two years later the first woman, Valentina Tereshkova. All this was presented as a new kind of threat to the west, a threat in a new dimension. At the same time, the Soviet Communists built a wall across the city of Berlin, and put missiles into Cuba aimed at the USA. Justifiably or not, Communism seemed to large numbers of people in Britain and the west an utterly baleful influence.

Theatre Workshop itself, which had been founded with such high Communist hopes, discovered some of the obfuscations and negatives of Soviet Communism for itself when it toured East Europe with *Macbeth* in 1957. Joan Littlewood records how in the Moscow Art Theatre the company's hosts wanted to know who was the 'leading lady'. The reply—'We don't have one—Lady Macbeth may be playing the skivvy tomorrow' echoed the original ideals of the tsarist founders of the Art Theatre, Stanislavsky and Nemirovich-Danchenko, who established their company on the premise that there would be no stars.[4] Ironically, to the Russian Communists, such egalitarianism seemed incomprehensible. Then, the critics wanted to know why the characters wore modern dress, and why there was no scenery, and advised Theatre Workshop members to visit Okhlopkov's production of *Hamlet*, then running in Moscow. Okhlopkov, trained by Meyerhold himself, had been a hero to the tyros of the 1930s Theatre of Action, but his *Hamlet* completely lacked the fire they had found in Communism, and was sadly slow and predictable. Later, in East Berlin, Joan Littlewood discovered that the function of a particularly important (perhaps self-important) member of the typical German theatre company, the 'dramaturg', actually only did what the troupe as a whole did at

Stratford East. And at the Maxim Gorky Theatre's New Year's Eve party, Littlewood refused to attend unless the uninvited stage staff, who were not on a par with the artists, also attended.[5] Communism in practice was not attractive.

At home, Harold Macmillan, the new prime minister, declared that the 'class war was obsolete'. This was, of course, somewhat disingenuous: in his 1957 cabinet, six of the sixteen members were Old Etonians, and only two had not been educated at private schools. Moreover, of the eighty-five members of the entire government, no fewer than thirty-five were related to Macmillan by blood or marriage. By the following year, seven of the nineteen members of his cabinet were related to him. Nevertheless, with Labour apparently split after Attlee's retirement between the old cloth-capped working class, epitomised by Aneurin Bevan, and a new non-ideological Labour Party typified by the patrician, Anthony Crosland, and especially his influential book, *The Future of Socialism*, published in 1956, the Tories were able to hold onto power. Macmillan may have resembled an Edwardian grouse-moor-obsessed upper-class twit, but he was also clever. Hire purchase restrictions were ended, taxes were cut and it was popularly agreed that 'we have never had it so good.' On the crest of this wave of economic confidence, Macmillan called an election in October 1959, and the Tories increased their majority significantly. Economic wellbeing produced complacency and Toryism. Home ownership was steadily rising: by 1964 it stood at 44 per cent. There were eight million cars on the roads. Over 90 per cent of homes had a television set. Consensus may have originally muffled the masses; now its materialism apparently entranced them.

In such circumstances, to continue to present a Marxist line, as Theatre Workshop had more or less been established to do, was impossible. The organisation was still nominally democratic, and the target audience of working-class East Enders suggested at least the dregs of the old political commitment, but this was in a sense the husk of their earlier ideals. Ironically, it was not Theatre Workshop but the dying Unity Theatre that revived overtly political theatre in late 1956 with a hard-hitting living newspaper, *World on Edge*, about Suez and Hungary. This even had contributions from Theatre Workshop stalwarts such as Howard Goorney, but Theatre Workshop was itself evolving. Its ideal of a permanent ensemble was becoming unsustainable, especially as some of the best actors, like Harry H. Corbett and George Cooper, were tempted away by wages more commensurate with their talent. It was the same story as that of Glasgow Unity when it came south to London in 1948. New actors arrived, untrained in Theatre Workshop's ways and ignorant of its ideology, attracted perhaps by its aura of experimental excitement, or seeing it as a means of reaching the West End, as more and more productions followed *The Quare Fellow* and *The Good Soldier Schweik* there in the late 1950s and early 1960s. But Theatre Workshop wages remained low, the theatre was still dingy (despite refurbishment in 1959) and the company faced bankruptcy several times. Moreover, the critics, though they now regularly noticed the company's work, were still patronising, as Tom Milne noted in 1958: '[They give] praise where praise is inevitable, but with an air of surprise that this enfant terrible (a *Leftist* enfant) should actually have produced something worthy of mature consideration, needing no excuse or special allowances.'[6]

Immediately after 1953, there had been a sense that Joan Littlewood was prepared to hang on, hoping that her co-founder and long-time artistic partner, Ewan MacColl, would return to Theatre Workshop. But with the success of MacColl's innovative Radio Ballads, and his emotional involvement with the non-theatrical Peggy Seeger, this gradually became less and less likely. Without MacColl, the company's playwright, the immediate need was for a retrenchment of the repertoire, which initially meant recourse to the classics. But this in itself was also unsustainable in the East End of London. A new company playwright—or company playwrights—were needed for Theatre Workshop, and in effect Joan Littlewood herself had to add this role to her others. After all, she had plenty of experience creating plays from other people's texts, having adapted *Alice in Wonderland*, *A Christmas Carol*, *Treasure Island*, Balzac's *Cruel Daughters*, Dickens's *The Chimes*, and more, for the company. Though she did not have MacColl's originality, she certainly equalled him in craft, and now she began to work with other playwrights to create a kind of drama suitable for the East End, and for the times. The plays for which Stratford East at last acquired a national reputation were instinctively radical, subversive, and produced and performed a version of the Cockney that, while lacking Ewan MacColl's political fury or analysis or imaginative metaphors, still achieved both theatrical punch and a political irreverence which suited the time. The aim now, as she made clear in a letter to *The Times* in July 1958, was 'a people's theatre'.[7] Ken Hill, who took over at Stratford East when Joan Littlewood quit, explained: 'She was trying to make theatre totally and completely accessible, to make it a people's art form.'[8] Indeed, there is some evidence that East End audiences responded more to the work presented at Stratford East during this third period of Theatre Workshop's history. The Cockney Joan Littlewood focused some plays specifically on Cockney attitudes and experiences, but more generally, following the successes of *The Quare Fellow* and *The Good Soldier Schweik*, and capitalising on the gradually growing disenchantment with all-embracing Tory philistinism, the work of this period celebrated outsiders and subversive misfits. In 1964 she explained:

> Shakespeare's company was made up of leary misfits, anarchists, out of work soldiers, and wits who worked at their ideas in pubs and performed them as throwaways to an uninhibited pre-Puritan audience. My company works without the assistance of smart direction, fancy dress, beards and greasepaint and was prepared for the wave of opposition which we knew would come. I hope the audience will enjoy our work as much as we do.[9]

Finding a new way, however, was not quite as simple as this statement might make it seem. For instance, Theatre Workshop's problems were compounded by the rise of the Royal Court Theatre as a darling of the fashionable left. The differences between Theatre Workshop and the Royal Court Theatre under the direction of George Devine were instructive, and explain why the Royal Court's subsidy was always so much greater than Theatre Workshop's. The Royal Court in the 1950s and 1960s was essentially a development from its earlier incarnation as the home of Fabian drama practised by George Bernard Shaw, John Galsworthy and Harley Granville Barker. It was a literary drama rooted in the concept that the playwright is the theatre's pivotal figure. Theatre Workshop's position, as Joan Littlewood explained in 1961, was very different:

> No one mind or imagination can foresee what a play will become until all the physical and intellectual stimuli, which are crystallised in the poetry of the author, have been understood by a company, and then tried out in terms of mime, discussion and the precise music of grammar; words and movement allied and integrated.[10]

This derived from the European *avant-garde* idea of total theatre, from Meyerhold and Mikhail Chekhov, especially. For them, true theatre was not to be found in a script, but in the living exchanges of actors in action on the stage. They insisted that a production was never a finished item, as a published script might be, but that if the actors were truly 'working in the present', every performance would be original and different. Joan Littlewood agreed. Thus, Theatre Workshop challenged ways of playmaking on a plane that was quite different from the concerns of the Royal Court. It was a plane that few understood then, or since, for the big establishment theatres of the second half of the twentieth century still continued to base their repertoires on the primacy of the playwright. But the plays in the repertoire of the Meyerhold Theatre in its greatest years, or those of Piscator's theatre of the 1920s, were comparatively undistinguished, comprising revivals of often unregarded old plays (Ostrovsky's *The Forest*, or Sukhovo-Kobylin's *The Death of Tarelkin*) and somewhat flimsy contemporary dramas (*The Magnanimous Cuckold* or Leo Lania's *Konjunktor*). Of course, both these directors did present some brilliant new plays (Meyerhold's production of Mayakovsky's *The Bathhouse*, for instance, or Piscator's of Toller's *Hoppla, Such is Life!*). But what was significant to these theatres was the experience of the audience, not the excellence of the playwrighting. They, like Theatre Workshop, urgently wanted communication with their spectators.

Joan Littlewood became, perhaps at second hand, the company playwright in order to develop a new kind of relationship between the company and the world. This still depended on the need to communicate, but what she communicated now was no longer a burning Communism, but rather, something that perhaps took itself less seriously, was more impertinent, more satirical, but, in the sense that Swift was satirical, no less angry than before. Theatre Workshop became a jester at the court of Harold Macmillan's kingdom of stuffy philistines. Methodologically, this required the Meyerholdian kind of total theatre, in which productions would have an unfinished quality, an ability to play in the present tense, which was a challenge both to a static society and to existing mainstream theatre practice. Littlewood still won awards—*The Hostage* won the Théâtres des Nations at Paris in 1959, she herself won the directing prize there, and *Fings Ain't Wot They Used T'Be* won the Evening Standard Best Musical award in 1960, for example—but Terence Rattigan put his finger on the quality of this work in a note he sent to Joan Littlewood after he saw *The Hostage* in 1958: 'I think *The Hostage* is the best directed modern play I have ever seen. I think the play is pretty wonderful, too, but it's you who have made it just as wonderful as it is, and it's you I want honestly and sincerely [to] thank for an evening of excitement and joy.'[11] Rattigan could see that it was the play-creation, which included the making both of the playscript and the production, that Littlewood—like Meyerhold—achieved. In this, she was as unique to the British theatre as Meyerhold was to the Russian.

Theatre-as-performance, as opposed to theatre-as-playscript, enabled Theatre Workshop to retain its uniqueness and its originality in the period of Macmillan's Tory ascendancy. The plays that Littlewood in effect co-authored, including *A Taste of Honey, The Hostage, Fings Ain't Wot They Used T'Be* and others, were subversive, frequently comical, presentations of what was often not seen or accepted in public society. They celebrated the power of laughter and the vitality of the excluded. They ensured that Theatre Workshop was very distinct from the more intellectual, more conventional Royal Court Theatre and explained something of the mutual antipathy between these two theatres. Andrew Davies suggested that this incarnation of Theatre Workshop 'indicates what an alternative theatre might look like: irreverent, sprawling, collective, improvisatory, spontaneous, topical—all that the West End usually was not'.[12] However, this process carried its own dangers, especially when compared to the earlier years when Ewan MacColl was the in-house playwright, because MacColl, like some of the better Royal Court dramatists, had specific ideas he wanted to communicate, and these could act as a source for self-discipline. This was partially lacking in some of the later Theatre Workshop plays, particularly those dealing with Cockney experience. Sometimes, they seemed too genial, too nostalgic, not keen enough to see the less happy side of living in the East End. For instance, in August 1963, Ian Nairn described Spitalfields, next to Bow, as 'London's worst slum',[13] and it was the period when both racketeering landlords like Peter Rachman and gangster crime such as that associated with the Kray brothers, was poisoning the quality of much local life. Yet at the opening of Joan Littlewood's film of *Sparrers Can't Sing* at the Bow Empire Cinema in March 1962, not only were Princess Margaret and Lord Snowdon honoured guests, so too were the notorious Kray twins. Nevertheless, Theatre Workshop's best plays of the period, including *A Taste of Honey, The Hostage, Fings Ain't Wot They Used T'Be, Make Me an Offer, Sam, the Highest Jumper of Them All* and *Sparrers Can't Sing* were, in the words of Alan Strachan, 'Popular in every sense, building a theatre of vigorous, trenchant style and often arousing what Littlewood called "race memories" in local audiences'.[14] Her work now seemed designed to open up the Establishment, to mock its pretensions and to dance with the deprived.

By 1960, the Tories, so recently re-elected, were tumbling from caricature into absurdity, symbolised by the crescendo of scandals that occurred. In March 1961 came the Portland spy scandal, in November the next year a civil servant, John Vassall, was convicted of spying for the Soviet Union in a case with undertones of homosexuality at the Admiralty, and two months later, Kim Philby apeared in Moscow, the 'third man' in the Burgess and MacLean spy ring. In the spring and summer of 1963, the 'Profumo scandal' unravelled, as it transpired that Macmillan's minister for war had been sharing a mistress with the Soviet military attaché, and had lied about the affair in the House of Commons. On 8 August 1963, the Great Train Robbery was carried out. With the economic 'boom' degenerating into 'bust' and the Conservatives losing by-elections, Macmillan lost his nerve as well as his head and in July 1962 sacked a third of his cabinet. When, early in 1963, the French president, Charles de Gaulle, vetoed Britain's entry into the then Common Market, Macmillan's time was clearly up. He resigned later that year and, amid farcical shenanigans at the Conservative Party conference, the fourteenth Earl of Home 'emerged' as the next Tory leader. Home owned 96,000 acres of farmland, forest and grouse moor in Scotland, and now he created a large cabinet of twenty-three members, ten of whom had been educated at Eton.

For a time it had appeared that no viable or principled opposition to all this was available. To some, the unexpected popularity of the Campaign for Nuclear Disarmament was a principal focus for dissent. This had grown out of the pre-war Peace Pledge Union, which evolved first into Operation Gandhi after the war, and then in February 1958 into CND, the creation of Bertrand Russell, Canon John Collins of St Paul's Cathedral, Michael Foot, J.B. Priestley and others. It attracted the intelligentsia, the young, trade unionists and non-affiliated progressives, including Iris Murdoch, Spike Milligan, Vanessa Redgrave, Henry Moore and A.J.P. Taylor, as well as 'New Left' radicals, Raphael Samuel, Ralph Milliband, Stuart Hall and others. CND was a kind of catalyst both for radical political thinking that emerged more clearly in the 1960s, and also for a newly politicised culture of folk song and radical theatre, which likewise grew stronger in the following decades. So-called 'satire' boomed, beginning perhaps with *Beyond the Fringe* and moving through television's Saturday night, *That Was the Week That Was*, to the magazine, *Private Eye.* In a position that was precisely the reverse of a decade earlier, upper-class accents became the butt of ridicule, while regional or working-class modes of speech were acceptable and interesting. New attitudes were to lead to 'flower power', the Beatles and so on to a drug culture. In all this, Theatre Workshop's self-created function as jester was gradually usurped.

Between 1959 and 1961 five Theatre Workshop productions transferred to the West End—*A Taste of Honey, The Hostage, Fings Ain't Wot They Used T'Be, Make Me an Offer* and *Sparrers Can't Sing*. Wolf Mankovitz's *Make Me an Offer* was created with the specific purpose of transferring. Though apparently a symbol of the company's success, these transfers in fact sucked out its lifeblood. Losing one or two actors from Stratford East each year, even actors as brilliant as Harry H. Corbett or George Cooper, was recoverable. To lose a whole company—or, worse, five whole companies—and at the same time to try to keep the home theatre alive was simply impossible. Theatre Workshop needed actors trained in its methods. Now it had lost them. Moreover, by 1961 Joan Littlewood was exhausted both artistically and physically in the face of seemingly endless financial inequities, and with the burdens she was carrying as author-collaborator, play director and creator of more and more new companies. She was, according to John Bury, 'burned out'.[15] She decided to leave, but before she did so, she declared: 'My objective in life has not changed; it is to work with other artists—actors, writers, designers, composers—and in collaboration with them, and by means of argument, experiment and research, to help to keep the English theatre alive and contemporary'. She went on to urge, in the light of her own experience at Stratford East: 'Each community should have a theatre; the West End has plundered our talent and diluted our ideas'.[16] Effectively therefore, 1961 marks the end of Theatre Workshop. The company broke up, and Littlewood herself departed to Nigeria, and new experiences. Kenneth Tynan was moved to write what sounded like an obituary:

As for Theatre Workshop, it is almost as if it had never been. Unknown in London ten years ago, and recently decapitated by the loss of Joan Littlewood, it has no West End memorial except what must by now be a fairly apathetic production of *Fings Ain't Wot They Used T'Be*. Theatrically, though not otherwise, Brendan Behan has been silent since *The Hostage*: Shelagh Delaney has not yet fulfilled the glowing promise of *A Taste of Honey*; and Alun Owen, all conquering on television, failed to conquer Shaftesbury Avenue with *Progress to the Park*.[17]

But Joan Littlewood had also promised: 'I'll be back'.[18]

She did return, two years later, to create with her reassembled company what was probably Theatre Workshop's most brilliant, most successful production, *Oh What a Lovely War*. In something of the style of Theatre Union's *Last Edition* and Ewan MacColl's *Uranium 235*, but with the insouciance of the jester to 1950s Toryism and the theatricalised ambience of a pier-end pierrot show, *Oh What a Lovely War* presented an unforgettable montage of the First World War to devastating effect—tears, smiles, heartbreak and cold anger. The manic sergeant-major, the sexy 'recruiting lady', the absurdly caricatured national leaders, and the French clown-*poilus* going like lambs to the slaughter, all appearing in front of evocative, Piscator-style projections of the war's reality, and the harsh facts of war flashing across the news panels, seemed almost a summation of thirty years of Joan Littlewood's endeavours. The nostalgia of the songs and the often simple clown comedy only enhanced the seriousness of the content, and thoughtful spectators came away ashen-faced, not just because of the perfidy of those who had trumpeted the First World War as a patriotic triumph, but also because of the unmistakable overtones of the war threat of their own times, a nuclear holocaust.

Ewan MacColl criticised *Oh What a Lovely War* because the audiences contained generals, and the widows of generals, muttering, 'Good show, damn good show'. MacColl continued: 'A show which deals with war and leaves the audience feeling nice and comfy, leaving the theatre in a roseate glow of nostalgia, isn't doing its job, it's failed. Theatre, when it's dealing with social issues, should hurt. They should send you out of the theatre furious.'[19] But the objection seems ill founded, and it may be noted that none of MacColl's own plays left their audiences feeling 'furious'. In truth, no-one with any sensitivity left *Oh What a Lovely War* feeling 'nice and comfy'. This is to mistake the reaction to the songs for the whole response. The 'nice and comfy' feeling is finely undercut by the scalpel of facts that surrounds the songs. In any case, the comment surely misunderstands the way theatre operates, which is not simply to make the spectator cross, but involves aesthetic, intellectual and spiritual responses as well as those of the emotions. On these counts, *Oh What a Lovely War* was a startling success, which was acclaimed equally by the locals of Stratford East and by the fashionable audiences of the West End, in continental Europe as well as in the USA. It has been revived by companies as diverse as school drama groups and large professional theatres continually for over forty years, and may have been the single most influential play of its time, inspiring decades of 'documentary' playmaking as well as a generation of radical theatre makers. In that sense it has been, perhaps, Theatre Workshop's, and especially Joan Littlewood's, most lasting monument.

CHAPTER FIFTEEN

The Royal Smut Hound

In 1965, Kenneth Tynan wrote a stinging diatribe against the Lord Chamberlain's power of censorship over British theatre under the title 'The Royal Smut Hound'.[1]

Censorship was indeed a particular obstacle to the progress of Theatre Workshop. The Lord Chamberlain possessed virtually unlimited powers over the live stage from 1737 until 1968, when those powers were abolished. The position had been created by Robert Walpole after a series of increasingly scurrilous and provocative attacks on him and his administration had been made in ballad operas, which began with the satire of John Gay's *The Beggar's Opera* in 1728, and culminated in the anti-government blast of Henry Fielding's *The Historical Register for the Year 1736*. Walpole's response was the Act of 1737 imposing the Lord Chamberlain as censor to the theatres, giving him powers that were further strengthened by the 1843 Theatres Act. Despite a fierce campaign led by Bernard Shaw, in 1909 a Joint Select Committee of Parliament concluded that such powers were necessary, and the then Lord Chamberlain promptly banned Herbert Beerbohm Tree's *Oedipus the King*! Sex, of which there was too much, religion, which was apt to cause great offence, and politics, which those in power preferred not discussed, were the main targets of the Lord Chamberlain's blue pencil. As Steve Nicholson has noted, the truth was no justification for allowing the performance of a play, when an application to stage a Soviet play was rejected because of the way the tsar and tsarina were presented, 'whatever truth there may be in the picture'. The Lord Chamberlain's memo adds that performance 'would obviously be deeply offensive to the King'.[2]

The Lord Chamberlain was democratically unaccountable, his appointment and therefore his allegiance being entirely due to the sovereign of the day. His staff consisted of a few examiners of plays, who first read the submitted scripts and commented on them, and two comptrollers, who received the scripts from the examiners, perhaps added their own comments, and then passed them on to the Lord Chamberlain himself. In the 1950s, the Lord Chamberlain was the eleventh Earl of Scarborough, educated at Eton,

Sandhurst and Oxford, and a former officer in the Hussars. Kenneth Tynan noted sarcastically of him, that 'he could boast first-hand experience of artistic endeavour, having written, in 1936, *The History of the Eleventh Hussars*'.[3] His two comptrollers were Sir Terence Nugent, later Lord Nugent, educated at Eton and Sandhurst, a former officer in the Irish Guards, and later to be lord-in-waiting to the queen, and Sir Norman Gwatkin, educated at Clifton and Sandhurst and a brigadier in the Coldstream Guards. The examiners included Sir Thomas St Vincent Troubridge, educated at Wellington and Sandhurst, a lieutenant-colonel in the King's Royal Rifle Corps, Geoffrey Dearmer, educated at Glasgow University, a writer and member of the Stage Society council, whose military background included fighting at Gallipoli in the First World War, and Charles Heriot, also educated at Glasgow University, a former actor and theatre director.

These men—and they were all men—permitted no mention in plays of eminent British people or their foreign friends or relations, alive or recently dead. Nor did they allow any reference to bodily functions, sexual or defecatory, though with regard to the latter, we find the Lord Chamberlain writing pathetically in 1955: 'I have read this play & do not feel certain in my mind what course to take. We have no rigid rule about plays in which immorality takes a prominent part—entire plays dealing with unnatural vice—and it is a question of where to draw the line.'[4] The comment is doubly silly in the light of the 1909 Select Committee's list of quasi-rules. A play, they said, should be licensed, unless it could be shown

a) to be indecent
b) to contain offensive personalities
c) to represent in an invidious manner a living person, or a person recently dead
d) to do violence to the sentiment of religious reverence
e) to be calculated to conduce to crime or vice
f) to be calculated to impair friendly relations with a Foreign Power
g) to be calculated to cause a breach of the peace[5]

It should be noted that all this extended not simply over what was said on the stage, but to the actions, too. The producer of Sartre's *The Respectable Prostitute* was heavily fined because a man was seen to lie on top of a woman at the end of one of the acts, an action which was not included as a stage direction in the script that had been passed for performance. One of the sillier aspects of the procedure was the bargaining the Lord Chamberlain often indulged in, as when he allowed Tom Thomas fifteen 'bloodys' in *The Ragged Trousered Philanthropists* in the 1920s.

The Lord Chamberlain's office always demanded a fee for reading the script, without which no licence was forthcoming, and today's permission did not imply that such permission would not be revoked tomorrow. In a position particularly threatening for Theatre Workshop, improvisation was strictly forbidden, since who could tell where it would lead? Performance of a play without a licence from the Lord Chamberlain rendered the guilty theatre liable to instant closure, though occasionally brave managers were prepared to turn their theatres into private clubs so that a play could continue. One of the most pernicious results of the system was the self-censorship playwrights imposed upon themselves, for what was the purpose of writing a play that would be banned? The sterility of so much British drama of the first half of the twentieth century, when European, American and Russian flourished so spectacularly, can surely be put down to the mere existence of the Lord Chamberlain.

Every year through the 1950s half a dozen or so plays were banned outright, including in that decade Sartre's *Huis Clos*, Hellman's *The Children's Hour*, Genet's *The Maids*, Miller's *A View from the Bridge* and Williams's *Cat on a Hot Tin Roof*; and every year significant changes or cuts were demanded in 15 to 20 per cent of the four or five hundred playscripts submitted before performance was allowed. Dominic Shellard, examining forty-two plays totally banned between 1945 and 1954, reported:

> 18 were refused a licence on account of alleged sexual impropriety; 14 because of their treatment of what the Lord Chamberlain was to refer to in 1957 as 'the forbidden subject', homosexuality; 4 because they included representations of Queen Victoria; 3 for referrring to living people; 2 because of political objections [. . .]; and 1 for being deemed offensive to christianity.[6]

It is against this background that one needs to weigh what sometimes seems like Theatre Workshop's cowardice in choosing its subject matter, and sometimes its courage. Ewan MacColl has been criticised, for instance, because his work seems homophobic, if only by omission. But whatever MacColl's attitude to homosexuality may have been, it seems certain that if he had wished to write about it, his work would have been banned, or at least greatly diluted. And when the company staged Friedrich Wolf's *Professor Mamlock*, about the persecution of the Jews in Nazi Germany, with—in a prologue written by Joan Littlewood—a comparison with anti-Semitism in 1940s Britain, the Lord Chamberlain excised the prologue and refused to allow any reference whatsoever to ongoing British persecutions.

But it was Littlewood's concern that productions should remain alive, with the implications for improvisation, or acting 'in the present', which was most dangerous, and the moment of truth arrived during the production of *You Won't Always Be on Top*. At a performance quite late in the run of this play, two men were seen in the audience jotting down various observations in their notebooks. They were the Lord Chamberlain's spies, and sure enough, some weeks later, during a rehearsal for *Celestina*, two plain-clothes detectives appeared in the theatre with arrest warrants for Joan Littlewood, as director of *You Won't Always Be on Top*, Gerry Raffles, as theatre manager, John Bury as designer and Richard Harris as actor. They, and the absent author, Henry Chapman, were charged that they did unlawfully present parts of the play before such parts had been allowed by the Lord Chamberlain, contrary to Section 15 of the Theatres Act of 1843. They were summoned to appear at West Ham Magistrates' Court on 16 April 1958.

As the run of the show had continued, Richard Harris had developed the comic 'official opening' of the public lavatory sequence far beyond Chapman's original conception. According to Murray Melvin, Harris 'put a watering can between his legs, raised his fingers in the V sign and, in Churchillian tones, said: "I declare this site open"'.[7] This combined smut with irreverence for a living person and had subversivce political implications. (It is worth noting that the earlier impersonation of Churchill in *Operation Olive Branch* had passed completely unnoticed by the Lord Chamberlain.)

The theatre was clearly threatened with action that could close it forever. A fighting fund was established, and well subscribed to, and public meetings called, though tellingly they were warned by friendly campaigners to avoid allowing known Commmunists to participate too visibly in their campaign. The Labour MP Harold Lever, who had been a supporter of Theatre Union in Manchester before the war, was able to obtain the services of a very high-profile barrister, Gerald Gardiner, later lord chancellor in Harold Wilson's government, and these two acted for Theatre Workshop for no fee. The case was something of a *cause célèbre* and the public gallery of the court was packed with supporters. As the witnesses for the prosecution read from their notebooks the offending passages—swear words and rude decriptions in deadpan, court-proceedured voices—the public became more and more amused. Besides which, it transpired that one of the magistrates was himself a builder, and thoroughly in sympathy with Chapman's play. It was clear that a breach of the Lord Chamberlain's licence had been committed—indeed the accused pleaded guilty—but the sympathies of the court, as well as the public, were wholly with them. The fine imposed was minimal and, together with costs, came to less than fifteen pounds, and the defendants were discharged.

Of course the company still had to submit plays to the Lord Chamberlain after this, and of course the Lord Chamberlain insisted on alterations. Brian Murphy recalled how, in *The Hostage*, when he as Mulleady had to 'goose' Ann Beach's staid Miss Gilchrist, the Lord Chamberlain insisted that Murphy's hand be kept horizontal at all times and the fingers were to remain straight. But Penelope Gilliatt suggested in

Encore that 'The licensing of this play may be a penance for the Henry Chapman affair. Lines of no reverence about such figureheads as the Queen, Dulles [the US Secretary of State], Peter Townsend [friend of Princess Margaret], Uffa Fox [a heroic British yachtsman] and the Virgin Mary are all there intact'.[8]

Fings Ain't Wot They Used T'Be also received his Lordship's attention, particularly after complaints from some members of the public (who, of course could in this way impede any stage work they did not approve of), but also because of the ongoing 'improvisation' that Joan Littlewood insisted on. One of his secretaries wrote: 'It is reported to his Lordship that numerous unauthorised amendments to the allowed manuscript have been made, and I am to require you to revert to it at once, submitting for approval any alteration which you wish to make before continuing them in use'.[9] The secretary then went on to list a number of the most abominable breaches of the licence, 'none of which would have been allowed had they been submitted'. These included:

> Indecent business of Rosie putting her hand up Red Hot's bottom.
> The interior decorator is not to be played as a homosexual and his remark '. . . Excuse me dear, red plush, that's very camp, that is,' is to be omitted, as is his remark, 'I've strained meself.'
> The builder's labourer is not to carry the plank in the erotic place and at the erotic angle that he does, and the Lord Chamberlain wishes to be informed of the manner in which the plank is in future to be carried.
> Tosher, when examining Red Hot's bag, is not to put his hand on Rosie's bottom with finger aligned as he does at the moment.
> Tosher is not to push Rosie backwards against the table when dancing in such a manner that her legs appear through his open legs in a manner indicative of copulation.[10]

It was clear that the Lord Chamberlain's spies had again visited Theatre Workshop, but perhaps also significant that this time no prosecution ensued. Even in 1967, a few months before his position as censor of plays was abolished by Act of Parliament, he was still interfering with Theatre Workshop, this time its production of *Mrs Wilson's Diary*, insisting that various anecdotes about government ministers be excised from the script, and that a half-naked statue of President Johnson be made more decorous.

But after 1958 and at least partly because of the laughing-stock the office of censor had become as a result of Theatre Workshop's case, the Lord Chamberlain's office was doomed. Joan Littlewood proclaimed, not inaccurately, that 'our victory was the first real blow at the ancient institution of censorship'. The significant consequence was the foundation of the pressure group, the Censorship Reform Committee, whose efforts really were instrumental in freeing British theatre from the arcane grip of the Lord Chamberlain's whims.

CHAPTER SIXTEEN

New Plays

If the first period of Theatre Workshop's existence was characterised by the political drama of Ewan MacColl, the third period was notable for a more eclectic series of new plays, largely discreetly co-authored by Joan Littlewood, approaching contemporary politics and society both more obliquely and more disrespectfully. In these plays, Theatre Workshop performed alternatives that did not so much confront the reality of the time as subvert it and hold it up to ridicule. Pretension in what was called 'the Establishment' seemed perhaps less a threat than an absurdity, and the viewpoint was not so much that of the industrial proletariat as that of the detached and deprived outsider. It was the Fool to Britain's King Complacency.

The series started in May 1956 with Brendan Behan's *The Quare Fellow*, set in Dublin's Mountjoy Gaol in the hours leading to a hanging. Originally written in Gaelic, and rejected by the Abbey Theatre, the piece has no 'plot' in conventional terms, but draws heavily upon Behan's own prison experience when his acquaintance, Bernard Kirwan, was hanged. In the play, the 'quare fellow' is not named, and this 'absence' is matched by the hole—the grave—that is the central symbol on the stage, as well as by the inarticulate off-stage howling and banging at the moment of the quare fellow's death. The prison is a sort of microcosm of society outside: the prisoners bet on whether the central character will be reprieved, and at the end they squabble for the dead man's letters like the soldiers quarrelling over Christ's clothes under the cross. The comparison with the outside world is emphasised by the matter-of-fact discussions of hanging, its problems and the necessary work processes it involves. This apparent normality, of course, masks the horror of what is to occur, enables the other characters to manage it, and on another level greatly increases the tension embedded in the trivial events depicted. The tension is further intensified by the reprieve of one of the condemned men, but not the other, and by the attempted suicide—a 'voluntary' death—of another prisoner.

Simultaneously, there is a good deal of gallows humour, such as when the prisoners are joshing Neighbour, and throw him into the open grave, a moment of supreme comic horror, as well as a kind of Brechtian 'alienation' important for Behan's dramatic strategy. The stylisation of the last meal sequence is also notably 'alienated':

> *(A Prisoner comes through the hospital gate and down the steps. He wears a white apron, carries a tray and is surrounded by an interested band [. . .] From the prisoners around the food an excited chorus:)*
>
> PRISONER A: Rasher and eggs.
> PRISONER B: He got that last night.
> MICKSER: Chicken
> NEIGHBOUR: He had that for dinner.
> PRISONER B: Sweet cake.
> PRISONER A: It's getting hung he is, not married.
> NEIGHBOUR: Steak and onions.
> MICKSER: Sausages and bacon.
> PRISONER B: And liver.
> PRISONER A: Pork chops.
> PRISONER B: Pig's feet.
> PRISONER A: Salmon.
> NEIGHBOUR: Fish and chips.
> MICKSER: Jelly and custard.
> NEIGHBOUR: Roast lamb.
> PRISONER A: Plum pudding.
> PRISONER B: Turkey.
> NEIGHBOUR: Goose.
> PRISONERS A, B AND
> NEIGHBOUR: Rashers and eggs.
> ALL: Rashers and eggs, rashers and eggs, and eggs and
>   rashers and eggs and rashers it is.
> COOK *(desperate)*: Ah, here, lads.
> PRISONERS: Here, give us a look, lift up the lid, eh, here, I never
>   seen it.
>
> *(The Cook struggles to protect his cargo, the prisoners mill round in a loose scrum of excitement and greed, their nostrils mad almost to the point of snatching a bit. There is a roar from the gate.)*
>
> WARDER DONNELLY: Get to hell out of that. Who do youse think you are
>   on?
>
> *(The prisoners scatter in a rush.)*
> *(The Cook with great dignity carries on.)*[1]

The play deals with its subject, capital punishment, at a tangent rather than head on, thereby subverting the death penalty's potency and asserting its contrary, life. It never preaches its case, preferring to present a series of incidents set around its unspoken horrific central act. These incidents are linked thematically, not as part of a sequential plot line, and focus on the quare fellow, and the hanging. It uses link montage, which may shift into something more confrontational, as when Jenkinson sings his absurd Salvation Army hymn while the Hangman makes his calculations:

JENKINSON (*sings*): My brother, sit and think,
                     While yet some time is left to thee,
                     Kneel to thy God who from thee does not shrink
                     And lay thy sins on Him who died for thee.
    HANGMAN: Take a fourteen stone man as a basis and giving him a
                     drop of eight foot . . .
    JENKINSON: Men shrink from thee but not I,
                     Come close to me, I love my erring sheep.
                     My blood can cleanse thy sins of blackest dye,
                     I understand if thou canst only weep.
    HANGMAN: Every half-stone lighter would require a two-inch
                     longer drop, so for weight thirteen and a half stone—
                     drop eight feet two inches, and for weight thirteen
                     stone—drop eight feet four inches.[2]

The montage is evident from the very beginning of the play. The curtain rises to disclose the barren geometry of the cells, the administrative building, the wall, and a blatant notice: 'SILENCE'. But we hear the sweet tentative voice of a prisoner singing:

> A hungry feeling came o'er me stealing
> And the mice were squealing in my prison cell,
> And that old triangle
> Went jingle jangle
> Along the banks of the Royal Canal.[3]

After another verse, the song is summarily truncated by the voice of a warder. But the battle lines are drawn: life against death, music against silence, joy against despair. After the performance, Kenneth Tynan 'left the theatre feeling overwhelmed and thanking all the powers that be for Sidney Silverman'.[4]

Tynan was equally enthusiastic about Behan's *The Hostage*, which he rightly labelled '*commedia dell'arte*'. 'A biting popular drama', he called it, 'that does not depend on hit songs, star names, spa sophistication or the more melodramatic aspects of homosexuality'.[5] Penelope Gilliatt, in *Encore*, concurred. Calling it 'Dublin's *Dreigroschenoper*', she concluded: '*The Hostage* is a huge belly-laugh that secretes enough morality for a satire'.[6] As in *The Quare Fellow*, there is little plot here—an Englishman is captured and held hostage by a fading and ludicrously outdated and inefficient IRA cell whose leader has declined into a brothel keeper. The hostage is held in order to force the release of an Irish patriot, whom we never see. The hostage develops a relationship with the maidservant, and in a comic-macabre climax, is accidentally killed. What is important, again, is the montage that Behan (or Littlewood) employs to construct this carnivalesque jig of a play. The technique is somewhat the same as in *The Quare Fellow* but now the characters are considerably more colourful and varied, from the homosexual navvy and his 'coloured' boyfriend, to the Russian sailor and the epicurean social worker. The love of Teresa and Leslie Williams, the English soldier, shines through all this, and is expressed in a traditional rhyme, with an unexpected theatricalised ending:

(They sing and dance.)

SOLDIER:	I will give you a golden ball, To hop with the children in the hall,
TERESA:	If you'll marry, marry, marry, marry, If you'll marry me.
SOLDIER:	I will give you the keys of my chest, And all the money that I possess,
TERESA:	If you'll marry, marry, marry, marry, If you'll marry me.
SOLDIER:	I will give you a watch and chain, To show the kids in Angel Lane,[7]
TERESA:	If you'll marry, marry, marry, marry, If you'll marry me. I will bake you a big pork pie, And hide you till the cops go by,
BOTH:	If you'll marry, marry, marry, marry, If you'll marry me.
SOLDIER:	But first I think that we should see If we fit each other.
TERESA *(to the audience)*:	Shall we?
SOLDIER:	Yes, let's see.

(They run to the bed.)[8]

There is an elegiac quality about this love story almost reminiscent of *Romeo and Juliet*. The ending of the play is also unexpected. After the English hostage is accidentally shot, as everyone turns away from the body,

(A ghostly green light glows on the body as Leslie Williams slowly gets up and sings:)
> The bells of hell
> Go ting-a-ling-a-ling,
> For you but not for me,
> Oh death, where is thy sting-a-ling-a-ling?
> Or grave thy victory?
> If you meet the undertaker
> Or the young man from the Pru,
> Get a pint with what's left over,
> Now I'll say goodbye to you.[9]

And the whole cast turns, and comes to the front of the stage, singing a last joyful chorus of 'The bells of hell'. It is a life-affirming ending, all the more powerful for its unexpectedness, when it seemed the boisterous and brilliant carnival was about to surrender to death.

Rather different was Henry Chapman's *You Won't Always Be on Top*, which preceded *The Hostage* chronologically, its first performance coming in September 1957. Chapman, a former building worker, dramatised building workers at work and, just as round a real building site gawpers lounge and stare, so the theatre audience was to play the part of the gawpers. It was an interesting way to fracture the 'fourth wall', yet simultaneously to re-emphasise the naturalism of the play's style, as alliances are built and quarrels explode or die, until, after the curtain call, when Albert, who has been digging a hole, emerges, rather like Firs at the end of *The Cherry Orchard*:

> Have they gone?—They've done it again, they have. (*He wanders across and off left mumbling to himself.*) I ain't going to have no more of this—Leaving me down that hole.—That's cold down that hole.—Tain't right.[10]

As startling as Behan's two plays, and making at least as deep an impression, was *A Taste of Honey* by Shelagh Delaney, presented by Theatre Workshop in May 1958. The author herself startled the critics: apparently the daughter of a bus driver, with Irish grandparents, and living in Salford, she was variously described as a photographer's apprentice, a cinema usherette and an engineering apprentice. What was most startling was that at the age of nineteen she had apparently seen *Variations on a Theme* by Terence Rattigan at the Manchester Opera House, and, convinced she could do better, had returned home and penned the first draft in a mere two weeks. Like Behan's plays, there is no real plot in *A Taste of Honey*. Jo and her mother, Helen, arrive in a dingy flat, Helen leaves with her male 'friend', Jo involves herself briefly in a relationship with a sailor, who leaves her pregnant. She is befriended by a caring gay student, who however leaves when Helen returns. Jo will have the baby. Will Geof return? What will Helen do? The questions are left unanswered.

Delaney's style is based in naturalism, though her psychological realism is more daring and more incisive than the better-patronised John Osborne. Indeed, there is something Chekhovian about this drama,[11] though Delaney plays in a different key. Like Chekhov, Delaney bursts the bounds of naturalism, for her characters owe as much to the theatre as they do to psychology.[12] The linking of the scenes with jazz riffs from the Apex Jazz Trio in Joan Littlewood's original production emphasised this, to the bewilderment of some critics, as did—obviously—the asides of the characters, especially Helen, to the audience. The play hints at the vexed problem of community, which continued to be a vital concept for Theatre Workshop, as Salford, Ewan MacColl's community, returns, but with an ambivalence that is distinct:

HELEN: The whole district's rotten, it's not fit to live in.
PETER: Let's go before we grow old sitting here.
HELEN: Shut up, the pubs will be open in ten minutes.
PETER: You're wrong there. (*Looking at his watch.*) They're open now.
          What time do you make it?
GEOF: There's one thing about this district, the people in it aren't
          rotten. Anyway, I think she's happier here with me than in that
          dazzling white house you're supposed to be so . . .[13]

The problem for all the characters in this play is that they exist beyond the
hold of the community. They are marginalised, feckless figures, moving
from one seedy flat to another, from one unsatisfactory relationship to
another, so that community becomes something perhaps not for them.

9. *A Taste of Honey* by Shelagh Delaney, with Murray Melvin (Geof),
Avis Bunnage (Helen), Frances Cuka (Jo) and John Bay (Peter),
Stratford East, 1958.

Such is frequently the experience of community for teenagers, and this play puts forward a teenager's view of the world. That, as well as the form, suggests its freshness. It lacks the disillusion of an older eye, but engages in an open-eyed waltz through reality, with time to reflect, and laugh, and cry. The freshness also derives, however, from the fact that it presents a woman's view of this marginalised world. Indeed *A Taste of Honey* might be the first significant play in British theatre history to be written by a woman and directed by a woman. As such, it takes an unconventional view of domesticity—the focal point of so much twentieth-century drama—with, as Michelene Wandor put it, 'no man to head [the family], [and] no secure, long-term home to house it.'[14] For these women, sex is often destructive, they must struggle for a meaningful morality, and issues of motherhood and caring assume a significance extremely rare, if not non-existent, in male-authored drama.

The press were confused, not to say contorted, when *A Taste of Honey* was originally presented by Theatre Workshop. T.C. Worsley, in the self-proclaimed progressive journal, the *New Statesman*, wrote that the play was '"about" a tart, a black boy giving a white girl a baby, (and) a queer. The whole contemporary lot, in short',[15] while Alan Brien, in the conservative *Spectator*, wrote: '*A Taste of Honey* still has the enormous advantage of being unlike almost any other working class play in that it is not scholarly anthropology observed from the outside through pince-nez, but the inside story of a savage culture observed by a genuine cannibal'.[16] The *Daily Mail* commented famously: 'Once authors wrote good plays set in drawing rooms. Now, under the Welfare State, they write bad plays set in garrets. If there is anything worse than an Angry Young Man it's an Angry Young Woman.'[17]

As succcessful commercially as *A Taste of Honey* was the production of Frank Norman's *Fings Ain't Wot They Used T'Be*, which opened in February 1959. The plot is as thin as it could be: it concerns a run-down gambling den, which is rescued by a fortuitously successful bet on a horse race. The den is redecorated and re-opened, a threatening rival gangster beaten off, and the hero hands over the running of his den to the policeman, who has always had a hankering to 'go crooked'. Joan Littlewood was delighted with the early sketched draft Norman presented to her, and suggested the play should become a musical. Lionel Bart, who had created a musical, *Turn It Up!*, at Unity Theatre, was contracted to provide the score.

The work deals with a group of 'loveable Cockneys', from the gay Horace, to the two tarts, Rosey and Betty, the failed burglar, Redhot, and the Honourable Percy Fortescue, the local lad made good, who has never forgotten his roots, and Myrtle, his upper-class fiancée. We may not believe in them, but they are clearly fun, and collector's items. The language is supposedly 'authentic' Cockney: here Redhot explains why he is not in gaol:

REDHOT:	Out for good behaviour.
FRED AND LIL:	Wot?
REDHOT:	Out for good behaviour.
FRED:	'E says 'e's out for good behaviour. I see you've still got yer old overcoat on.
REDHOT:	Course I 'ave. Brass monkey wevver, ain't it?
FRED:	Wot?
REDHOT:	Brass monkey wevver.
FRED:	'E says it's brass monkey wevver.
LIL:	Want a cup of splosh, darling?
REDHOT:	Got anything stronger?
FRED:	Wot?
REDHOT:	Anything stronger?
FRED:	Stronger? No.
REDHOT:	I fort I was going to touch yer.
FRED:	Touch me?
LIL:	Some 'opes![18]

This is fast-paced and amusing, and Littlewood was consistently adamant that she wanted only 'authentic' working-class speech in her theatre. As J.M. Synge remarked, peasant language in itself is not enough, and this has a kind of theatricality about it that makes most listeners laugh. Language, and especially dialect, is one means of defining community, and one of this play's aims is to define a particular kind of Cockney community, which may have never existed, yet is somewhere in the subconscious of many of those born within the sound of Bow bells. The dream of community takes over in the fairy-tale ending of the play, when the copper turns croupier and faithful Lil, the charlady, marries the boss.

It may be that this sentimentalises a culture which was in fact dangerous and anti-social. This was the East End of the Kray twins, it may be recalled. The women in this play are either tarts who belong to their pimps, or 'decent' women who are the property of their husbands or bosses. The economics of prostitution or the gambling den are never explored, as they are in *The Beggar's Opera* or even *The Threepenny Opera*, to which *Fings Ain't Wot They used T'Be* has sometimes been compared. But it has a zest and energy which subverts po-faced moralising and refuses to accept either the need for social responsibility or economic justice. Again, the critics were exceedingly puzzled as to how to receive it. *Queen* magazine asserted patronisingly: 'The whole thing wouldn't last a minute in the West End',[19] a prognostication belied by its long and highly successful run at the Garrick Theatre, followed by further success on Broadway.

Make Me an Offer, a musical by Wolf Mankowitz set among the East End's Cockney and Jewish street traders, followed *Fings* to the West End, but *Sam, the Highest Jumper of Them All* by the American poet, William Saroyan, was less successful. Sam is a bank clerk, and when the bank is robbed, Sam leaps over the counter to stop the thief. But the police assume he is the robber and beat him over the head. This affects his brain, for he decides to become a high jumper, the highest jumper in the world. If he can jump so high, imagine what he could think! Sam's temporary madness makes him into a sort of holy fool. The play is intended as satire on capitalism, on good social order and conformism, and on hierarchies of all sorts. Jumping becomes an image for subverting good order, it turns the world upside down, it distracts and destabilises. However interesting the idea, the production was poorly focussed and badly received. Even worse was the reception afforded to James Clancy's play, *Ned Kelly*, a month later in May 1960. The production saw the return to the company of Harry H. Corbett in the title role of the Australian outlaw hero. Though his performance attracted some attention for its dashing romanticism, the play was too long and too loosely constructed to make an impact.

Sparrers Can't Sing by Stephen Lewis, opening in August 1960, was much more successful. Set once more in the East End of London, this play has some interesting affinities with Elmer Rice's *Street Scene*. Once again the plot was not significant, but the play presented a group of people, a community, interacting, as the young seek mates and those who are married squabble and bawl at each other. When Jack wins money at the races, everyone is invited to the celebrations; everyone makes fun of Peanut's *outré* hairstyle; they all try to exclude George, the outsider, when he comes courting Nellie. The Stratford East programme implicitly linked this fictional community with local reality: it contained much information on the 'Metropolitan Borough of Stepney', including population changes over twenty years, notes of the main industries and discussion of the mixed population—Jewish, Irish and Buddhists and 'Mahommedans', who co-existed with a 'large floating population of sailors, and people catering for sailors' needs'. Like *Sparrers Can't Sing*, *Progress to the Park* by Alun Owen, which opened in November 1960, directed by Harry H. Corbett, focused on community: both plays were ideal for ensemble playing, and had no 'star' roles. This time the community was Liverpool, riven by hostility between Protestant and Catholic and between older and younger generations. The main interest was reserved for Teifion, a Welshman with a black girlfriend, and Mag, similarly an outsider, hanging onto herself as best she can in desperate circumstances.

In January 1961, Theatre Workshop presented Marvin Kane's *We're Just Not Practical*. Conceived as a television play, the author objected to Joan

Littlewood's treatment of his script, and the two quarrelled fiercely. Later that year, Littlewood presented the last of these new plays, *They Might Be Giants* by James Goldman. But in spite of her faith in this play, and her good relations with its author, despite too the presence of Harry H. Corbett as Sherlock Holmes and Avis Bunnage as Watson, the play failed. Littlewood wound up the company and departed for Nigeria.

In 1963, on her return, Theatre Workshop presented a new play that was also in a sense a new type of play—though it clearly had its models and predecessors, from Piscator's *Rasputin, the Romanovs, the War and the People Who Rose Against Them* to Ewan MacColl's *Uranium 235*. Yet this was a remarkable and distinct drama. Exactly whose idea *Oh What a Lovely War* was remains a matter of controversy. What seems certain is that Gerry Raffles heard a radio programme, *The Long Long Trail*, a compilation of First World War soldiers' songs made by Charles Chilton, with linking commentary spoken originally by Andrew Faulds, but in the repeat, slightly modified broadcast, by Bud Flanagan. Raffles contacted both Joan Littlewood and Charles Chilton, and the play was made. The convolutions of this process, and the unquantified input from other writers, including Jim Allan, Gwyn Thomas and the members of the original cast themselves, are discussed in detail by Derek Paget in an article published in *New Theatre Quarterly*.[20] Suffice to say that several court cases were fought over the vexed question of authorship, though this was probably an unavoidable upshot of the Theatre Workshop method of work. It does, however, make Littlewood's claim in the revised text, published in 2000, seem disingenuous, if not distinctly ungenerous: 'The idea came from Gerry Raffles, who had heard a BBC programme of songs from the First World War, the plot from Joan Littlewood, and the rest was worked out with the company.'[21]

Oh What a Lovely War owes part of its success to the fact that the subject matter of the piece taps into something deep within the British psyche and 'race memory', as this extract from *The Classic Slum*, the picture of the Salford in which Ewan MacColl grew up, indicates:

> One evening [. . .] my eldest sister came home, placed a page of sheet music on the piano and began to play and sing, 'Oh, oh, oh, it's a lovely war!' The old man sat much amused; but at about the third rendering, with the whole family gathered round intent on learning the words and tune of this rollicking new song, my mother, who had not joined in, got up, took the sheet from the stand, rolled it into a cylinder and returned it to my sister. We stood astonished . . .
>
> 'I won't have it,' she said quietly, 'not in this house—such carnage! And people sing "it's a lovely war!"'
>
> 'Don't you see?' said my father. 'It's skitting! It's ridicule! "Up to the waist in water!"' he sang. '. . ."Up to the eyes in slush!" . . .'

'I see well enough,' she said, 'but some things are too terrible for ridicule.'

My sister got up, tossed the music on top of the piano and flounced out.[22]

Here is everything Theatre Workshop's drama aimed for: something intangible, 'feelings as profound and strange as yours and mine'[23] co-existing with documented 'facts' culled from a long list of sources printed at the end of the published text.

Littlewood's procedure was inherently collaborative. She and a group of actors, including Brian Murphy, George Sewell, Avis Bunnage, Victor Spinetti, Murray Melvin and Griffith Davies, researched the material that Chilton's songs implied, often in Chilton's archive, and then improvised 'scenes' in whatever style seemed appropriate for the content. This produced 'a medley of different styles which the genius of Littlewood and the invention of the ensemble [. . .] welded into one'.[24] Thus there was agit-prop next to naturalism, stylisation next to a presentational style that often included direct address to the audience. As Littlewood explained, it was 'all in the juxtapositioning', reminiscent of MacColl's 'contrasts' and Benjamin's 'interruptions', juxtapositions that were made here not only through time, that is, through a sequence of scenes, but also through space, as the pierrots performing the scenes were set against giant projections of First World War soldiers, scenes of battles, or perhaps absurd advertisements for items such as 'Carter's Liver Pills—for Active Service'.[25] This visual complexity was further intensified by a news panel, across which flashed essential 'facts', such as the numbers of casualties and the gains or losses in yards of particular actions. And all was contained within a frame of brightly coloured fairy lights. The show's approach therefore was similar to that explained by Leo Lania of the Piscator collective in the 1920s:

This basic attitude towards historical drama means a complete revision of traditional dramatic form; not the inner arc of dramatic events is important, but the most accurate and comprehensive epic account of the epoch from its roots to its ultimate ramifications. Drama is important for us only where it can be supported by documentary evidence. Film, the constant interruption of external events by projections and film clips, are a means of achieving this documentary breadth and depth; they are inserted between the acts and after decisive turns of events and provide areas of illumination as the searchlight of history penetrates the uttermost darkness of the times.[26]

Piscator listed his source material for *Rasputin, the Romanovs, the War and the People Who Rose Against Them* in exactly the way source material for *Oh What a Lovely War* is listed.

The juxtapositioning of projections, jokes, 'facts', songs and more, the way each interrupts the other, was dialectical in the best sense. In her introduction to the script in 2000, Joan Littlewood instructs that 'essential to the play' is that 'the Pierrots, the screen and the newspanel must all be in the same field of vision. If either the newspanel or the screen is suspended elsewhere, at the side of the auditorium for example, the audience will simply not look at them'.[27] This is a perfect example of what Eisenstein meant by 'collision montage', and results in emotion checked by thought, understanding undermined by horror, brutality confronted by 'civilisation' and cheeriness by degradation. It is hard to decide whether this is a satire against those who control our society or a celebration of the stoicism of those who receive the orders, harder still to say whether the songs are nostalgic or bitter, and whether the characters are cartoons or representative types. Part of the reason for this, and for the seeming freshness of the form, is that Theatre Workshop here was in no way interested in the exploration of style or form as such, but was driven to seek the most effective means of communicating something important. In other words, the material, and its social function—that is, its effect on the spectators—drove its technique.

Audiences were absorbed, not as with a thriller to find out what would happen next, but by the presentation of the material. Bernard Levin reported how 'there were uneasy stirrings in the house at some of the things that were being done with the Union Jack'[28] and Derek Paget records how a recording of a performance in April 1963 reveals the audience response to the scene of the troops fraternising at Christmas 1914:

> There is *total* silence from the house—no sounds of coughing, fidgeting, or any of the markers of audience inattention. At the final freeze, the prolonged and vigorous applause confirms how undivided the audience's attention has been. This applause cuts very suddenly—presumably as they took in the Newspanel.[29]

It is true that the original ending—a bitter comment about the ongoingness of war—was changed when the play transferred to the West End,[30] but even the 'safer' version was extraordinarily effective. It was probably to the latter that Jackie Fletcher responded:

> Joan Littlewood's production made me understand. The slide projections depicting the reality of trench warfare in all its grotesque and horrid waste of human life, juxtaposed to scenes in which upper-class twits, aggrandised with military titles, flounder in incompetence, and fat-cat industrialists rub their hands with glee at their growing bank balances, finally made sense of a war which sacrificed the working-classes of all nationalities for the benefit of the status quo. The texts projected [. . .] pushed the sheer scale of the atrocity, the utter insanity of the military strategy, home. And yet I

was uplifted. I came out singing the songs, delighted with the physicality of the performances.[31]

Forty years after its composition, the power of *Oh What a Lovely War* remained. Michael Billington, after seeing a professional production in Regent's Park open-air theatre in 2002, wrote: 'Seeing the show again nearly forty years on, I find it still brings a tear to the eye while making one's gorge rise'.[32] The original production, as 'political' as anything from the Theatre Workshop of Ewan MacColl's time, summed up much of the company's, and especially Joan Littlewood's, development. In it can be seen, not only the European *avant-garde* influences mentioned, but also the culmination of a process that began with *John Bullion* and *Newsboy*, and developed first through *Classic Soil*, *Johnny Noble* and *Uranium 235*, then through *Volpone*, *Macbeth* and *The Dutch Courtesan* and finally through the later sequence of plays, including *The Quare Fellow*, *A Taste of Honey* and *The Hostage*. *Oh What a Lovely War* performed not only an alternative version of the First World War, but an alternative model of social—and theatrical— reality.

All the new plays, from *The Quare Fellow* to *Oh What a Lovely War*, have something in common. This is not simply a certain coherence of outlook, a shared attitude to life and social reality, but also a common process of creation that is what dictates the common attitude. The first element in the process is the absorption of the playwright into the collective. The examples to be followed were Shakespeare and Molière, and it was they whom Ewan MacColl, when he was Theatre Workshop's playwright-in-residence (as it were) certainly followed: like Shakepeare and Molière, he wrote scripts but also acted in them. The process worked best when the author's original script, the starting point of the process, was fairly raw, as *A Taste of Honey* was: according to Littlewood, this had 'two believable characters and a lot of splendid lines all mixed up with stuff that might have come straight from *Peg's Paper*'.[33] The first work on the play involved a wide-ranging exploration of ideas, themes and possibilities that the material suggested. For *You Won't Always Be on Top*, this meant the actors going round building sites, watching bricklayers and others at work, then finding a friendly 'ganger' and talking to him in a pub, while for *The Hostage* the company listened to Brendan Behan's songs and stories of Ireland. This beginning gives depth to the ensuing improvisation work, 'the basis for a sort of *commedia dell'arte* improvisation', as Littlewood put it.[34] The improvisations might be generated from the skeletal script, perhaps with different situations for characters to explore, or they might introduce new characters whom the 'author' had not considered. For the final act of *The Hostage* there was virtually no script to work from, and the actors effectively created it:

> We sat there, imagining it was the dead of night, that we were waiting for news of the prisoner in Northern Ireland. If they hanged him, the young hostage sitting there with us would die.
>
> One couldn't sustain such a mood for the whole act. Brendan's characters would burst into hilarity if they were on their way to the scaffold. That would work, but let the I.R.A. guard be seen and there would be half-spoken fears, fragments of prayers . . . Kate O'Connor at the piano started playing moody music in these breaks. It helped.[35]

Often this work proceeded through mime or movement without words, seeking the physical heart of the episode. Thus, an actor's truth was established which might then require revision of the script. Frank Norman, author of *Fings Ain't Wot They used T'Be*, found this hard to accept: 'On the first morning the cast foregathered on stage and the peculiar process began. The famous extemporizing of the actors that had been infused into the text of *The Hostage* and *A Taste of Honey* was now permitted to run riot in *Fings*.'[36] The process was able also to incorporate chance happenings or references to contemporary events, like that to the Russian Sputnik in *You Won't Always Be on Top*, or the remark of the woman who came out of her flat during the filming of *Sparrers Can't Sing*, and asserted, 'They're putting all the old ones at the top, you know, to kill 'em off', which was immediately included in the script.[37] From this process, a final production script was reached—though it must be noted that this was not sacrosanct or untouchable during the play's run.

This process undoubtedly clarified and sharpened many playtexts. For example, Act II Scene 2 of *A Taste of Honey* begins in the published text with Geof 'dancing' in with a mop and a bucket, and cleaning the room, an engagingly physical demonstration of his arrival, not just in Jo's flat, but in her life. In the original version, however, the scene begins with Geof 'busily knitting', giving an altogether different impression. Similarly, in the original ending, no sooner does Helen return to the flat than Jo goes into labour. The ambulance men arrive and take Jo off, leaving Helen and Geof together for the final scene. Geof says he may join a ballet company, and informs Helen that the baby may be black. Their exchanges are somewhat forlorn, even inconsequential, as they fail to establish any *rapport*, and Helen leaves. Geof starts to tidy the room:

> (*He picks up the rubber doll.*) A rubber doll—a life-size replica of a rubber doll! Like me—the nearest I'll ever get to a son and heir. Never mind, Geoffrey—you've got an empty room—all the curtains drawn (*He pulls the curtains together.*)—the doors locked (*He locks the door.*)—all the fires put out. (*He lies back on the couch, the doll in his hand.*)
> Curtain
The End[38]

The published ending, the one used in performance, is much more satisfactory. Here Jo is left alone on the stage, and she sings to herself Geof's fantasy nursery rhyme: 'As I was going up Pippin Hill'.[39]

The same kind of sharpening can be seen in *The Hostage*. For instance, Act II begins with the hostage and his two guards, the former asking for a cigarette and about his next meal. The guards leave, and Teresa enters with the tray. In the first performed version, something like a game of Grandmother's Footsteps (or London) takes place in this scene.

> *The house appears to be still, but in the dark corners and doorways, behind the piano and under the stairs, people are hiding, waiting for an opportunity to contact the prisoner, to see what he looks like and to take him comforts like cups of tea, Bible tracts, cigarettes and stout. As soon as the Officer and the Volunteer turn their backs, a scurry of movement is seen and hisses and low whistles are heard. When the I.R.A. men turn to look there is silence and stillness.*

After the IRA guards leave, and before Teresa enters with the tray –

> *All hell breaks loose and everyone tries to get to the Soldier at once. People hare through the room at breakneck speed, leaving the Soldier with stout, hymn sheets, aspidistras, and words of comfort.*[40]

This version then continues:

COLETTE: Five minutes—upstairs—I won't charge you.
                              (*Teresa enters with tray.*)
ROPEEN (*lifting a lid*):   Rashers and eggs!
       GRACE: Oh, the two eggs, the yolk in the middle, like a
                    bride's eye under a pink veil (*stealing a bit of bread*)
                    and the big black rashers all greasy.

Then, despite the Volunteer's attempts to stop them, the other characters gather round, steal bits of the hostage's breakfast and generally make nuisances of themselves until they are chased away by Pat. When the play transferred to Wyndham's Theatre, this sequence changed again. Now, after Colette's line, 'Five minutes—upstairs—I won't charge you', the Volunteer attempts fruitlessly to stop them mobbing the hostage, until finally Pat enters and drives them away. When they have gone, Pat calls Teresa in. He goes, leaving the hostage and Teresa alone together. In other words, the business of the other characters mobbing Teresa and the hostage together, and stealing bits of the breakfast, was jettisoned, presumably to retain the purity of their relationship. Yet the 'Grandmother's Footsteps' business was retained from the second version, because it made a significant point, as well as giving the montage additional dynamic.[41]

For *Oh What a Lovely War*, for which no script existed before rehearsals (apart from Charles Chilton's radio programme), there was more emphasis initially on research. Actors were asked to read some relevant work assigned to them, and report back to the group. Thus Brian Murphy read Liddell Hart's *A History of the First World War*, and this reading informed subsequent improvisations. These began with the actors simply 'being' soldiers in trenches—'somebody would take on the role of being the witty one, or somebody would play cards, or somebody would just want to play a mouth organ'[42]—but gradually specific possibilities were introduced. At one rehearsal recalled by Brian Murphy, all the lights were extinguished, and all the actors sat or lay on the stage. Then, one group of them had to make their way to the back of the auditorium in absolute silence. Any noise was challenged. Colin Kemball, an actor who had originally been a member of the BBC singers who had recorded *The Long Long Trail* radio programme, then climbed to the flies and started singing, 'Stille Nacht'. Later the scene was extended forwards, so that the soldiers are seen chatting before nightfall, and the use of several quotations from the trench newspaper, *The Wipers Times*, which their research had uncovered, were introduced. Furthermore, in the early rehearsals for this scene in the trenches, it was clearly envisaged that there would be a good deal of naturalistic 'clutter', a fire step, sandbags, a brazier for boiling tea and so on on stage, and this was only removed comparatively late in the process of making the scene. At another rehearsal, as the scene seemed to flag somewhat, Victor Spinetti walked forward, singing quietly; 'Brother Bertie went away, / To do his bit the other day . . .'. Act I had its conclusion.[43]

This method was open to abuse. As Toni Palmer said: 'If Joan likes what you're doing, she may fill out your part. But you daren't go down with 'flu. You may not have a part left when you get back.'[44] On the other hand, as Murray Melvin recounted about *Sparrers Can't Sing*, 'I began rehearsals playing a character who isn't even in the play, he's only referred to as a "bloke with red boots". In the end I had a major part, that of Knocker Jug'.[45] In another dimension, it was possible that, even a day before opening, the script would still not be finalised, as happened with *The Hostage*. Joan Littlewood's presence throughout was crucial to the process, as she retained a sort of overall skeleton of the play in her head. This was the case, for instance, for *The Hostage*, which was a fairly conventional one-act play, written in Gaelic, when Littlewood began work on it, and gave it not only three acts, but also its special music-hall character, its deliberate flouting of conventions and, indeed, its moving finale. With *Oh What a Lovely War*, it was she who edited the projection sequences, and decided about the contents of the newspanels, as well as providing what might be called the 'through line' of the performance. Though this was never to become a constriction, it did provide a rhythm.

None of this should suggest that Joan Littlewood or the Theatre
Workshop company lacked respect for the playwright's contribution.
Littlewood may have added jazz sequences and direct address to the
audience to *A Taste of Honey*, and even changed its ending, but it was all
intended to help Delaney's play to speak in its true voice: according to
Frances Cuka, the original Jo, 'Joan said it was a young girl's play and we
mustn't wreck the flavour of it'.[46] After the first night of *The Quare Fellow*,
Brendan Behan told the audience, 'Miss Littlewood's company have
performed a better play than I wrote'.[47] Henry Chapman's *You Won't Always
Be on Top* was compared with Robert Tressell's *The Ragged Trousered
Philanthropists*. But not all authors were delighted. Frank Norman, author of
Fings Ain't Wot They Used T'Be, complained:

> The moment of a play's acceptance [at Theatre Workshop] was very often
> the moment of departure from it. The journey from page to stage was
> fraught with hazards for the unwary playwright. Powerless to do anything
> about it, short of call the whole thing off, a forlorn author would sit
> hunched in the stalls and gaze up at a stage littered with discarded pages as
> Littlewood tore his play to bits with her bare hands, cut out the heart, gave
> it the kiss of life and tossed it to the assembled company of improvisers.
> With the raw material of ad libs she would then proceed to remodel the
> flesh in her own image.[48]

Whatever justification Norman may have had for this diatribe, it remained
true that the Theatre Workshop playwrights—Frank Norman himself,
Brendan Behan, Shelagh Delaney, Henry Chapman, Stephen Lewis and
others—had virtually no playwrighting successes beyond their work with
Joan Littlewood's company.

Partly because of their shared process of creation, these Theatre
Workshop plays shared certain stylistic features and certain attitudes that
were a major part of their strength. For instance, they tended to deal with
groups of people rather than individuals. Partly a result of the collective
nature of much of the creative process, partly because of Theatre
Workshop's communal ideals, Behan's plays, Chapman's *You Won't Always
Be on Top*, *Sparrers Can't Sing* by Stephen Lewis and *Oh What a Lovely War*
itself all demand ensemble playing, with no star parts. Each provides a
variety of viewpoints on its subject matter, something akin to Bakhtin's
'polyphony', in which no voice is particularly privileged and spectators
must make their own connections, interpretations, conclusions. This in
turn creates the 'collective hero'—the building workers, the Tommies in
the trenches, the prisoners in Mountjoy Gaol—that is a significant feature
of this drama.

The plays also tend to employ a variety of styles that contrast with or
interrupt each other in order for each to make its maximum impact. Thus,

speech gives way to song, dialogue to monologue, there is 'acting out'—the opening of the public lavatory in *You Can't Always Be on Top*, for instance, or Jo and the Boy in *A Taste of Honey* playing Desdemona and Othello—and 'theatricalisation'—*The Quare Fellow*'s hanging party presented as a horse race, the soldiers in *Oh What a Lovely War* seen as pierrots. There is persistent recourse to something like a documentary use of facts, even in the case of apparently fictional plays. One element of this is the use of songs that were familiar to the audience, such as music-hall numbers and nursery rhymes, which bring something apparently authentic from the outside world into the drama. The documentary form and its accompanying structural feature—montage—derives largely from the agit-prop of the inter-war years. Compare this short scene from Tom Thomas's 1930 agit-prop piece, *Their Theatre and Ours*, with the opening of *Oh What a Lovely War*:

> (*The group gather round like a chorus on stage or film 'plugging' a 'cheer-up' song. A satirical picture of the way this stuff is put across. Faces ghastly with forced happiness. 2nd leads them in the song:*
> 'Happy days are here again, The skies above are clear again'. (*Straight on to*)
> 'There's a good time coming, So keep your sunny side up, up'—
> (*All break off singing suddenly and become a worker audience coming out of a show.*)

1ST (*enthusiastic*):	Good show, that!
3RD (*wearily*):	Not bad.
1ST:	Nice and cheerful!
3RD:	It's about the only thing that is!
4TH:	Don't I know it? I've been out nearly two years. Just lost one of my little ones—couldn't feed her properly.
5TH:	And we're all working short time—and speeded up like mad while we're there.
6TH:	Yes, and by the time you've paid the landlord and the clubs there's nothing left to live on.
4TH:	What we want is a revolution!
1ST (*still cheerful*):	Cheer up, mate, there's a good time coming!
3RD (*laughing sourly*):	So keep your sunny side up, eh?
1ST (*sings softly to himself*):	Sing Hallelujah, Hallelujah, and you'll shoo your blues away.
2ND (*breaks into scene; the others go off quickly*):	And that's how they do it on you. There's always a good time coming—but the workers never get it.
3RD:	And when in 1914 the bosses drove us to fight their bloody war for them, to increase their profits—their theatres and cinemas did the dirty work.

GIRL (*enters and sings to audience in heavily emphasized*
       music hall style):   For we don't want to lose you, but we think
                    you ought to go, for your king and your
                    country both need you so.
     ANOTHER GIRL: And one million men who were caught like
                    this never came back but died ghastly tortured
                    deaths for the profits of the capitalist class.
          MAN: And thousands who did come back are
                    tramping the streets—unemployed—
                    unwanted—outcasts—And what do the king
                    and the country care?[49]

We are reminded irresistibly of *Oh What a Lovely War*, partly of course by
the subject matter here, but even more so by the dramatic rhythm with its
powerful interruptions, and by the use of factual material and period songs.
Oh What a Lovely War is far more sophisticated than this, with its
newspanel, the circus parade of the main players of the 'War Game', and the
projection of the Kitchener poster, 'Your Country Needs You' over the
singer of 'For we don't want to lose you'. But the ability to swing the mood
of the performance from satire, through pathos to anger is striking, as are
the technical switches from conventional drama, through direct address to
the audiencec and the introduction of song.

    This reminds us of another feature of the Theatre Workshop plays—the
use of minor and illegitimate forms of drama. Agit-prop, pierrot clowns,
music hall, all oppose the dominant naturalism of the contemporary stage,
and give the plays a flavour of rebellion, or subversion, even in their form.
This is compounded by the use of meta-theatrical devices. The pierrots, of
course, draw constant attention to the theatricality of *Oh What a Lovely War*
but other plays are similarly self-conscious. In *The Hostage*, after Rio Rita,
Mulleady and Princess Grace sing 'We're here because we're queer, /
Because we're queer because we're here', Princess Grace remarks to the
audience: 'The trouble we had getting that past the nice Lord
Chamberlain,' and then: 'This next bit's even worse'.[50] As Colbert Kearney
has pointed out, '*The Quare Fellow* is a play within a play [. . .] There are
two audiences: those in the theatre watch those on the stage who witness
the externals of the closet-drama'.[51] *You Won't Always Be on Top* reverses this
process, making the theatre audience into street 'gawpers'.

    From all this we can deduce that these Theatre Workshop plays also
share certain attitudes or assumptions. Conventional hierarchical order is
usually perceived as sterile, whereas disorder is likely to be creative. *The
Hostage* may be the obvious example of this, but it is true, too, of *Oh What a
Lovely War* and *You Won't Always Be on Top*. The plays demystify or challenge
accepted narratives, especially historical narratives which explain current
society. This is again best seen in *The Hostage's* challenges to Irish

mythologised history, and *Oh What a Lovely War's* rewriting of the First
World War. It is clear, in fact, that these plays all fracture hegemonistic
viewpoints, provide scandals and eccentricities, and thus share a
carnivalesque approach that marks them as subversive and celebratory
simultaneously. The contradictions of Bakhtin's carnival are nicely
summarised in a statement Joan Littlewood made in 1964:

> Hate made me write [. . .] *Oh What a Lovely War*. But I hope it turns into
> love because the political commitment is joy and the word almost for voice
> is joy in Greek. Theatre is expression in laughter; laughter gets you by in a
> very desperate situation; living on this planet, which isn't much fun.[52]

According to Bakhtin, carnival's typical tactic to break down hierarchies
and subvert authority is parody. The Theatre Workshop plays illustrate this
with almost textbook precision. Thus, in *The Quare Fellow* the solemn
procession to the gallows is portrayed as a horse race:

> We're ready for the start, and in good time, and who do I see lined up for
> the off but the High Sheriff of this ancient city of ours [. . .] We're off, in
> this order: The Governor, the Chief, two screws Regan and Crimmin, the
> quare fellow between them, two more screws and three runners from
> across the Channel, getting well in front now, the Canon. He's making a
> big effort for the last two furlongs. He's got the white pudding bag on his
> head, just a short distance to go. He's in . . .[53]

In *A Taste of Honey*, as Michelene Wandor points out, it is gender roles that
are subverted. Jo is 'deeply ambiguous' about her pregnancy, she 'hates
babies' and cannot bear the thought of breastfeeding, which she compares
to 'having a little animal nibbling away at me', while Geof is a kind of
mother, caring for Jo better than Helen ever did and preparing a cot for the
baby. Apparently this 'comes natural' to him.[54] And the use of parody is
pervasive. The church service sequence in *Oh What a Lovely War* is one
example, the parody of civil war and terrorism in *The Hostage* another. In
You Won't Always Be on Top, a Churchill figure takes the guided tour round
the public lavatory, while *Fings Ain't Wot They Used T'Be* ends with a
parodied marriage.

Like carnival, these plays assert the values of community as opposed to
hierarchy, even if the communities presented are communities of the
dispossessed: the East End of London, the working-class areas of Liverpool
or Dublin, or the communities made by the inmates of prison or the
Tommies in the trenches. And in these communities of the dispossessed,
marginal figures are made central, as Teifion and Mag are in *Progress to the
Park*, or Jo and Geof in *A Taste of Honey*. Even Peter in that play, apparently a
representative of the middle class, seems to have become *déclassé*, with his
eye-patch and his *penchant* for older women. In these plays, the outsider

becomes a valid subject, not simply an 'other', a nominative, not necessarily the accusative she or he usually is. Woman—that is, in Theatre Workshop's context, Joan Littlewood—is the essential outsider, as Monique Wittig has asserted,[55] and this helps the beam of these plays to focus, but what is equally plain—and impressive—is that none of the outsider-protagonists are pinned down to a containable identity. Jo in *A Taste of Honey* is probably the best example of a shifting identity on the Theatre Workshop stage, but Sam, the high jumper, is another, as is Fred in *You Won't Always Be on Top*, Leslie in *The Hostage*, and others, too.

Finally, and again as with carnival, these plays affirm the values of the body, not the spirit, they assert the scatological and see the indecent as regenerative. In the time when the Lord Chamberlain wielded his blue pencil with some persistency, this was not easy to assert, yet the wild jigs, love making and outrageous partying that characterises *The Hostage*, create something genuinely Rabelaisian, and Mag, the alternative heroine of *Progress to the Park*, finds renewal in attempting neither to preserve her virginity nor to practise fidelity. The plays break many taboos of the time, some of which are still with us. The transvestism of *The Hostage's* IRA men who become nuns is still capable of causing a *frisson* of outrage, while the clown-*poilus* who go like lambs to the slaughter in *Oh What a Lovely War* also still resonate. *A Taste of Honey*, however, breaks most taboos most boldly, presenting a young girl taking her life into her own hands, having sex with, and getting pregnant by, a black man, and finding comfort with a gay man. Was it only people in the 1950s who found such behaviour truly offensive?

Theatre can animate carnivalesque images, though it is not carnival, because carnival makes no distinction between performer and audience. In carnival everyone joins in, whereas in the theatre the spectators can only do so vicariously. Nevertheless, some of the accounts of Brendan Behan's behaviour, especially during *The Hostage*, when he was very likely to leave his seat and clamber on stage, probably singing some Irish drinking song, may have brought the Theatre Royal, Stratford East, as close to the reality of carnival as any British theatre has ever come. Certainly, that building in the 1950s was the heart of British carnivalesque theatre.

CHAPTER SEVENTEEN

Joan Littlewood, Director

The living link through all Theatre Workshop's creative existence, what gave its varied achievements coherence, vitality and drive, was the person of its artistic director, Joan Littlewood, who was responsible for production from the company's inception. 'A solidly built sympathetic woman in a woolly hat, chain smoking Gauloises',[1] Littlewood's refusal to conform, her intractable ultraism—she was utterly uninterested in working with the John Osbornes of the day because they could find their voice in an 'Establishment' theatre—led Kenneth Tynan to suggest that 'a few centuries ago [. . .] such a woman might easily have been burned as a witch'.[2] Settling at Stratford East undoubtedly unloosed a new dynamic into her work. She may have lost Ewan MacColl, but she had found Gerry Raffles, and his reliability, and his energy as a theatre manager, while still playing a large number and wide variety of parts on stage, was obviously highly significant for her. She was simply able to direct the plays which excited her, as she rummaged through, for example, the Elizabethan repertoire and found plays like *The Dutch Courtesan* and *Arden of Faversham*, to say nothing of the plays of Ben Jonson, which have probably never had a finer interpreter. It should be remembered, too, that she acted in many of the productions as well as directing them. She was Marinette in *The Flying Doctor*, Lil in *You're Only Young Once*, Maisie Madigan in *Juno and the Paycock*, Lady Would-be in *Volpone*, Alisa in Fernando de Rojas's *Celestina*, Amanda Wingfield in *The Glass Menagerie*, directed by Clifford Williams, and more. And she was a superb actress. Patience Collier, seeing her rehearse as a peasant woman in *Fuente Ovejuna*, exclaimed to her companion, 'Why isn't this woman playing great leading parts in the West End?' to which the reply was, 'She doesn't want to, she's not that sort of woman'.[3] Ewan MacColl recalled half a century later the impact that his first view of her on stage as the conventional Maid at a provincial repertory theatre had made on him.

> Joan had all the makings of a superb actress. It wasn't merely that she had a
> voice which could charm birds out of trees; it was the sense of truth which
> informed everything she did. She invested even the smallest walk-on with
> the deep, shining passion of real art, so that one felt impelled to watch the

10. Images of Joan Littlewood.

maid collecting teacups and loading them on to a tray, when one should
have been watching the mistress stabbing her lover.[4]

Patience Collier was told Joan Littlewood was not 'that sort of woman'
because Littlewood preferred to start a radical theatre company of her own.
It was the creation and nourishing of that company that was her life's work.
At first a touring political theatre, Theatre Workshop metamorphosed
under Littlewood's artistic direction into a 'people's theatre', at base an
anarchist conception, but shot through with socialism. The first
implication of this, which Joan Littlewood energetically endorsed, was that
creation in the theatre was a collective business. 'I do not believe in the
supremacy of the director, designer, actor or even of the writer. It is
through collaboration that this knockabout art of theatre survives and
kicks.'[5] This anti-elitist viewpoint implies a popular style, with a particular
attitude towards the audience. On the one hand, as Stephen Lacey has
pointed out, it can incorporate into its style audience interjections,[6] and on
the other it is a place in which an 'ordinary person' can feel comfortable. In
other words, this is a theatre with a relation to a community. Joan
Littlewood pleaded for 'each community' to have its own theatre, and
railed against the fact that Stratford East's theatre had been continuously
'plundered' for its talent by the West End, and commercial television.[7]

Her concept of community was perhaps more fluid than she would have
cared to admit: it included the children living near the theatre, for whom
she always had time, as well as all the employees of the theatre—the
Theatre Royal, Stratford East, was the first to include the names of its
cleaners (Mrs Chambers, Mrs Parham, Mrs Snell and Mrs Woolmer), bar
staff (Ruth Parham) and box office (Monica Patterson), in its programme.
Littlewood's insistence that the national anthem would only be played
when royalty were physically present in the theatre—a policy greeted with
raised eyebrows in many quarters, and something considerably worse in
some others—was really part of the same attempt to define 'her'
community. For the term now no longer referred, as it had in Ewan
MacColl's day, to class; but nor, in fact, did it refer to place, for Alun
Owen's *Progress to the Park*, a play about community if ever there was one,
was based in Liverpool, not the East End. There was something shifting,
something temporary in Littlewood's latest—and perhaps most potent—
'communities'. *The Quare Fellow* defined its community as the population
of the prison; in *Oh What a Lovely War*, it was perhaps the British army, or at
least the group of Tommies who fought the battles and forged a kind of
community whose strength was to be wondered at. What Littlewood
effectively did, in fact, was to discover how to *perform* community, depicting
the forging of community through the work of a very specific
community—the Theatre Workshop company itself. Clive Barker, an

alumnus of the company, writing about it in 2003, noted the deaths of two of his former colleagues at Stratford East, Fanny Carby and Richard Harris. 'There are fewer of us left', he commented,[8] implicitly acknowledging that there was 'something special' about these graduates of Joan Littlewood's community. Without that sense in the company, perhaps the notion would have had less validity in the work.

The audience that feels itself free to make 'interjections' suggests other significant parts of the Littlewood heritage. She was the director in British theatre who abolished the 'fourth wall'—perhaps originally of necessity, since the concept is simply impractical in many miners' welfare halls. But in the theatre proper, she did away with the front curtain, she threw out the footlights, relic of the eighteenth century, she expelled the prompter so her actors had to know what they were doing, and her actors went on stage without make-up. All this seems almost conventional now, but in the 1940s and 1950s it was revolutionary. 'When I was twenty', she told an interviewer in 1964, 'I was talking about new structures, about breaking down walls and having new theatres', adding ruefully, 'and I found myself in this place', that is, the Victorian Theatre Royal at Stratford East.[9] What she did echoes what Meyerhold did in the Russian theatre, but the influence of the continental theatre was wider than that. One perceptive critic noted in 1959 that 'Her approach to acting derives from Stanislavsky, and she works along Method lines. [But] her stagecraft is boldly Brechtian, breaking through the fourth wall of naturalism and speaking directly to the audience (but she thinks Brecht has many bourgeois faults).'[10] The idea of the theatre company as the basic community is continental, too, as Irving Wardle noted: '[Joan Littlewood was] the only British director in the great Continental tradition: the absolute ruler of an egalitarian ensemble, for whom the creation of fine work on stage is inseparable from the creation of a freely co-operating collective.'[11]

Littlewood—again like Meyerhold—liked to note, in contrast, the influence of popular theatres, often pointing to the *commedia dell' arte*, the Chinese theatre, and the nineteenth-century street theatre of Britain, from which, she claimed, Charlie Chaplin sprang—in itself a fascinating lineage, since Meyerhold and Brecht both claimed Chaplin as a particular inspiration. The *commedia* influence was consciously present from the 1930s, and shows, for instance, in *The Flying Doctor*, an amalgam of Molière's *Le Médecin Volant* and the *commedia* scenario, *Il Medico Volante*. As for the use of Chinese theatre techniques, Clive Barker described how they were used in the production of *Arden of Faversham* in scenes we have already seen being rehearsed using Laban's movement techniques. The scenes in which Black Will and Shakebag stalk Arden would, in the Elizabethan theatre, Barker points out,

[be] played in broad daylight and a lot of the comedy arose out of the visible actors playing as though in the dark. Modern staging techniques make this stylised acting unnecessary and a lot of the fun is lost in modern recreations. Amalgamating two scenes from two Peking Operas, 'The Fight in the Dark' from *The Inn at the Cross-roads* and the set piece of *Crossing the Autumn River*, Littlewood staged the scenes in two (non-existent) boats in the middle of the river.

and thereby retained not only the fun, but also the theatricality, of the original. As Barker comments, this was 'characteristic of Littlewood's refusal to stay within naturalistic techniques but to use a wide range of stylised techniques.'[12]

The English nineteenth-century street actors were brothers to those who played the East End penny gaffs whom James Grant described in 1838, and whose grubby and gaudy crudeness is revealed in Henry Mayhew's *London Labour and the London Poor*, the four volumes of which were published between 1851 and 1862. It was to this theatre 'of runaway clerks and chimney sweeps' that Littlewood's theatre claimed kinship, with their ability to 'sing, dance, mime swimming and flying, and survive poverty'.[13] They were clearly multi-skilled, and adept at improvisation:

> A strolling actor is supposed to know something of everything. He doesn't always get a part given to him to learn, but he's often told what character he's to take, and he's supposed to be able to find words capable of illustrating the character; in fact, he has to 'gag', that is, make up words.[14]

Much of the performance was polished by observation; the actor interviewed by Mayhew who created his own clown character 'Silly Billy' had spent nearly two years observing boys playing, fighting, singing and coining sayings before he actually performed the part, which soon became hugely popular with the street audiences. They, for their part, responded by accepting conventions. Another 'strolling actor' recorded that in the play *The Bottle Imp*, 'The imp is always acted by a man in a cloak with a mask on. You see his cavalier boots under his cloak, but that don't matter to holiday folk when once they know it's intended to be a demon'.[15] The audience, in other words, do not *believe* this is an imp, they take the performance as a crude version, this particular actor's version perhaps, of the imp. These street performers were the artistic parents of those who performed melodramas at the Victorian Theatre Royal, and the grandparents of the pierrots, who performed on makeshift stages on the beaches of Edwardian England (and later), who could 'sing and dance and make you laugh' and were 'the great joy of the seaside'.[16] Joan Littlewood remembered such a troupe on Ramsgate beach in 1928, singing:

I wasn't born in Africa,
I wasn't born in France,
I wasn't born in sunny, sunny Spain,
I was simply born to dance.[17]

Unlike the street performers a hundred years before her time, however, Joan Littlewood believed in extremely thorough and meticulous rehearsals. In fact, her thoroughness and care, built as they were on the foundations of the training her actors—and she herself—continued to work at, was unprecedented in the British theatre, and even today has—and has had— very few, if any, imitators. Ewan MacColl felt his work with her was 'a great voyage of discovery',[18] for she was always unpredictable, always one step ahead of other people, and yet always carried forward on a huge wave of enthusiasm. She was violently opposed to 'type casting', and a glance at the variety of parts her actors performed vindicates her attitude powerfully. She was tireless, and had the ruthless ability of the true artist to destroy volumes of her own work if she saw it was failing to penetrate to the truth she sought. 'She would come in and watch something we'd spent three days on and say, "Scrap it, it's awful, it doesn't work." And she'd start again.'[19] She could be harsh with others, but she was harsher with herself, and so her actors forgave her and worked on.

Joan Littlewood's rehearsal methods and procedures were probably unique, but they were not particularly mysterious. They combined many of the elements of Stanislavsky's system with Laban's theory of movement, to which was added Littlewood's own penchant for games and improvisation. She went into rehearsal with no pre-conceived ideas, at least as far as stage movements ('blocking') were concerned, or how the dynamic of any specific scene would work out. The first rehearsals were usually devoted to shaking out the play, rather as one might shake the feathers out of a pillow. Themes, ideas, historical contexts, social pressures, characters' psychology and much more, might be unravelled. Actors were frequently asked to research a topic of particular relevance, and return prepared to give a more or less formal talk about it.

Usually before the play was cast, a good deal of exploratory work was done. First, and perhaps most significant, as with Stanislavsky, was to discover and discuss the play's 'final objective', what Stanislavsky calls the 'superobjective'. This had to be clear and strong, and to be remembered at all times, because all the action related to it. Then, characters might be discussed, but not as parts for actors, rather as human beings, and often their characteristic movements would be the focus or key. This would probably deploy Laban's principles: is the character typically heavy or light, direct or indirect, fast or slow? Is she high, or low, does she flow or stutter?

Round the table, the play was split into 'units', and then the objectives, or intentions, within the units explored. Why does the character say this? Why does the other character respond in that way? This analysis is often the crux of rehearsing because people (and therefore dramatic characters) rarely say exactly what they mean. But the analysis in Theatre Workshop was frequently carried out physically rather than through discussion. This is unusual and important. It shows how Littlewood found her own way to something unexpectedly like Stanislavsky's 'Method of Physical Action', where the actor must stand up and walk through the action without first trying to work it out intellectually. This physicalisation often uncovers the heart of the action rapidly, and without the kind of cerebration which can become self-defeating, sterile or exhausting. It can work in reverse as well, of course: the objectives may be clear from the start, and thus govern the action. Intention and action are two sides of the same coin. But physicalisation was usually Littlewood's preferred means of reaching beyond any but the most superficial reading of the text, and in her company the use of the shared Laban technique provided the perfect means for this. Henry Livings spoke of Littlewood's 'relentless analysis of what is *really* going on',[20] and Murray Melvin described her 'teasing out the truth below the lines [. . .] especially as she was an experienced writer herself'.[21] We have some glimpses of how this worked in the shape of Littlewood's notes, for instance those scribbled in the margins of the typescript of *The Travellers* which indicate how each unit has a title to indicate the action, and then intentions, articulated usually in imperatives, for each character. Thus, from the beginning of the play, Enrico Goriano is waiting 'in a state of extreme nervous tension'. Finally Kari Nielson, his girl friend, arrives. The italicised words in the following extract are Littlewood's annotations:

KARI'S LATENESS

ENRICO (*I must not hurt her*): Kari!

KARI (*I must hold him off*): I was delayed at the passport office. They asked me so many questions.

ENRICO: I am going crazy thinking you are not coming.

KARI: Nothing could stop me.

(They embrace again.)
Oh, Enrico, we are really going! I didn't really believe it would come true.

GORIANO'S HAPPINESS

ENRICO (*I will show her I am sorry for having suspected her*): But of course I, Enrico Goriano, say we go and we go. Now we must hurry. Here, I carry your bag.

KARI (*I must hold him off*): No, I'll take it.

After the scene when Katherine discovers her husband, Lorentz's perfidy, she enters the compartment where MacLean sits alone, reading. The first unit is entitled '*KATHERINE'S INTRUSION ON MACLEAN*', and each character is given a number of objectives at the outset. For Katherine these are: '*I must dump my bag*'; '*I must overcome my caution*'; '*I must sit down*'. For MacLean, '*I must be alone*'; '*I must show this woman she isn't welcome*'. The dialogue proceeds, and each character has further modifying intentions:

KATHERINE: May I share your compartment?
MACLEAN (*apologetic politeness*): Of course. Let me help you.
(He lifts her case onto the rack.)
KATHERINE: Thanks.

AVOIDING CONTACT
MACLEAN: Excuse me but . . . are you feeling all right? You're trembling.
KATHERINE (*I must keep hold of myself*): Please . . . it's nothing.
MACLEAN (*I must end this woman's grief*): If you are in some kind of trouble . . .
KATHERINE: I've had a shock. I'll be all right presently.
MACLEAN: An accident?
KATHERINE (*I must be sane*): Part of me has just been murdered.
MACLEAN (*I must be normal*): If you'd rather be alone I dare say I could find another carriage.

What is interesting about this sequence is the way that the two characters come together, almost coalesce, in their intentions, ending with '*I must be sane*' and '*I must be normal*', while the action is '*AVOIDING CONTACT*'. Without the use of this method, could this paradox be realised?

This reproduction is in danger of making the method seem over-academic. It is almost impossible to find an equally coherent pattern in her notes anywhere else in the typescript. Even if these notes were the results of analysis, it is important to reiterate that Littlewood's method was largely through action, that is, improvisation (any kind of acting without prepared lines or actions pre-considered) or games, and scenes were most often worked out spontaneously. These notes, however, indicate the way she thought about scenes. As a corrective, it is worth remembering what one observer recorded: 'Improvisation was first used in preparatory work on the classics, as when drawing you might try several lines before finding the exact one. Ad lib was only used in certain passages, as in jazz.'[22] Actors often found the method difficult and challenging because, instead being able to retreat behind the author's words and preconceived notions of character, they had to draw on their own internal selves, their own honesty and emotional experience. But as he worked with Littlewood, Nigel

Hawthorne found to his surprise that his 'fear of launching forth into unfamiliar territory without knowing what was going to come out of my mouth slowly began to disperse. I even began to find improvisation helpful.'[23] The work might be conducted first in mime, which was an excellent way of finding the physical essence of the scene, and then perhaps at a rapid tempo; actors might be asked to exchange roles, or to try the scene as a dance, or to approach it by the use of a 'parallel scene', that is, a scene that explores and exploits an equivalent emotional impact, but involves quite different characters. Nigel Hawthorne describes the process during rehearsals for *Oh What a Lovely War*:

> There was a tiny scene in which she felt that the actresses playing French country girls were being too modern in their approach to the Tommies. They were gathering round a group of soldiers, bringing them gifts of bread and wine and flirting with them [. . .] The band begins to play 'Mademoiselle from Armentiers' and they pair up and, whirling round and round, totally at ease in one another's company, dance off into the distance. So Joan invented an imaginary convent, just a few chairs and a table for the altar, and with the rest of us pretending to be devout nuns chanting in the background, each girl was asked to bring a posy of flowers down the aisle of the 'chapel', shyly present her gift to the Mother Superior and receive her blessing. Then Joan made them return to the scene itself. The difference was remarkable—it made sense for the first time. It sounds simple enough, I know, and there'll be cries of 'Anyone can do that!' The painful truth is that anyone can't.[24]

This leads to the kind of games Littlewood liked to employ, such as memory games, Blind Man's Buff or the sort of Wild West game that involved everyone's imagination, quick responses and wholehearted commitment. When games were inclusive of everybody and were fun in themselves, it was found that they could be extremely productive. And, of course, by employing everybody in these games and exercises, nobody was relegated to the role of spear-carrier, nor was anyone elevated to stardom.

Rehearsals for *Richard II* provided examples of this kind of rehearsal work: Howard Goorney describes how

> the initial rehearsals of *Richard II* were devoted to capturing the feeling of the period in quite basic terms. Improvisation exercises aimed at developing the enmity between the characters, the sudden outbreaks of violence, the suspicions, the ever present fear of the knife in the back. For example, Joan would say, 'You're in a market-place and it's full of people. You're getting your shopping and a fight breaks out!' We would fight each other, go beserk, jump on each other. Then she would say, 'Now you're stabbed in the back . . . You're on horseback, you're knocked off, you're dragged along, you shout and scream and sweat.'[25]

The emphasis was always on the physical. Thus, Richard strikes John of Gaunt with his glove at the climax of one scene; in the garden scene, emphasis was placed on the handling of the fruit by the gardeners.

A typical Littlewood production proceeded in this manner, introducing new complications, examining and improvising round possible contradictions and alternatives, sometimes using music in rehearsals, sometimes using unexpected lighting, always probing for new solutions with restless dissatisfied energy. At its best, this approach produced unmatchable brilliance, as with the finale of Act I of *Oh What a Lovely War*, the making of which is described above, and about which one reviewer wrote: 'It takes an unusually well-developed sense of truth to stage a scene like the Christmas night fraternization in no-man's-land without becoming mawkish. Here, if anywhere, one senses Miss Littlewood's finest qualities as a director.'[26] As with her performance as the Maid in Rusholme Repertory Theatre in 1934, it was Littlewood's 'sense of truth' which was so incisive.

At Theatre Workshop, at no time during rehearsals did an actor ask how to move, or where to go on the stage. The training and the method together produced a kind of organic quality that led actors almost to develop their own antennae so that they would move in response to rhythms, Laban-like efforts, and out of the deep well of work around the idea. They listened to each other, paid honest attention, and responded. Even Littlewood's best-trained actors sometimes found themselves 'acting' or doing something 'in the past tense'. One requisite for this rehearsal method is that the director must able able to think fast—faster, in fact, than anyone else in the rehearsal. It was a trait Meyerhold had in abundance, and so did Joan Littlewood. Both these directors were accused of tyrannising their actors, but in fact that was a misapprehension: they simply reached better solutions more quickly, partly as a result of their greater experience, but partly, too, because they had an intense flair and feeling for truth on the stage. As Joan Littlewood herself put it when her *Richard II* caused the critics such problems: 'When we play *Richard II*, the critics can't stand it because we're playing in what they call a vulgar fashion—we're playing it for action and dynamic rather than for decoration'.[27]

Littlewood's approach also cemented the group. They became a team. The *Glasgow Herald's* review of *The Imaginary Invalid* reported:

> The salient quality of the acting was teamwork. Even the most subsidiary character had something to contribute and was encouraged to do so. The leading parts were woven into the play's texture with easy authority without monopolising the limelight. The highly satisfactory result was the impression of a fellowship of players sharing an enjoyable experience with the audience.[28]

Penelope Gilliat, writing almost a decade later about *Sparrers Can't Sing*, commented, 'The plot [. . .] is minimal; but the ensemble playing is superlative'.[29] One advantage of working as an ensemble was that most of the discussion of the play, and the early rehearsals, could be carried on before actors were cast in roles, so that all were involved in reaching the ultimate meanings to be conveyed, and the methods for conveying them. Theatre is always at its best when it is collaborative, however much one or two restless individuals may carry an ultimate responsibility, as Shakespeare might have done at the Globe, or Stanislavsky at the Moscow Art Theatre. Certainly Joan Littlewood was *prima inter pares* rather than a dictator to her company: 'I never told anyone to "Move over there"; we didn't do that. We'd all work on a script and analyse it [. . .] I love that term, "the composite mind"'.[30]

What this meant can be exemplified by Littlewood's practice in *Johnny Noble*, the first Theatre Workshop production, and in *Oh What a Lovely War*, almost its last. When rehearsing the scenes at sea in *Johnny Noble*, Littlewood asked the actors each to suggest one sound, a single sound, which would express its essence. Someone suggested the slapping of the halyards, someone else the drone of the engine screw. These were used to stimulate the actors' movements. David Scase as Johnny sat on a box, swaying slightly back and forward, while his companion swayed from side to side. This movement in slightly different directions created the pitch and toss of the ship with uncanny expressiveness. Littlewood then added a green and a red light at the sides of the stage, also moving up and down, and this effect, two actors swaying, with the small coloured lights also swaying in the darkness, and the throb of the engine, was so effective that spectators were even left feeling seasick. It is notable how Littlewood effectively orchestrated ideas that originated with the actors. According to Hugh McDiarmid, 'it was a perfect example of team work and it was doubtful if groupings had ever been more naturally achieved.'[31] Littlewood's own description of the process of making *Oh What a Lovely War* suggests the same methods in action:

> Part of the good that has come out of this show is the way which a group of young people have worked together. Each brought a different point of view. They hated some of those songs. They didn't want to do propaganda, so they argued their way through each scene, and you've got, in the piece, the points of view of many people [. . .] There were no rehearsals as they are known. There was a collection of individuals, more of an anti-group than a group, working on ideas, on songs, on settings, on facts.[32]

Though this underplays Littlewood's own part in the creation of this piece, the process is clear from it. Harold Hobson said that the first thing he noticed about Theatre Workshop was the way the production was created collaboratively, and Littlewood herself expressed the idea with considerable animation at the 1963 Edinburgh Festival:

> I say to hell with geniuses in the theatre. Let's have the authors by all means, the Lorcas and the Brendan Behans, but let's get them together with their equals, the actors, with all their wit and stupidity and insight. And this clash, this collaboration, this *anti*-collaboration will create an explosion more important than any bomb.[33]

Such an approach requires actors who are prepared genuinely to trust themselves, to trust the other actors, the material, the play, the rehearsals and, above all, the director. With Littlewood in charge, the process often seemed agonising. Each rehearsal seemed to jettison the previous day's hard-won gains, and Littlewood cheerfully proclaimed, 'If we don't get lost, we'll never find a new route'.[34] 'When artists or scientists set out', she argued, 'they don't know what the end product will be. It changes. It changes in collaboration, each man [*sic*] trusting and mistrusting the people he works with'.[35] There is also the implication, of course, that no member of the group, actor or director, can be precious, but all must allow input from others.

Such a company requires multi-skilled actors, which was why Littlewood insisted on training, and why, when she was faced with the necessity in the early 1960s of training yet another group, she resigned. At the height of her career, however, her actors displayed a versatility which may have been unique in the history of British theatre. Of *A Christmas Carol*, staged in December 1958, one critic wrote: 'The cast's lightning transitions from straight dramatic acting to audience-shared jokes, songs and a variety of winks and nudges, as usual with this company, were admirable in effect and neat evidence of the professionalism behind them.'[36] *Uranium 235*, the company's third production presented in 1946, required actors who had a mastery of agit-prop techniques as well as 'straight' naturalism, who could play a variety of parts with little or no time to consider the changes during performance, who could dance, sing, clown, declaim, speak as part of a chorus and mime. In *Oh What a Lovely War*, almost two decades later, at least these skills were still demanded by Joan Littlewood. In *A Taste of Honey*, Avis Bunnage 'managed most skilfully to combine the broadest eye-on-the-gallery caricature, with straightforward detailed naturalism'.[37]

The versatility of the players was carried over into the versatility of the production. In *A Taste of Honey* the acting was complemented by the three-piece jazz band and the symbolic lighting effects. In *The Other Animals* there were surprising costumes, inventive choreography and a complicated sequence of sound effects. Joan Littlewood's gifts as a visual artist were carried over into her theatre work, too, as is clear from many production photographs, including those included in this book. Many of the 'pictures' she created on the stage have an arresting shape and often these pictures in themselves tell a story which subtly comments on the content of the play. In the photograph of *A Taste of Honey*, for example, the symmetrical grouping is noteworthy, having, tellingly, the apparently weakest character (Geof) at the top, and the apparently strongest, Peter, at the bottom. In the centre, Jo and Helen dispute. Note, too, how the lighting and decor highlight the effect achieved. Littlewood's handling of the stage picture and the juxtapositions she could achieve reached their finest in *Oh What a Lovely War*. Here the soldiers were framed by the fairy lights, they clowned under the huge slide projections of wounded soldiers, and all were set against the newspanel flashing its facts. This suggests a theatre of synthesis that goes beyond mere contrast to rely on a sophisticated form of collision montage, the balance and power of which was the director's greatest achievement.

Montage (*pace* Eisenstein) is also open-ended, pushing the responsibility for making meanings onto the spectator. Littlewood understood this. She also understood that actually there are no final meanings in a form as complex as drama, especially montaged drama. And just as the rehearsals never seemed to come to the point of fixity, when the actors knew that here was the finalised production, so her productions were never finished pieces either, but continued to evolve no matter how long they ran for. Keeping them alive, open-ended, was an unalterable part of Littlewood's theatre practice. She wanted the company to be like a jazz ensemble, each player acting 'off' the others, rather than a symphony orchestra under an all-powerful conductor—herself.[38] Kenneth Tynan reported her insistence that 'as soon as a production is fixed, it is dead',[39] and Alexander Frater reported that 'in her view, no two nights of a play should be the same. Lines should be given new emphases, calling for a new emphasis in the response.'[40] It was not simply that, as Brian Murphy put it, 'we didn't do the same thing every night',[41] it was a deliberate policy pursued to extremes. 'If something worked brilliantly, she'd change it, just to stop actors recreating it.'[42] 'Theatre is *today* [. . .] The excitement I'm talking about—today and tomorrow—that is the present tense. Would you like to repeat this conversation again an hour from now? Could you, would you like to do it tomorrow and tomorrow?'[43] This 'improvisation in performance', something advocated and practised by the greatest Russian masters, Stanislavsky, Meyerhold and Mikhail Chekhov, was and still is virtually unknown in British theatre. It is perhaps the key to Littlewood's theatrical significance, and the reason why she needed to train her actors. If they were unable to play 'in the present' as she put it, they were unsuitable for the Theatre Workshop company. Richard Harris recalled her saying: 'Don't practice how to say a line—it's whatever comes out tonight', and 'You're getting used to that, change it'.[44] The actors must watch and listen, and pay absolute attention to each other. Then they may be able to grope towards what Harry H. Corbett described as the ideal: for the actor to be able to enter the stage, properly motivated ('I must go and do such-and-such'), but 'from that point [. . .] to play only off his reaction to the other actors'.[45]

In order the keep productions free from the curse of 'remembered rehearsal', Joan Littlewood watched performance after performance, assiduously taking notes throughout. These notes were relayed to the actors, and became something of a by-word. When the company was touring in its early years, Harry H. Corbett recalled: 'Squashed in amongst the scenery, Joan was striking matches, giving notes at twelve-thirty in the bloody morning. This was a regular occurrence. You felt as if you were in a dressing-room [. . .] Her notes were copious, but good and to the point.'[46]

The result was a series of productions that were startling, unconventional and daring in the face of the prevailing British theatre culture of the two decades after the Second World War. In *Oh What a Lovely War*, as Derek Paget has pointed out, audiences were confronted not with 'performers-pretending-to-be-people' but with 'performers-pretending-to-be-pierrots-pretending-to-be-people'.[47] In *The Hostage*, 'there was no "fourth wall" between the actors and the audience, and the music hall style of the production made it easy to involve anything untoward that happened in the auditorium',[48] including Behan's own frequent interjections. In *Every Man in His Humour*, the slapstick, the speed and the contemporaneity of Ben Jonson caused grave misgivings. And yet these productions were disturbingly immediate. One anti-capital punishment critic wrote of *The Quare Fellow*: 'Joan Littlewood has directed the play with eloquent simplicity and integrity, and her company have been rightly inspired [. . .] If anyone leaves this Theatre Workshop production regretting Sidney Silverman's success in abolishing the death penalty, it will be no fault of players or author.'[49]

The contemporary relevance was one of the features, perhaps the most telling feature, which some critics found hard to stomach. Thus, of *Macbeth* one critic wrote: 'If it had to be done, it has been done brilliantly,' while another complained of 'Macbeth in winter-warm leather leggings and Sam Browne belt.' While the *Manchester Guardian* found this 'a driving, inventive production', *The Times* railed against 'the insensitive arrogance of the production.' The reviewer continued: 'What staff officers would chat to old men in the rain, where private executions were carried out by homberg-hatted hatchet men, where coronation robes and the uniform of a commissar were jumbled together?'[50] Indeed, Littlewood's productions attracted almost as much vituperation as they did praise. John Elsom complained of 'excessive jollity' in *The Hostage* and Lindsay Anderson suggested the work suffered from 'a kind of intellectual limitation'. Michael Coren asserted that there was 'a certain naivete' about *Oh What a Lovely War*, and reported concerns that some of Littlewood's productions were 'facile'.[51]

The comparison between the Old Vic's *Richard II* and Theatre Workshop's version of the same play illuminates contemporary difficulties with Littlewood's work. The beautiful Old Vic voices, the pageantry of the staging, the elegance of the costumes, all of which highly delighted most theatregoers who saw them, were anathema to Littlewood, whose show created a unique kind of low-budget intensity. Her 'style' was rooted in 1930s agit-prop, experiments with *commedia dell'arte*, German expressionism and profound work with the ideas of Stanislavsky and Laban. Consequently, it had all the hallmarks of the hybrid—and hence, orginal—which critics always find hard to assess. Jack Reading pointed out that the staging of *A Taste of Honey* was 'revolutionary': 'Littlewood's direction methods resulted in a style, acceptable, workable, but more direct and real than any acting to be seen further to the west in London'.[52] Irving Wardle remembered *Johnny Noble* as 'marvellous and beautiful until, in the middle of the bombardment, Miss Littlewood herself stepped forward, her huge forehead glistening under the wing spots, and delivered a rhetorical lament on behalf of bereaved proletarian womanhood. At that moment [. . .] everything turned false.'[53] It was not, of course, the play which 'turned false', but rather Wardle's preconceptions, his assumptions of dramatic decorum, which were undermined. Theatre Workshop's actors played, preached, illustrated and demonstrated, and their audiences in reciprocation escaped, confronted, were amazed and were stimulated to protest or think or laugh. 'The vital methods of Theatre Workshop make the average production look like a Victorian charade', according to Hugh McDiarmid,[54] and, according to a Swedish critic, 'as an artist, she (Joan Littlewood) is worth the entire Old Vic'.[55]

Theatre directors leave little behind them. Many who worked with Joan Littlewood have left glimpses of her at work. Brian Murphy said: 'If rehearsals were going badly, she would come in like a charge of electricity. You knew you'd be okay.'[56] A perhaps-offended playwright asserted that in rehearsals, she 'bellowed instructions through a megaphone in terms that would shame a Fascist traffic cop',[57] though most of her actors would probably find such a comment hard to recognise. To Sylvester McCoy 'she was wonderfully frustrating, joyful and annoying',[58] while Ben Ellis said: 'She had an extraordinary power of being able to get out of an individual the one spark they possibly had in them'.[59] Nigel Hawthorne said that Littlewood was 'the most important influence of my life. I owe her everything, even though sometimes what was achieved struggled through the swirling mists of confusion—and was frequently acrimonious. Her encouragement stimulated me and transformed my work as an actor. She taught me to be truthful.'[60] She clearly loved actors, but she bequeathed them a serious attitude to their art, which can be seen, for example, in the written work of former Theatre Workshop actor, Peter Bridgmont. She had courage, a vivid imagination and an extraordinary eye for detail, as well as endless patience and a ruthless determination that never accepted second best. Perhaps she was possessed of what the great artist is said to need—a heart of ice—though anyone who has read her letters to Gerry Raffles might doubt that. To her actors she sometimes seemed like a 'mother hen'[61] and Jean Vilar asked why it was a woman who was resurrecting the British theatre.[62] Perhaps Kenneth Tynan characterised Joan Littlewood most aptly when he called her 'a wily holy innocent'.[63]

CHAPTER EIGHTEEN

The *Mise-en-Scène*

The Workers' Theatre Movement of the 1930s boasted proudly that it was a 'propertyless theatre for the propertyless class'. Its costumes were at most symbolic—a cloth cap for a worker, a top hat for a capitalist—and its plays were performed on open platforms that encouraged a presentational style and a sense of 'performing' a story. Once the agit-prop players decided that their work would be more effective indoors, some form of stage setting was required, along with the requirement that it be lit. In Manchester, this sent Alf Armitt and Ewan MacColl to the public library, where they discovered the work of Adolphe Appia. It was also at this time that Joan Littlewood arrived in Manchester from London, where a year or two earlier she had been impressed by a performance of Michel Saint-Denis's Compagnie des Quinzes. This French group were noted for the poetic spirit of their work, and the physicality of its expression, but they also used striking lighting effects, apparently derived from Appia's ideas.

The basis of Appia's philosophy was that a stage setting was not some kind of 'reality', nor was the purpose of lighting it merely to illuminate it. Setting and lighting, according to Appia, made their own contribution to the meaning of the drama, forming a vital dimension of their own that complemented the movement of the performers and the use of music and sound. Appia conjectured 'rhythmic spaces', symbolic and architectural scenery, light used in combination with shadow to emphasise the stage's volumetrics, and all these combined to focus on the dynamic human form. His ideas implied the death of traditional proscenium arch staging, the end of the 'stage picture', and its replacement by the stage as three-dimensional space filled by light, which was not to provide illumination so much as to accentuate, provoke and even conceal.

Littlewood and MacColl's companies never had much money for stage sets, and Appia's brilliant modernism suggested something not only financially more viable, but artistically more vibrant. 'The fact that you could throw light, that you could make parallel beams or you could make arcs and circles of different sizes, that one could use light for the purpose of controlling space—for expanding and limiting space—was a revelation to us.'[1] The new freedom was supported by Littlewood's 'painter's eye, [her] instinct for colour and composition',[2] as well as by Alf Armitt's predatory skills. He 'went out and pinched road-lamps, took the lenses out of them, and made spotlights out of biscuit tins'.[3] As time went on, other colleagues 'lifted' other components from their various places of work, and Armitt was able to build a surprisingly sophisticated portable lighting system. Meanwhile, what was now Theatre Union was working with local artists, who helped to make their productions notable for progressive *mises-en-scène*. Perhaps the first of these was *Fuente Ovejuna*, with its sculpted ram towering over a well in front of a hessian backcloth in the muted colours of Spain. This was followed by the use of back projections and a surprisingly advanced sound plot for *The Good Soldier Schweik*, a production that was technically at least as successful as Erwin Piscator's more famous one in Berlin a decade earlier. *Lysistrata* used a series of ramps, strikingly lit from the side, in front of black drapes, while *Last Edition* had action on three sides of the audience, and a complex lighting plot.

It seems likely that by 1940 Theatre Union's *mises-en-scène* were as advanced as any in the country, and this determination not to slip into a lazy illusionism continued after the Second World War, even though the company was touring to often primitive venues. Thus, when Max Gorelik's *New Theatres for Old* was published in 1947, Joan Littlewood pointed her company members specifically to the following paragraph:

> In design [. . .] the process of thought is purely *inductive*. The designer does not imagine a room for the characters, or a striking atmosphere. Instead he supplies all necessary properties, sections of doors or windows or steps, and arranges for these to function with workmanlike precision. Of course beauty is not excluded, since the resultant arrangement may possess its own beauty of form, and since beauty and color in some or all of the properties may be specifically necessary.

She also noted Gorelik's comments on what, following the Russians as well as Brecht, he termed 'Epic' theatre: 'It is the *function* which is essential. Hence Epic design, instead of reproducing the object (as in the Naturalistic method), or symbolizing it by means of a significant part (as do the Symbolists), represents the object by means of its function'. She also noted Gorelik's references two pages later, to Piscator's theatre, and his quotation from the latter's *The Political Theatre*: 'His chief technician, Richter, has visualized, in place of present stages, steel and electric structures of ample size, "with mobile bridges, elevators, cranes, motors, great scene docks and moving platforms"'. Gorelik concludes: 'There are very few stages indeed which have the mechanical precision and efficiency of an ordinary modern factory'.[4] The implications of this are seen in Littlewood's design for *The Other Animals* the year after Gorelik's book was published. Noting her

11. *Operation Olive Branch*, adapted from Aristophanes' *Lysistrata*, Stratford
East, 1953. The photograph emphasises the stark stage design and the
lighting, which complements it.

principle that 'sets were never finalised till we'd analysed the play and
decided on the essential visual elements', and the conditions which
constricted her—'mostly we had to re-work materials already used'—
Littlewood's construction for this play was both functional and factory-like.
It consisted of a silver disc suspended in space from which a series of steel
rods decended, fanning out to make a circular cage-prison for Hanau. The
lighting by John Bury contrived to give the impression that this structure
sometimes moved, and the bars, or rods, seemed to disappear, to reveal an
arch which at times seemed so small it almost disappeared, but at others
was tall and imposing.

Earlier Theatre Workshop touring sets did not quite match this but,
given the financial constraints under which the company operated, they
were still impressive. For *The Flying Doctor*, for instance, wood was obtained
from a friendly timber yard and Bill Davidson constructed a portable stage
that included a small revolve operated by the actors in full view of the
audience. Across the revolve's diameter was a canvas flat held in place by
metal sockets. One side of this flat was painted to represent a house on a
street, with a front door and open window and a 'floating' cloud, and the
other side represented the interior of the house, front door and open
window. This simple stage was light (for easy carriage) and creaks were

prevented by an arrangement of taut wires like those between a biplane's wings. It was elegant and functional. *The Flying Doctor's* companion on Theatre Workshop's double bill was *Johnny Noble*, and this was staged on a bare stage in front of black drapes. Lorca's *The Love of Don Perlimplin and Belisa in the Garden* used a more sensual approach, with velvet curtains in emerald and crimson, wrought-iron furniture and surrealist decoration in the style of de Falla and Grandos. *The Travellers*, which was presented after *The Other Animals*, was more elaborate, but while depending on the functional and epic principles outlined by Gorelik, it also harked back to earlier Littlewood–MacColl productions, like *Last Edition* and Friedrich Wolf's *Professor Mamlock*, which used 'two sloping platforms, with brilliant overhead spotlighting'.[5] As mentioned before, the stage in *The Travellers* was used as the station platform, while the train itself was built down the centre of the auditorium, so that the audience sat on either side.

Importantly, these functional settings, conceived as Appia had desired, to use the stage as a three-dimensional space, were complemented, again as Appia aimed, by a sophisticated use of light and sound. Even though

12. *The Other Animals*, Theatre Workshop, 1948. Hanau (Ewan MacColl) and Robert (David Scase) imprisoned in steel rods, designed by Joan Littlewood.

equipment had to be collected as and where it could be found, including from the wreck of a crashed plane carrying equipment intended for the entertainment of troops in 1948, the company achieved an extraordinarily high level of artistic execution. This was partly due to the creative abilities of some of the company members, notably John Bury and David Scase. The latter, later to become a notably successful and uncompromising theatre director in his own right, had been invalided out of the merchant navy when his ship was torpedoed, and had become a BBC sound technician. He built a sound system for the company, and created one of the most memorable sequences in *Johnny Noble*, when Johnny's ship was being dive-bombed in the dark. The production also used passages of recorded instrumental music to counterpoint the live singing and later the dramatic perspective.[6] Foreign critics who saw Theatre Workshop's performances constantly praised this area of their work. In Czechoslovakia in 1948, *Johnny Noble* was commended for its 'witty sound effects [and] excellent lighting', while in Sweden one newpaper noted that the 'use of light' in these productions was 'especially important', and another noted that the company's 'use of sound is wonderful, full of nuance'.[7]

Most of the lamps from the air crash were put into the care of John Bury, at that time playing small roles and operating the lighting board. Bury came into his own with the move to Stratford East, which created a new and urgent need for stage design. He had no training but at Stratford he began designing lighting in earnest, which led naturally to his designing the stage setting as well, and by the mid-1950s he was directing shows, including *The Duchess of Malfi*, *The Playboy of the Western World* and *Treasure Island*. By now he was effectively second in the company's artistic hierarchy after Joan Littlewood herself. But directing was not his *forte*, any more than acting was, though he played many parts over the years, including Charlie Bentham in *Juno and the Paycock*, William Dudgeon in *The Devil's Disciple* and Lord Cheny in *Arden of Faversham*. This experience was invaluable, however, when he concentrated solely on design. He learned from being on stage the value and problems of performance without make-up, with no front curtain, and no footlights, in a theatre that considered the proscenium arch an obstacle, and where the settings were often—for want of money—made of found objects and discarded pieces from previous sets.

He often found, in his early designs, that he would begin with light and develop a stage design later. He worked very closely with Joan Littlewood in the early stages of a production, seeking an idea or an image to encapsulate in solid, probably sculptural, terms, the core of the production. He sought colours, tones, textures for the image, so that the stage itself would provide a dynamic part of the meaning, as the building of the wall was in *You Won't Always Be on Top* and the fairy lights, projections and newspanel were in *Oh What a Lovely War*. These sets commented in their own terms on the action. Bury's stages were often stark, 'platforms from which [Joan Littlewood's] productions are launched at the audience',[8] but they used the full range of the stage, as Appia commended, both vertically and horizontally, and were unprecedentedly versatile in the possibilities they offered to actors. Typical of Bury were the partially completed environments—rooms, yards, halls, whatever—which enabled actors to move freely and rapidly between 'realism' 'in' the set, and a more presentational style on the forestage to address the audience directly. Thus, even comparatively naruralistic plays tended to be characterised by a lack of 'clutter', the context being suggested by a dominant image that allowed the narrative its own metaphorical space. These stage settings were often dependent on Bury's unique abilities as a lighting designer. His images relied heavily on spatial relationships defined by lighting, which was most likely to be directed from above, or the sides, or even the back. Clive Barker noted how Bury's practice was

> in contradiction to the majority of British theatre practice which relied on painted two-dimensional flats, lit with bland, smooth illumination. The tendency in the 1950s and 1960s was towards smooth, multi-lantern settings. Theatre Workshop used lanterns sparsely, in settings in which shadows and darkness were as important as lit areas.[9]

One observer wrote:

> [John Bury's] sets, dark, cavernous, cold and often ugly, contained a minimum of scenery and a maximum of acting space, enabling scenes to follow one another in rapid continuity. He liked to light the actors from overhead, or from the back, creating black voids from which they would emerge into pools of light.[10]

In 1958, Tom Milne asserted that Bury was 'probably the finest designer and lighting director working in the English theatre today',[11] and in 1961, when it seemed Theatre Workshop was breaking up, Gerard Fay wrote that, if he left 'it may be quickly proved that he is a greater loss [than Joan Littlewood], that he has always been the greater artist, but concealed as it were by the greater conviction radiating from Miss Littlewood'.[12] However that may be, his value was undisputed, and when he went on to the Royal Shakespeare Company and then the National Theatre, he was instantly recognised as by far the most dynamic and original—not to say influential—designer of his generation.

Even before the company settled at Stratford, John Bury's value as a practical designer was noted. For the doomed *Alice in Wonderland* production, for instance, he discovered 'a form of spun latex' to cover the oversize mushrooms and flowers that adorned Alice's dream.[13] One of his

earliest, and most significant, successes came with *Arden of Faversham*, which
won acclaim in Paris partly because Bury lit it frequently from the back,
thus imparting an intrinsically nightmarish quality to the farcical horror of
the piece. In 1956, in *The Quare Fellow*, he added real-life railings and lamp-
posts to the theatre's own brick back wall with its fat heating pipes, to create
the effect of the prison, while at Christmas that year, for his own
production of *Treasure Island*, he created something completely different. A
judicious *Times* reviewer, revealing incidentally both the problems
contemporary critics had with Theatre Workshop, and also something of
Bury's own artistic struggle in combining the roles of director and designer,
wrote:

> The Admiral Benbow in the new production is not a place where a retired
> pirate might hope to lie low. Its walls are mere screens and it is open to the
> sky, for Mr John Bury, the producer, wants speed and continuity in the
> action generally rather than the realistic presentation of one stage of it. The
> picture of the schooner at sea is the same as that of the schooner in dock.
> On the island itself the attempt is to suggest that we are in the presence not
> of danger or hardship but of beauty, and that is achieved. A freshness in the
> tropical colours, a strangeness in the light, speaks to the imagination.[14]

The next year saw one of Bury's most noted triumphs, the creation of the
building site for Henry Chapman's *You Won't Always Be on Top*. Audiences
were amazed by the part-constructed three-storey building Bury presented
to them, and the brick wall that was built during the course of the
performance. Around these were scaffolding, a real workman's hut,
ladders, planks, tarpaulins, wheelbarrows, buckets and even puddles in
what Kenneth Tynan described as an 'astonishing' creation. His 1957 set for
Macbeth sounds almost like a stripping down of this building site: a bare
stage at the back of which were rough wooden pillars supporting a long
scaffolding balcony, under which gloomy recesses disappeared into
darkness. *The Times* described it as 'an unlovely permanent setting',[15] but
the *Manchester Guardian* called it 'a skilful net of light and dark'.[16]

The Hostage in 1958 was designed by Sean Kenny, but very much along
the lines of Bury's post-Appia design principles, with the main room
suggested rather than presented, and giving easy access for the actors to
emerge from it into a more presentational 'performance' mode for direct
speeches to the audience or 'production numbers'. This was the first stage
design created by Kenny, 'a young Irish architect', according to Joan
Littlewood. She found his work 'tremendously evocative',[17] while Kenneth
Tynan stated simply: 'Sean Kenny's setting is, as often at this theatre, by far
the best in London'.[18]

John Bury continued as the leading designer. For *Sam, the Highest Jumper
of Them All*, he created an open stage, quasi-Expressionist set with distorted

furniture set on the different levels in front of a stylised map of the London Underground, ironically echoing his own earlier design for *Edward* II, with its stylised map of England. And for *Oh What a Lovely War*, he created an entirely electrical set, with fairy lights, the electric newspanel, and slide projections. In this production, there were no fewer than 324 lighting cues, as well as 110 sound cues, employing four synchronised tape recorders. Derek Paget indicated how important the lighting was, for instance to the scene of the fraternisation of British and German troops:

> The scene was staged on the diagonal, with the 'trench' in a downstage corner. The German soldiers came from the opposite upstage corner, and thus had to travel a large distance, relative to the stage space available. This stage distance, in addition to the thoughtful use of stage time, supplied eloquent emblems for the real distance covered by the real participants in the 'real time' of the 1914 Christmas truce. Stratford East's lighting style contributed effectively, isolating the trench from the rest of the stage. It also ensured that the Germans emerged from the shadows upstage, creating a sense of danger (because it was not clear initially whether they were armed or not).[19]

After *Oh What a Lovely War*, John Bury took his talents to the Royal Shakespeare Company, and then to the National Theatre. But it was, as Alan Strachan noted, at Stratford East, that Bury, although 'often working on miniscule budgets [. . .] helped redefine stage design in Britain.'[20]

PART FIVE

After Theatre Workshop, 1963–88

Society and the Stage

CHAPTER NINETEEN

Times A-Changing

In the early 1960s, as Bob Dylan sang, the times they were a-changing. Significantly, the old men—Macmillan, Eisenhower and others—were giving way to a younger generation—Wilson in Britain, Kennedy in the USA. The dull, dreary 1950s were fading away and with them, sadly, Theatre Workshop. The energy, finance and talent required were virtually exhausted, and new fashions and new fears were appearing. Even Theatre Workshop's place as a permanent company, whose repertoire was in the 1950s 'remarkably like the repertory one would hope to find at our hypothetical National Theatre',[1] was threatened by the foundation, first, of the Royal Shakespeare Company as a permanent ensemble in 1960, though the ensemble ideal lasted for a very short time, and then in 1963, of the National Theatre itself. Theatre Workshop may have begun to look almost redundant.

The early 1960s saw the spring blossoming of 'youth culture', embodied in pop music and personified by the Beatles. 'Pirate' radio stations were listened to, apparently illegally, and the BBC was prompted to establish its own pop channel, Radio 1. Youthful disrespect became fashionable, along with the denims, floral patterns and mini-skirts of Carnaby Street, and style—to some extent at least—became generational rather than class-based. Education for young adults expanded with the establishment, after the 1963 Robbins Report, of a flurry of new universities—there were no less than fifty-six universities in all by 1968, and the Open University offered a fresh chance to those who had missed out earlier.

The Open University was self-consciously the creation of Labour's prime minister, Harold Wilson, who was sharp, alert and dryly witty—a new kind of politician for the new television age. Wilson dominated the politics of the early 1960s, presenting an attractive classlessness that the Conservatives under the fourteenth Earl of Home were wholly incapable of matching. In 1962 unemployment was creeping up, and the economy was slowing down. People wanted change, and though the 1964 general election was extremely close, it was Wilson's Labour Party which won it, with a majority of five. The ensuing economic crisis, culminating in the devaluation of the pound in 1967, was largely blamed by Wilson on his Tory predecessors. Whatever Wilson's competence or otherwise in the economic sphere, however, his government had—and still has—a proud record in the field of social reform. During the 1960s a number of matters that had been of particular concern to Theatre Workshop, were legislated on, including in 1965 the abolition of the death penalty and in 1968 the abolition of the Lord Chamberlain's power to censor stage plays.

In 1968, of course, much more than that happened. Indeed, 1968 is often considered one of those years in which the world changes. Internationally, Czechoslovakia instituted its 'Communism with a human face' experiment, also known as 'the Prague Spring', which was mercilessly crushed by the Soviet Union. In France, students and workers combined in *les événements* and almost toppled their Government. With the Vietnam War at its height, 1968 was also the year when the Democratic Party Convention in Chicago ended with tear gas and tanks in the street, when Martin Luther King and Robert Kennedy were assassinated, and Richard Nixon elected to the White House. In Britain, 30,000 people demonstrated against the Vietnam War in Grosvenor Square, the housing charity, Shelter, was founded, and students at Hornsey College of Art and the London School of Economics 'sat in'. Random happenings, perhaps, straws in the wind, but they suggested that the older world of Labour and Tory consensus and a country existing on smug complacency was gone for ever.

It was that old world which Theatre Workshop had been created to contest. Now the company's relevance was no longer clear.

CHAPTER TWENTY

The End of Theatre Workshop

After *Oh What a Lovely War*, Theatre Workshop under Joan Littlewood stuttered on for almost a decade more. There was a widely admired *Henry IV*, which premiered at the official Edinburgh Festival in 1964, as opposed to the Fringe, before *Oh What a Lovely War* was taken to New York for a successful run.

Meanwhile, Joan Littlewood herself had become increasingly excited by the possibility of creating what she called a 'Fun Palace', a kind of twentieth-century equivalent to the eighteenth-century pleasure gardens, but contained within an extraordinary changeable and changing building designed by the visionary architect, Cedric Price. Price's 'space-age utopianism', his championing of an architecture of 'autonomy, impermanence and social wellbeing',[1] made him Littlewood's ideal partner for this scheme. Her conception was for a 'university of the streets' with a strong community link, which would include the possibility for people to either watch or participate in games, music, science activities, theatre, art and more, and which would provide places to stroll, have coffee and relax. In a completely original proposal, large television screens would be mounted for people to watch, and the place would also be suitable for rallies, concerts and the like. The whole was to be characterised by informality and flexibility. Price's design used ramps, catwalks and escalators, and divided areas by air currents, static vapour zones and lightweight blinds, all moveable and changeable according to whim or need. Initially proposed in 1961 for Lea Valley, north London, the project's supporters spent four or five years seeking suitable sites including one in Camden Town and another at Mill Meads, Tottenham, before problems with cost, legal obstructions, suspicious locals or planning regulations always got the better of it, and it was never established. Though it partly inspired the Pompidou Centre in Paris, the Fun Palace was probably too radical, too innovative for those who might have helped it into being in England: the very word 'fun', deliberately used to be provocative by Joan Littlewood, may have doomed the project. After all, how could 'fun' be docketed and filed by a government bureaucrat?

In 1965 Joan Littlewood began working with the Centre Culturel in Hammamet, Tunisia, returning in the spring of 1967 to direct two shows at the Theatre Royal, Stratford East, *Macbird* and *Intrigues and Amours*, adapted from Vanbrugh. She and other members of the company also became involved in a Playground Project with local children, which created play spaces out of the slum demolitions of the Stratford East locality. In the autumn of 1967, Theatre Workshop presented *Mrs Wilson's Diary* and the provocative *Marie Lloyd Story* about the famous Cockney entertainer, another tenacious outsider. According to Alan Strachan,

> Dan Farson's script was never quite tight enough, but with just a few essential elements—a dressing room screen, trunks and skips at Crewe Station, a row of footlights—Littlewood bewitchingly evoked the world of train calls and the music halls, while from Avis Bunnage as an ageing but battling Marie and Nigel Hawthorne in several roles including the shrewd impresario Oswald Stoll, she drew some of the most truthful character work in the company's history.[2]

In 1968 Joan Littlewood went to Calcutta to work for Image India, returning to continue the Playground Project before the end of the year. In the early 1970s she directed her last shows, faintly stirring old memories, and working with actors who were paid at last a reasonable wage. Her last production was *So You Want to Be in Pictures* by Peter Rankin in November 1973. By now industrial unrest dominated British social and political life, the state against the traditional working class, with a three-day working week and ministers urging people to brush their teeth in the dark to save electricity. Theatre Workshop no longer participated in these struggles, and Ken Hill, who had not been a member of the company for long, took over its running. Gerry Raffles left, and died in France on 11 April 1975. He was only fifty-one years old, but suffered from both a weak heart and diabetes. This was, perhaps, the moment that Joan Littlewood's theatre died, too. Certainly, she never again set foot in the Theatre Royal, Stratford East, and never directed another production. Perhaps, as Brian Murphy said, 'the commercial people breathed a sigh of relief,'[3] but British theatre, which had tried to ignore her for so long, was immeasurably the poorer. Littlewood lived out the rest of her days in Paris under the name of Mme Petitbois. Remarkably soon, nobody knew much about her or about Theatre Workshop. Perhaps they never had.

CHAPTER TWENTY-ONE

The Making of Modern British Theatre

Theatre Workshop changed—and failed to change—British theatre in extraordinary ways. It may be that without Theatre Workshop, the theatre in Britain would still be languishing in the drawing-room representationalism and the decorative plangency of escapist Shakespeare that was the norm before Theatre Workshop appeared. Theatre Workshop's modernism was often rejected, but by the 1960s its influence was pervasive.

This can most easily be identified perhaps in the later career of John Bury. He worked first with the Royal Shakespeare Company, where his designs for *Hamlet* and *The Homecoming* by Harold Pinter were among the most powerful the company has ever used, and then for twelve years was head of design at the National Theatre. He designed opera for Glyndebourne and Covent Garden, as well as in Europe, Japan and the USA, he spent eighteen years, in two separate stints, on the Arts Council Drama Panel, and was for ten years chairman of the Society of British Theatre Designers. Other old alumni of Theatre Workshop may have been less eminent, but were nevertheless influential, too. David Scase, for instance, who married Theatre Workshop's early teacher of movement, Rosalie Williams, was a director of outstanding distinction, especially in regional theatre, most notably in his years as artistic director of the Manchester Library Theatre, where he gave debuts or early opportunities to, among others, Patrick Stewart, Robert Stephens, Anthony Hopkins, Leonard Rossiter, Richard Griffiths and Alan Rickman. Margaret Walker, John Bury's first wife, opened the E15 Acting School in 1961, basing its syllabus on Theatre Workshop's practice. Perhaps the only theatre school to have emerged from a professional theatre company, E15 School, which since 2000 has been part of the University of Essex, still follows Joan Littlewood's method, basing its curriculum on a co-ordinated approach through the philosophies of Stanislavsky and Laban. Clive Barker also spent a lifetime propagating his Littlewood-influenced approach to theatre in a career that unusually bridged the gap between academic theatre studies and professional theatre, and his influence was also seen in his long period as an active co-editor of *New Theatre Quarterly*. The list of actors who worked with Theatre Workshop is long and distinguished, and includes—a very small sample—Miriam Karlin, James Booth, Patience Collier, Barry Humphries, Dudley Foster, Sylvester McCoy, Roy Kinnear and Henry Livings. Clive Barker suggested that

> The clearest signs of Littlewood's presence in the British theatre [. . .] lie in sitcoms and soaps—Harry H. Corbett in *Steptoe* [. . .]; Yootha Joyce and Brian Murphy as the Ropers; Glyn Edwards, a most undervalued and sensitive actor, propping up the bar in *Minder*; Barbara Windsor in *Eastenders*; Stephen Cato in so much.[1]

Ewan MacColl's career after Theatre Workshop was also significant. Between 1958 and 1964, with Peggy Seeger and Charles Parker, he created the series of internationally acclaimed Radio Ballads, employing many of the techniques he had used as Theatre Workshop's playwright. Most significantly, these works deploy the 'contrast', or montage, of his most successful plays, but with the significant difference that, instead of using actors, all the 'voices' are 'actuality' recorded 'in the field'. This provides a particularly piquant referencing to reality. Thus, *The Travelling People* of 1964 opens:

CHILDREN (*singing*):   My mother said I never should
Play with the gypsies in the wood.
If I did she'd surely say,
'Naughty lad to disobey!'
VOICES :   (Kate Cole) They call us the wild ones . . .
(Belle Stewart) The pilgrims of the mist . . .
(James Adams) Romanies, gypsies, Didekais, mumpers, travellers . . .
(Charlotte Higgins) Nomads of the road . . .
(Scotsman) Black-faced Diddies . . .
(Minty Smith) Because we gypsies are dark they call us card-boshers, black men . . .
(Charlotte Higgins) Gangrel bodies! Some said it more politely than others.
(J.Hilton) In Carlisle they call you potters. Dirty potters this and dirty potters that.
SINGER :   On a rock on the shore is the cormorant's dwelling,
The wild warbling blackbird has its nest in the tree,
The birds of the air and the fish of the ocean,
Each has its own place—but there's no place for me.
VOICE :   (Alderman Watton) They seem to come almost from nowhere overnight. They are a bit like the starlings in Birmingham. They're here—and they're making a mess.[2]

The battle lines for the drama of gypsy life are clearly drawn.

Between 1968 and 1974, MacColl worked with the Critics Group, mostly semi-professional folk singers, to create an annual review, *The Festival of Fools*, perhaps like Fielding's *Historical Register*. They were topical, comic, cynical, and satirical, using song and speech, with sketches covering topics from the death penalty through mini skirts and unemployment, to the Vietnam War. These reviews ran four nights per week for five weeks in New Merlin's Cave, Margery Street, near King's Cross, and by 1974 the shows used three stages simultaneously, complex lighting and sound plots, and the (amateur) performers were expected to do voice and movement training as part of the preparation. In the end, the participants revolted, and the theatrical experiment was over, but not without leaving its mark. *The Festival of Fools* showed, for example, the potential of 'pub theatre'.

The Radio Ballads and *The Festival of Fools*, like *Oh What a Lovely War*, both traced their origins back to the living newspapers of the 1930s and Piscator's theatre of the Weimar Republic. In turn, *Oh What a Lovely War* inspired the Royal Shakespeare Company's most hubristic exercise, a documentary about the 1926 General Strike, directed by Trevor Nunn, called (like Eisenstein's film) *Strike*. The humiliating failure of this work demonstrated several things: first, that without a knowledge or sympathy with the subject matter, failure was inevitable; second, that the techniques of *Oh What a Lovely War* were considerably more sophisticated than had been imagined; and third, that with the levels of subsidy granted to the Royal Shakespeare Company, such a failure was inconsequential. It failed to deflect even temporarily the special status of the company or the career of its Oxbridge-educated director.

Much more significant, though considerably less well rewarded, was the work in this tradition by John McGrath at the Everyman Theatre, Liverpool, where a conscious effort was made to attract working-class audiences, and by Peter Cheeseman at the Victoria Theatre, Stoke-on-Trent, where involvement with the local community was central to the thrust of the work. This led, in Cheeseman's case, to the creation of a number of original and popular documentary dramas that acknowledged the influence of Joan Littlewood and Ewan MacColl but never slavishly copied either of them. For instance, Cheeseman put the focus of his work on the actor 'as the principal instrument of the documentary',[3] rather than, as in *Oh What a Lovely War*, the tension between the actor and the projection on a screen. (That this would have been problematic in a theatre-in-the-round such as the Victoria was not ultimately relevant.) Cheeseman's method included up to six months for preliminary research, the creation of a story-line from the edited researched material, and the development of this into specific scenes during a four- to five-week rehearsal period. Cheeseman insisted on the use of primary material only in what was spoken on stage—comparable to the use of 'actuality' in the Radio Ballads—because, he asserted, this allowed for a multiplicity of voices. He also used song rather as Theatre Workshop did, as a voice in a different register, something outside the action, and usually he preferred authentic period songs to new, composed works. Finally, he insisted on an acting style that was open, but restrained and objective, unlike Theatre Workshop's more flamboyant theatricality; but it should be noted in this connection that Cheeseman never had a permanent company which existed for a number of years and which he himself had trained. Nevertheless, the Victoria Theatre's series of documentary plays, including *The Jolly Potters* (1964), *The Staffordshire Rebels* (1965), *The Knotty* (1966), *Six into One* (1968), *The Burning Mountain* (1970), *Hands Up for You the War is Ended* (1971) and *Fight for Shelton Bar!* (1974), made a significant contribution to British theatre.

Other work followed in this tradition, notably Alan Plater's *Close the Coalhouse Door*, John Hipkin's *The Massacre at Peterloo* and Albert Hunt's more extravagant *John Ford's Cuban Missile Crisis*. Perhaps as significant was the development in the 1960s of Theatre in Education, which saw the creation of a number of dedicated companies, at the Belgrade Theatre, Coventry, the Octagon Theatre, Bolton, London's Cockpit Theatre and others, taking dramas—very frequently documentary dramas inspired by *Oh What a Lovely War*—into schools. The impact of this work on young people is inevitably impossible to calculate, but may have been extremely significant. Improvisation, audience participation, the use of montage scripts were only some of the Theatre Workshop-derived practices which these companies deployed continually and creatively in their work, and which seeped into school drama lessons as well as a surprisingly large number of school productions, often replacing more traditional 'school plays' to excellent effect.

Unity Theatre in the 1960s also owed a debt to Theatre Workshop. Apart from presenting a musical version of Henry Chapman's *You Won't Always Be On Top* in 1960, they created their own post-*Oh What a Lovely War* documentary in 1963 with Charles Chilton, called *Oh Freedom* telling the story of black people in the USA. At this time, Unity shared some of Theatre Workshop's personnel, including Lionel Bart, Howard Goorney, Clive Barker, Brian Murphy and Amelia Bayntum, but, as Ted Willis remarked, it needed someone like Joan Littlewood to rescue it from its slide into oblivion. No such person appeared, and soon it was more likely to be hosting shows like John Arden and Margaretta D'Arcy's *Harold Muggins Is a Martyr* presented by Cartoon Archetypal Slogan Theatre (CAST) than mounting its own shows. Unity continued until two fires, the first in

November 1975, and another a little over a year later, effectively ended its existence.

Another significant attempt to realise some of the ideals of Theatre Workshop was Centre 42, a self-proclaimed Socialist project set in motion by left-wing artists dissatisfied with the contemporary commercialisation of art and culture. Centre 42 aimed to bypass both the whims of the free market, and the dangers of state subsidy, and to explore new forms of patronage, hoping their support would come from the organised Labour movement. Prime movers behind Centre 42 included Arnold Wesker, Clive Barker, Doris Lessing, Jennie Lee, John McGrath, Beba Lavrin, Clive Exton, Ted Kotcheff, Gareth Wigan and Charles Parker. They mounted a series of arts festivals, including drama, poetry, folk music, jazz and exhibitions, the first at Wellingborough in 1961, followed by five more the following year, as well as presenting events in factory canteens, arts centres, pubs and other places. But financially the enterprise was quite impractical and it had effectively collapsed with serious debts by 1963.

The failure of Centre 42 and the Fun Palace, along with the steep decline in the fortunes of Theatre Workshop itself as well as Unity Theatre meant that when the tumultuous year of 1968 arrived, the theatrical response was unexpected and original. CAST organised a meeting at Unity Theatre from which an AgitProp Information Service emerged, and the Information Service itself soon transformed into AgitProp Street Players, a group not unlike those of the Workers' Theatre Movement nearly forty years before. Five years later, the AgitProp Street Players became Red Ladder Theatre Company, while other more or less politically motivated 'fringe' theatre groups, including Welfare State, 7:84, Joint Stock, General Will and Portable Theatre, all established after 1968, made up something not unlike a Workers' Theatre Movement. The differences were significant, however. On the one hand, almost all the new groups were middle class and their members University-educated; and secondly, they all required—and received—financial support from the state, which more and more they came to rely on. Would this have solved Theatre Workshop's perennial problems? It implied a compromise that Joan Littlewood was never realistically asked to make. By contrast, in 1973, its first year in that form, Red Ladder received £4,000, an amount that within five years had risen tenfold to over £40,000.[4] Nevertheless, its productions were often similar to the earlier socialist theatre. *Strike While the Iron is Hot*, for example, which Red Ladder toured between 1974 and 1976, used plenty of songs and dance, and rejected all forms of naturalism out of hand. The play concerned a woman who makes a journey across England not dissimilar to Johnny Noble's journey, and it debates the efficacy of politics, its ability to effect change.

Although Harold Hobson doubted 'if there would have been any Fringe without Theatre Workshop and Joan Littlewood',[5] how much of their predecessors the leading figures of this new political and theatrical fringe knew is debatable. David Edgar apparently believed that '1968 can be taken as the starting date of political theatre in Britain',[6] but Kathleen McCreery and Richard Stourac of Red Ladder acknowledged the Russian, German and British agit-prop theatre of the 1920s and 1930s, and published a book on it.[7] Derek Paget wrote, rather more soberly: 'Dramatic practices which fed off the methodological model of *Lovely War* became especially important after 1968, when the theatre became overtly politicised in the aftermath of the so-called "student revolution" of 1968'.[8] One group that overtly acknowledged the influence of Theatre Workshop, and especially of Ewan MacColl, and his later work, was the Birmingham-based Banner Theatre of Actuality, headed by MacColl's BBC producer on the Radio Ballads, Charles Parker. Between 1974 and 1977, they created a series of powerful performance pieces, using 'actuality' rather than written dialogue, about coal miners, the fascist dictatorship in Chile, racism, sexism and more, and toured them to working class halls, arts centres and open air rallies.

The most significant of these Theatre Workshop-influenced companies, however, was probably 7:84, formed in 1971 by John McGrath and only finally dying after McGrath resigned in 1988. This is not the place to rehearse 7:84's triumphs and trials.[9] It became widely known with the success of the extraordinary and extraordinarily powerful *The Cheviot, the Stag and the Black, Black Oil*, a highly original work, which yet clearly grew out of McGrath's understanding of *Oh What a Lovely War*, as well as much of the earlier radical theatre described in this book. A series of other plays were also toured, especially to the Highlands of Scotland, where no tradition of theatre existed, and the people were often derided and usually ignored. The company continued heroically with their policy of touring for many years longer than Theatre Workshop did, but at least they always had a grant—though not necessarily a generous one—and it was when the compromise between receiving the grant and doing what the grant awarders wanted became no longer acceptable that McGrath resigned. Among other achievements of the company should be noted the 1982 'Clydebuilt' season, when the company staged a number of seminal socialist dramas from earlier in the twentieth century, including Ewan MacColl's *Johnny Noble*, directed by David Scase.

Theatre Workshop brought much more that was intangible to the theatre, and more than any other organisation or person the company was responsible for making British theatre modern. This was at least partly as a result of the move to Stratford East, without which its work would perhaps not have been noticed. As it was, a critic as influential as Kenneth Tynan could write: 'It now seems quite likely that when the annals of the British theatre in the middle years of the twentieth century come to be written, Joan's name will lead all the rest. Others write plays, direct them, or act in them; she alone "makes theatre".'[10] In this, she was like Meyerhold: he, too, 'made theatre'. We can say that this was partly because of her uniquely collaborative methods, which meant actor, director, author and designer all working together in ways that were literally not dreamed of before Joan Littlewood worked in the theatre. The company was one without stars, and though today a genuine theatre ensemble is very hard to find, the whole apparatus which revolved around the 'star' in the 1930s, and after, has now gone for ever, probably more because of Joan Littlewood's example than for any other reason. The acting style that Littlewood introduced is now also generally accepted—if not practised always with the skill and dedication of the Theatre Workshop actors. She encouraged actors to express themselves through physical skills, insisting that the whole body be involved in the process of acting. Her concept of 'actors' versions' of characters gave them confidence to create, and what they created was in the nature of a mask. Theatre Workshop actors 'performed' character, thereby putting power into the hands of the spectator and undermining accepted readings and traditional 'business'. Her actors, too, were expected to act 'in the present', to listen to their partners on the stage and to react honestly to what those partners said or did. Never was a Theatre Workshop actor to serve up memories of rehearsals. This was epic acting in the proper sense, not 'representationalism'. Littlewood's process started at the sessions round the table, which she was probably the first to use in Britain, but which are now frequently found in professional theatre—though how democratic this procedure usually is, how much of a collaborative exploration, even today, may be questioned.

Theatre Workshop introduced what are now accepted as modern forms of stage design and lighting, and the modern use of the open stage, often attributed to Brecht, was actually pioneered in Britain by Joan Littlewood and Ewan MacColl. The notion of a 'theatre of synthesis' was theirs, too, as was the method of structuring a play by montage techniques. What was once revolutionary becomes commonplace, but *Oh What a Lovely War* is still influential, and it can claim what few plays can—that it did change people's minds. Theatre Workshop was a theatre that wanted its spectators to engage at all levels with the material of the play, and found a style of production and performance that enabled that to happen. It was what is sometimes called 'Brechtian', but it is important to remember that Littlewood's theatre was working in this style in Britain years before Brecht's ideas had infiltrated British theatre, which did not happen in any significant way until after the Berliner Ensemble's second visit to London in 1966.

Theatre Workshop, and in particular Joan Littlewood, posed a threat to the established theatre. Part of the reason for this was that she was a woman—and that was part of the reason why the Establishment tried to marginalise or ignore her. She was dangerous because she refused to be stereotyped: women are supposed to have children, be docile, amenable. Joan Littlewood was childless, and she was abrasive, unbowed and impossible to dominate. No doubt her swearing was exaggerated in many male minds, but she certainly used it to maintain her independence. Women are not supposed to be tough: she was. They are not supposed to lead: she did. By marginalising her, paradoxically the Establishment may have helped her creativeness. Her emphasis on collaboration may also have derived from her gender, though Michelene Wandor has denied that this is a female quality in the theatre, which is inevitably collaborative. But Joan Littlewood's collaborativeness was of an altogether different, and more real, kind than the perfunctory necessities that Wandor describes.

From this, the question inevitably arises: was Joan Littlewood—is she now—an inspiration for other women theatre workers? Perhaps. Events that began to propel women into more significant roles in the theatre, however, had little input from her. Micheline Wandor dates this change from a conference at Ruskin College, Oxford, which, she argues, jerked the Women's Liberation Movement into life in 1970. The next year, 1971, the Women's Street Theatre Group was founded. In 1973 the first Women's Theatre Festival was held, and in 1975 the best-known women's group, Monstrous Regiment, began. Joan Littlewood was not involved in any of this. Ann Jellicoe was virtually the only serious woman playwright (apart from Shelagh Delaney) in the 1950s and 1960s, and even in the 1970s there were only a few—Caryl Churchill, Pam Gems, Maureen Duffy and Mary O'Malley. As for female stage designers, Jocelyn Herbert was virtually alone. When Judith Cook published *Directors' Theatre* in 1974, of the fourteen leading theatre directors she interviewed, only Littlewood was not male. Of course, in the following decades, women made some progress, and there have been more playwrights, designers, company managers and directors. But still, when a new artistic director of the National Theatre was appointed in the third millennium, it was perhaps not insignificant that the post was given to an Oxbridge-educated man, and that the leading female contender, with a less prestigious background, but probably a stronger career record, was passed over. In this area, Littlewood seems to have had little influence.

But her theatre practice did effect a complete change in the British theatre, and she—or Theatre Workshop as a whole—dragged Britain into the age of modernism. What had been long taken for granted in Germany, or Russia, or France, or the USA, was evident in her practice, and came to be adopted—however belatedly—in Britain. In 1949, one journalist noted:

> The vital methods of Theatre Workshop make the average production look like Victorian charades. This young company has worked hard and made many sacrifices to hew out a new technique of presentation and production which has the stamp of contemporary life. The lively methods of this company reflect the determination of the young to pull up the dead wood; to grow from the seed instead of pruning plants which are better dead.[11]

Looking back on Theatre Workshop in 1984, Norman Buchan, a Labour MP and experienced observer, said that Theatre Workshop was 'as important as the coming of Ibsen to the theatre of Europe',[12] and Harold Hobson, speaking a decade earlier, asserted that Joan Littlewood 'broke up the fabric of British theatre'. He continued: 'She began an internal revolution in the theatre in the way plays were produced and the sort of plays that were produced, in the way that they were written, in the way the director and the players were operating with the author, and this has gone through the whole British theatre'.[13] Looking at Joan Littlewood's work and Theatre Workshop's achievement in the 1970s, Hobson could see what time has perhaps obscured for us. We take for granted what he described. But when today someone enquires where almost any admirable matter of theatre practice in Britain originated, the answer is very often—in Theatre Workshop.

The director whose work Littlewood's most reminds us of is Vsevolod Meyerhold, the Russian theatre 'master' whose life was ended by a firing squad in one of Stalin's gaols. Littlewood's creative life was not ended by a bullet: it was killed by a philistine establishment's indifference to—or rejection of—her work.

Notes

Chapter One

1. Thomson, David, *England in the Twentieth Century*, Harmondsworth: Penguin, 1965, p. 130.
2. MacColl, Ewan, *Journeyman*, London: Sidgwick & Jackson, 1990, pp. 19–20.
3. Lloyd, A.L., *Folk Song in England*, London: Lawrence and Wishart, 1967, pp. 358–59.
4. Quoted in Nicholson, Steve, *British Theatre and the Red Peril*, Exeter: University of Exeter Press, 1999, p. 69.
5. Greenwood, Walter, *Love on the Dole*, Harmondsworth: Penguin, 1969, p. 170.
6. Hannington, Wal, *Unemployed Struggles, 1919–1936*, London: Lawrence and Wishart, 1977, p. 268.
7. Ibid., pp. 190–91.
8. Ibid., p. 234.

Chapter Two

1. Nicoll, Allardyce, *The English Theatre*, London: Nelson, 1936, p. 188.
2. For an incisive discussion of this play and its context, see Nicholson, Steve, *British Theatre and the Red Peril*, Exeter: University of Exeter Press, 1999.
3. All quotations from: Moussinac, Leon, *The New Movement in the Theatre*, London: B.T. Batsford, 1931. The pages of this book are not numbered. For further discussion, see Paget, Derek, 'Theatre Workshop, Moussinac, and the European Connection', *New Theatre Quarterly*, vol. XI, no. 43, August 1995, pp. 211–24.
4. Sinclair, Upton, *Singing Jailbirds*, Long Beach, CA: Upton Sinclair, 1924, *passim.*
5. Wilder, Thornton, *Our Town, The Skin of Our Teeth, The Matchmaker*, Harmondsworth: Penguin, 1962, p. 21.
6. See Nicholson, Steve, *op. cit.*, pp. 22–24.
7. Marshall, Norman, *The Other Theatre*, London: John Lehman, 1947, p. 53.
8. Ibid., p. 50.
9. Sidnell, Michael, *Dances of Death*, London: Faber and Faber, 1984, p. 50.
10. Auden, W.H., and Isherwood, Christopher, *The Dog Beneath the Skin*, London: Faber and Faber, 1935, p. 146.

Chapter Three

1. *Red Stage*, no. 3, February 1932.
2. Edwards, Ness, *The Workers' Theatre*, Cardiff, 1930, quoted in Samuel, Raphael, MacColl, Ewan, and Cosgrove, Stuart, *Theatres of the Left*, London: Routledge and Kegan Paul, 1985, p. 194.
3. 'The Workers' Theatre Movement', an interview with Philip Poole by Jon Clarke and David Margolies, in *Red Letters*, no.10, p. 9.
4. Samuel, Raphael, *et al.* (eds), *op. cit.*, p. 84.
5. *Red Stage*, no.7, September 1932.
6. Gottfried, Martin, *Arthur Miller: A Life*, London: Faber and Faber, 2003, p. 26.
7. *Red Stage*, no. 3, February 1932.
8. 'The Basis and Development of the Workers' Theatre Movement (1932)', in Samuel, Raphael, *et al.* (eds), *op. cit.*, p. 101.

9 *New Red Stage*, nos. 6 and 7, June–July 1932.

10 *Red Letters*, no. 10, p. 6.

11 'Something for Nothing', *Red Stage*, no. 5, April–May 1932; 'Their Theatre and Ours', quoted in Samuel, Raphael, *et al.* (eds), *op. cit.*; 'Speed Up', *New Red Stage*, no. 7, September 1932.

12 Samuel, Raphael, *et al* (eds)., *op. cit.*, p. 106.

13 See Roberts, Robert, *The Classic Slum*, Manchester: Manchester University Press, 1971, p. 14.

14 Davies, Andrew, *Leisure, Gender and Poverty*, Buckingham: Open University Press, 1992, p. 158.

15 Roberts, Robert, *op. cit.*, p. 26.

16 Ibid., p. 119.

17 Quoted in Davies, Andrew, *op. cit.*, p. 25.

18 Priestley, J.B., *English Journey*, London: William Heinemann, 1934, p. 262.

19 See Cohen, Anthony P., *The Symbolic Construction of Community*, London: Routledge, 1993; Crow, Graham and Allen, Graham, *Community Life: An Introduction to Local Social Relations*, Hemel Hempstead: Harvester Wheatsheaf, 1994; Benedict Anderson, *Imagined Communities*, London: Verso, 1990.

20 Samuel, Raphael, *et al.* (eds), *op. cit.*, p. 14.

21 Ibid., p. 231.

22 Ibid., pp. 213, 222.

23 MacColl, Ewan, *Journeyman*, London: Sidgwick & Jackson, 1990, p. 200.

Chapter Four

1 *Manchester Guardian*, 1 January 1934.

2 Untitled typescript by Ewan MacColl, Ewan MacColl and Peggy Seeger Archive, Ruskin College Library, Oxford.

3 Goorney, Howard, *The Theatre Workshop Story*, London: Eyre Methuen, 1981, p. 8.

4 Eddershaw, Margaret, *Performing Brecht: Forty Years of British Performances*, London: Routledge, 1996, p. 43.

5 MacColl, Ewan, *Journeyman*, London: Sidgwick & Jackson, 1990, p. 211.

6 Littlewood, Joan, *Joan's Book*, London: Methuen, 1994, p. 91.

7 See Leach, Robert, *Revolutionary Theatre,* London: Routledge, 1994, pp. 82–84.

8 Goorney, Howard, and MacColl, Ewan (eds), *Agit-Prop to Theatre Workshop*, Manchester: Manchester University Press, 1986, p. 14.

9 Ibid., p. 15.

10 See ibid., p. xxx; however, in *The Theatre Workshop Story*, Goorney says the name of this actor was Bunny Bowen.

11 Mann, Emily, and Roessel, David, (eds), *Political Stages*, New York: Applause, 2002, p. 353.

12 Ibid., pp. 384–85.

13 Davies, Cecil, *The Plays of Ernst Toller: A Revaluation*, Amsterdam: Harwood Academic, 1996, p. 381.

14 Ibid., pp. 376–78.

Chapter Five

1 Thomson, David, *England in the Twentieth Century*, Harmondsworth: Penguin, 1965, p. 157.

2 Billingham, Peter, *Theatres of Conscience, 1939–53*, London: Routledge, 2002, p. 21.

3 Pimlott, Ben, *Labour and the Left in the 1930s*, Cambridge: Cambridge University Press, 1977, p. 155.

4 Tynan, Kenneth, *Tynan Right and Left*, London: Longmans, 1967, p. 320.

5 Goorney, Howard, and MacColl, Ewan (eds), *Agit-Prop to Theatre Workshop*, Manchester: Manchester University Press, 1986, p. xxxix.

6   *Theatre Workshop*, BBC Radio, 1978, tape in Ewan MacColl and Peggy Seeger Archive, Ruskin College Library, Oxford.
7   Littlewood, Joan, *Joan's Book*, London: Methuen, 1994, pp. 763–64.
8   Ibid., p. 764.
9   Goorney, Howard, *The Theatre Workshop Story*, London: Eyre Methuen, 1981, p. 25.
10 Goorney, Howard, and MacColl, Ewan (eds), *op. cit.*, p. xlii.
11 Benjamin, Walter, *Understanding Brecht*, London: NLB, 1973, p. 3.
12 Goorney, Howard, and MacColl, Ewan (eds), *op. cit.*, p. xlii.
13 Transcript of interview with Ewan MacColl, supplied by Clive Barker.
14 Willis, Ted, *Whatever Happened to Tom Mix*, London: Eyre and Spottiswoode, 1970, pp. 150–51.
15 *Theatre Workshop*, BBC Radio, 1978, tape in Ewan MacColl and Peggy Seeger Archive, Ruskin College Library, Oxford.
16 Goorney, Howard, and MacColl, Ewan (eds), *op. cit.*, p.xlvii.
17 Joan Littlewood and The Theatre Workshop Collection, Harry Ransom Humanities Research Center, University of Texas at Austin, box 1, folder 5.
18 See Billingham, Peter, *op. cit.*
19 Joan Littlewood and The Theatre Workshop Collection, Harry Ransom Humanities Research Center, University of Texas at Austin, box 1, folder 5.

Chapter Six

1   Littlewood, Joan, *Joan's Book*, London: Methuen, 1994, p. 167.
2   Christopher Mayhew, in Thompson, Alan, *The Day Before Yesterday*, London: Granada, 1971, p. 17.
3   Mass Observation Archive, University of Sussex, quoted in *When Peace Broke Out: Britain 1945*, London: HMSO, 1994, p. 93.
4   Chambers, Colin, *The Story of Unity Theatre*, London: Lawrence and Wishart, 1989, p. 277.
5   Ibid., p. 337.
6   Quoted in Billingham, Peter, *Theatres of Conscience, 1939–53*, London: Routledge, 2002, p. 89.
7   Littlewood, Joan, *op.cit.*, p.157.
8   MacColl, Ewan, *Journeyman*, London: Sidgwick and Jackson, 1990, p. 244.
9   Theatre Workshop publicity leaflet, undated, but c. 1945.
10 Quoted in Goorney, Howard, *The Theatre Workshop Story*, London: Eyre Methuen, 1981, p. 194.
11 Ibid., p.77.
12 Littlewood, Joan, *op.cit.*, p. 255.
13 Ibid., p. 413.
14 Transcript of interview with Ewan MacColl, supplied by Clive Barker.
15 Ibid.
16 MacColl, Ewan, *op.cit.*, p.251.
17 Goorney, Howard, 'Political Theatre in Britain, 1928–1986', available at Working Class Movement Library website: http://www.wcml.org.uk/culture/hgepilogue.htm.
18 Transcript of interview with Ewan MacColl, supplied by Clive Barker.
19 Gladkov, Aleksandr, *Meyerhold Speaks, Meyerhold Rehearses*, Amsterdam: Harwood Academic Publishers, 1997, p. 165.

Chapter Seven

1   See Sissons, Michael, and French, Philip, *Age of Austerity*, Harmondsworth: Penguin, 1964, p. 173.
2   Typescript, 'The Theatre and Communism by Joan Littlewood', Joan Littlewood and the Theatre Workshop Collection, Harry Ransom Humanities Research Center, University of Texas at Austin, box 1, folder 3.

3   Joan Littlewood and the Theatre Workshop Collection, Harry Ransom Humanities Research Center, University of Texas at Austin, box 2, folder 9.
4   Quoted in Littlewood, Joan, *Joan's Book*, London: Methuen, 1994, p. 295.
5   Quoted in Goorney, Howard, *The Theatre Workshop Story*, London: Eyre Methuen, 1981, p. 65.
6   Joan Littlewood and the Theatre Workshop Collection, Harry Ransom Humanities Research Center, University of Texas at Austin, box 2, folder 9.
7   Clurman, Harold, *The Fervent Years*, London: Dennis Dobson, 1946, p. 229.
8   Transcript of interview with Ewan MacColl, supplied by Clive Barker.
9   *Theatre Workshop*, BBC Radio, 1978, tape in Ewan MacColl and Peggy Seeger Archive, Ruskin College Library, Oxford.
10 Goorney, Howard, *op. cit.*, p. 48.
11 MacLennan, Elizabeth, *The Moon Belongs to Everyone*, London: Methuen, 1990, p. 31.
12 Littlewood, Joan, *op. cit.*, p. 191.
13 Ibid., p. 425.
14 Quoted in Goorney, Howard, *op. cit.*, p. 83.
15 Ibid., p. 83.
16 MacColl, Ewan, *Journeyman*, London: Sidgwick and Jackson, 1990, p. 264.
17 Joan Littlewood and the Theatre Workshop Collection, Harry Ransom Humanities Research Center, University of Texas at Austin, box 2, folder 9.
18 For full details of this proposal, see Joan Littlewood and the Theatre Workshop Collection, Harry Ransom Humanities Research Center, University of Texas at Austin, box 15, folder 6.

Chapter Eight

1   Jack Pulman, quoted in Goorney, Howard, *The Theatre Workshop Story*, London: Eyre Methuen, 1981, p. 89.
2   See MacColl, Ewan, *Journeyman*, London: Sidgwick and Jackson, 1990, pp. 22, 47, 53–54.
3   Ibid., p. 213.
4   *The Travellers*, typescript, p. 40.
5   Goorney, Howard, and MacColl, Ewan (eds), *Agit-Prop to Theatre Workshop*, Manchester: Manchester University Press, 1986, p. 85.
6   *Rogue's Gallery*, typescript, p. 28.
7   *The Travellers*, typescript, pp. 13–14.
8   Goorney, Howard, and MacColl, Ewan (eds), *op. cit.*, p. 195.
9   *Hell Is What You Make It*, typescript, p. 60.
10 Goorney, Howard, and MacColl, Ewan (eds), *op. cit.*, p. 63.
11 *Rogue's Gallery*, typescript, pp. 22, 92.
12 Chambers, Colin, and Prior, Mike, *Playwrights' Progress*, Oxford: Amber Lane Press, 1987, p. 35.
13 Goorney, Howard, and MacColl, Ewan (eds), *op. cit.*, p. 161.
14 McDiarmid, Hugh, Introduction to MacColl, Ewan, *Uranium 235*, Glasgow: William MacLennan, n.d.
15 See Seeger, Peggy (ed.), *The Essential Ewan MacColl Songbook*, New York: Oak Publications, 2001, p. 8.
16 Samuel, Raphael, MacColl, Ewan, and Cosgrove, Stuart, *Theatres of the Left*, London: Routledge and Kegan Paul, 1985, p. 254.
17 MacColl, Ewan, *op. cit.*, p. 379.
18 Ibid., p. 269.
19 Transcript of interview with Ewan MacColl, supplied by Clive Barker.
20 Seeger, Peggy (ed.), *op. cit.*, p.8.
21 Ewan MacColl, in *The Voice of Experience*, tape, published by the Charles Parker Archive Trust.
22 Samuel, Raphael, *et al.* (eds), *op. cit.*, p. 211.

23 Bauman, Zygmunt, *Community: Seeking Safety in an Insecure World*, Cambridge: Polity, 2001, p. 3.
24 Sissons, Michael, and French, Philip, *Age of Austerity*, Harmondsworth: Penguin, 1964, p. 44.
25 *You're Only Young Once*, typescript, pp. 13–14.
26 Ibid., p. 54.
27 Ibid, p. 54.
28 Transcript of interview with Ewan MacColl, supplied by Clive Barker.
29 *Rogue's Gallery*, typescript, p. 93.
30 Wilder, Thornton, *Pullman Car 'Hiawatha'*, London: Samuel French Ltd, n.d., p. 5.
31 Quoted in MacLennan, Elizabeth, *The Moon Belongs to Everyone*, London: Methuen, 1990, p. 33.
32 Paget, Derek, *True Stories? Documentary Drama on Radio, Screen and Stage*, Manchester: Manchester University Press, 1990, p. 83.
33 Goorney, Howard, and MacColl, Ewan (eds), *op. cit.*, p. l.
34 *Operation Olive Branch*, typescript, p. 84.
35 Ibid., p. 5.
36 Goorney, Howard, and MacColl, Ewan (eds), *op. cit.*, p. 83.
37 *The Travellers*, typescript, p. 27.
38 Goorney, Howard, and MacColl, Ewan (eds), *op. cit.*, pp. 58–59.
39 See especially 'The Montage of Attractions' and 'The Montage of Film Attractions' in Eisenstein, S.M., *Selected Works*, vol. 1: *Writings, 1922–34*, ed. Richard Taylor, London: BFI Publishing, 1988, pp. 33–58.
40 Goorney, Howard, *The Theatre Workshop Story*, London: Eyre Methuen, 1981, p. 34.
41 Goorney, Howard, and MacColl, Ewan (eds), *op. cit.*, p. 36.
42 *Landscape with Chimneys*, typescript, p. 2.
43 *Ours the Fruit*, typescript, p. 1.
44 *Landscape with Chimneys*, typescript, p. 39.
45 Goorney, Howard, and MacColl, Ewan (eds), *op. cit.*, p. 82.
46 Ibid., p. 53.
47 Ibid, pp. 56–57.
48 Seeger, Peggy (ed), *op. cit.*, p. 364.
49 Goorney, Howard, and MacColl, Ewan (eds), *op. cit.*, p.121.
50 MacColl, Ewan, *op. cit.*, p. 252. See also Littlewood, Joan, *Joan's Book*, London: Methuen, 1994, p. 174.
51 Goorney, Howard, *op. cit.*, pp. 52–53.
52 Quoted in Bannister, Winifred, 'New Scottish Drama', in *Scottish Music and Drama*, August 1950, p. 13.

Chapter Nine

1 Goorney, Howard, *The Theatre Workshop Story*, London: Eyre Methuen, 1981, p. 4.
2 Ibid., p. 20.
3 Littlewood, Joan, *Joan's Book*, London: Methuen, 1994, pp.252, 254–55.
4 Murray Melvin, in conversation with the author, 1 March 2005.
5 Joan Littlewood and the Theatre Workshop Collection, Harry Ransom Humanities Research Center, University of Texas at Austin, box 1, folder 1.
6 Joan Littlewood and the Theatre Workshop Collection, Harry Ransom Humanities Research Center, University of Texas at Austin, box 1, folder 6.
7 Ibid.
8 See Gorelik, Mordecai, *New Theatres for Old*, London: Dennis Dobson, 1947, pp. 303–5.
9 It is preserved in Joan Littlewood and the Theatre Workshop Collection, Harry Ransom Humanities Research Center, University of Texas at Austin, box 1, folder 2.
10 Joan Littlewood and the Theatre Workshop Collection, Harry Ransom Humanities Research Center, University of Texas at Austin, box 1, folder 5.
11 Ibid.

12   Joan Littlewood and the Theatre Workshop Collection, Harry Ransom Humanities Research Center, University of Texas at Austin, box 1, folder 3.
13   Littlewood, Joan, *op. cit.*, p. 772.
14   Newlove, Jean, and Dalby, John, *Laban for All*, London: NHB, 2004, p. 13.
15   Littlewood, Joan, *op. cit.*, p. 772.
16   Howard Goorney, in conversation with the author, 25 November 1990.
17   Jean Newlove, in conversation with the author, 8 November 2004.
18   Newlove, Jean, *Laban for Actors and Dancers*, London: Nick Hern Books, 1993, p. 13.
19   Bridgmont, Peter, *Liberation of the Actor*, London: Temple Lodge, 1992, p. 25.
20   Jean Newlove, in conversation with the author, 8 November 2004.
21   Goorney, Howard, *op. cit.*, p. 160.
22   MacColl, Ewan, *Journeyman*, London: Sidgwick and Jackson, 1990, p. 389.
23   Joan Littlewood and the Theatre Workshop Collection, Harry Ransom Humanities Research Center, University of Texas at Austin, box 1, folder 3.
24   Joan Littlewood and the Theatre Workshop Collection, Harry Ransom Humanities Research Center, University of Texas at Austin, box 1, folders 1, 2 and 3.
25   Joan Littlewood and the Theatre Workshop Collection, Harry Ransom Humanities Research Center, University of Texas at Austin, box 1, folder 1.
26   Joan Littlewood and the Theatre Workshop Collection, Harry Ransom Humanities Research Center, University of Texas at Austin, box 2, folder 9.
27   Newlove, Jean, *op. cit.*, p. 8.
28   Bridgmont,. Peter, *The Spear Thrower*, Ireland: An Gianan, 1983, p. 29.
29   Goorney, Howard, *op. cit.*, p. 19.
30   *The Voice of Experience*, tape, published by the Charles Parker Archive Trust.
31   Joan Littlewood and the Theatre Workshop Collection, Harry Ransom Humanities Research Center, University of Texas at Austin, box 1, folder 5.
32   MacColl, Ewan, *op. cit.*, p. 349.
33   Joan Littlewood and the Theatre Workshop Collection, Harry Ransom Humanities Research Center, University of Texas at Austin, box 1, folder 6.
34   *Guardian*, 26 February 2003.
35   Newlove, Jean, *op. cit.*, p. 11.
36   Littlewood, Joan, *op. cit.*, p. 211.
37   Joan Littlewood and the Theatre Workshop Collection, Harry Ransom Humanities Research Center, University of Texas at Austin, box 1, folder 1.
38   Ibid.
39   Ibid.
40   Tynan, Kenneth, *Tynan Right and Left*, London: Longmans, 1967, p. 317.
41   Joan Littlewood and the Theatre Workshop Collection, Harry Ransom Humanities Research Center, University of Texas at Austin, box 1, folders 1 and 5.
42   Joan Littlewood and the Theatre Workshop Collection, Harry Ransom Humanities Research Center, University of Texas at Austin, box 1, folder 5.

Chapter Ten

1   Shellard, Dominic (ed.), *British Theatre in the 1950s*, Sheffield: Sheffield Academic Press, 2000, p. 69.
2   Billingham, Peter, *Theatres of Conscience, 1939–1953*, London: Routledge, 2002, p. 85.
3   Jean Newlove, in conversation with the author, 28 February 2005.
4   MacColl, Ewan, *Journeyman*, London: Sidgwick and Jackson, 1990, p. 265.
5   *Theatre Workshop*, BBC Radio, 1978, tape in Ewan MacColl and Peggy Seeger Archive, Ruskin College Library, Oxford.
6   Ibid.
7   Jean Newlove, in conversation with the author, 28 February 2005.
8   Transcript of interview with Ewan MacColl, supplied by Clive Barker.
9   Jean Newlove, in conversation with the author, 28 February 2005.
10   Littlewood, Joan, *Joan's Book*, London: Methuen, 1994, p. 434.

11   *Omnibus*, BBC Television, 19 April 1994.

Chapter Eleven

1   Palmer, Alan, *The East End*, London: John Murray, 2000, pp. 145–46.
2   Quoted in Sheridan, Paul, *Penny Theatres of Victorian London*, London: Dennis Dobson, 1981, p. 8.
3   Quoted in Coren, Michael, *Theatre Royal*, London: Quartet Books, 1984, pp. 4–5.
4   *Observer*, 30 March 1947.
5   *The Times*, 25 March 1947.
6   Littlewood, Joan, *Joan's Book*, London: Methuen, 1994, p. 301.
7   Murray Melvin, in conversation with the author, 1 March 2005.
8   *Theatre Workshop*, BBC Radio, 1978, tape in Ewan MacColl and Peggy Seeger Archive, Ruskin College Library, Oxford.
9   Ibid.
10 Barker, Clive, 'Closing Joan's Book: Some Personal Footnotes', *New Theatre Quarterly*, vol. XIX, no. 2, (*NTQ* 74), May 2003, pp. 99–100.
11 *Independent*, 23 September 2002.
12 Marowitz, Charles, Milne, Tom, and Hale, Owen (eds), *The Encore Reader*, London: Methuen, 1965, p. 84.
13 *Sunday Times*, 23 January 1955.
14 Quoted in Goorney, Howard, *The Theatre Workshop Story*, London: Eyre Methuen, 1981, p. 151.
15 Ibid.
16 Tynan, Kenneth, *Tynan on Theatre*, Harmondsworth: Penguin, 1964, p. 229.
17 *Sunday Times*, 3 July 1955.
18 Quoted in Goorney, Howard, *op. cit.*, p. 154.
19 Shellard, Dominic (ed.), *British Theatre in the 1950s*, Sheffield: Sheffield Academic Press, 2000, p. 37.

Chapter Twelve

1   Littlewood, Joan, *Joan's Book*, London: Methuen, 1994, p. 184.
2   Transcript of interview with Ewan MacColl, supplied by Clive Barker.
3   Joan Littlewood and the Theatre Workshop Collection, Harry Ransom Humanities Research Center, University of Texas in Austin, box 2, folder 9.
4   See Littlewood, Joan, *op. cit.*, p. 389.
5   MacColl, Ewan, *Journeyman*, London: Sidgwick and Jackson, 1990, p. 265.
6   For further details, see Holdsworth, Nadine, '"They'd Have Pissed on my Grave": The Arts Council and Theatre Workshop', *New Theatre Quarterly*, vol. XV, no, 1, 1999, pp. 3–16.
7   Coren, Michael, *Theatre Royal*, London: Quartet Books, 1984, p. 37.
8   MacColl, Ewan, *op. cit.*, p.252.
9   Quoted in MacLennan, Elizabeth, *The Moon Belongs to Everyone*, London: Methuen, 1990, pp. 161–62.

Chapter Thirteen

1   Marowitz, Charles, Milne, Tom, and Hale, Owen (eds), *The Encore Reader*, London: Methuen, 1965, p. 66.
2   *Guardian*, 28 November 2001.
3   Quoted in Coren, Michael, *Theatre Royal*, London: Quartet Books, 1984, p. 59.
4   *The Times*, 9 December 1957.
5   Barker, Clive, 'Joan Littlewood', in Hodge, Alison (ed.), *Twentieth Century Actor Training*, London: Routledge, 2000, p. 123.
6   Goorney, Howard, *The Theatre Workshop Story*, London: Eyre Methuen, 1981, p. 168.
7   *Daily Herald*, 10 July 1961.

8   MacColl, Ewan, *Journeyman*, London: Sidgwick and Jackson, 1990, p. 245.
9   *Guardian*, 7 December 2001.
10   Ibid.
11   *Independent*, 12 May 1993.
12   Ibid.
13   See *Daily Herald*, 19 July 1961.
14   Littlewood, Joan, *Joan's Book*, London: Methuen, 1994, p. 693.
15   Goorney, Howard, *op. cit.*, pp. 169–70.
16   *Independent*, 26 March 1994.
17   See Hodge, Alison (ed.), *op. cit.*, p. 121.
18   MacColl, Ewan, *op. cit.*, p. 211.
19   *Independent*, 12 May 1993.
20   *Guardian*, 25 September 2002.
21   *Independent*, 12 May 1993.
22   Ibid.
23   *Independent*, 26 March, 1994.
24   *Independent*, 12 May 1993.
25   Bridgmont, Peter, *Liberation of the Actor*, London: Temple Lodge, p. ix.
26   Littlewood, Joan, *op. cit.*, p.275.
27   *Independent*, 26 March 1994.
28   Joan Littlewood and the Theatre Workshop Collection, Harry Ransom Humanities Research Center, University of Texas at Austin, box 1, folder 2.
29   Littlewood, Joan, *op. cit.*, p. 431.
30   Goorney, Howard, *op. cit.*, p. 167.
31   Shellard, Dominic (ed.), *British Theatre in the 1950s*, Sheffield: Sheffield Academic Press, 2000, p. 34.
32   Joan Littlewood and the Theatre Workshop Collection, Harry Ransom Humanities Research Center, University of Texas at Austin, box 1, folder 3.
33   Littlewood, Joan, *op. cit.*, p. 469.
34   Ibid., p. 165.
35   Newlove, Jean, *Laban for Actors and Dancers*, London: Nick Hern Books, 1993, p. 8.
36   Quoted in Davies, Andrew, *Other Theatres*, London: Macmillan, 1987, pp. 153–54.
37   Goorney, Howard, and MacColl, Ewan (eds), *Agit-Prop to Theatre Workshop*, Manchester: Manchester University Press, 1986, p. xlix.
38   Hawthorne, Nigel, *Straight Face*, London: BBC Audiobooks, 2004, p. 218.
39   See, for example, reviews of Chapman's *You Won't Always Be on Top*.
40   Littlewood, Joan, *op. cit.*, p.199.
41   *Observer*, 6 March 1955.
42   Littlewood, Joan, *op. cit.*, pp. 430–31.
43   Marowitz, Charles, *et al.* (eds), p. 133.
44   First and third quotations are from unidentified press cuttings in the Victoria and Albert Archive, Theatre Museum Collection, Stratford East box; the second is from *Stratford Express*, 23 February 1954.
45   Unidentified press cuttings, Victoria and Albert Archive, Theatre Museum, Stratford East box.
46   Ibid.
47   *Daily Telegraph*, 31 March 1954.
48   *The Times*, 26 May 1954.
49   *Daily Telegraph*, 4 March, 1955; *Observer*, 6 March 1955.
50   Littlewood, Joan, *op. cit.*, p. 776.
51   *Observer*, 6 March 1955.
52   *Daily Mail*, 29 September 1954; *The Times*, 29 September 1954; *Observer*, 2 October 1954.
53   *Stratford Express*, 23 February 1954. John Blanshard was also known as 'Joby'.
54   Unidentified press cuttings, Victoria and Albert Archive, Theatre Museum, Stratford East box.

55 *Daily Mail*, 10 November 1954.
56 *Evening Standard*, 10 November 1954.
57 *Observer*, 14 November 1954.
58 *Guardian*, 25 June 1984.
59 *The Times*, 18 January 1955.
60 Unidentified press cuttings, Victoria and Albert Archive, Theatre Museum, Stratford East box.

Chapter Fourteen

1   Shellard, Dominic (ed.), *British Theatre in the 1950s*, Sheffield: Sheffield Academic Press, 2000, p. 69.
2   Tynan, Kenneth, *Tynan on Theatre*, Harmondsworth: Penguin, 1964, p. 57.
3   *Manchester Guardian*, 5 November 1956.
4   See Stanislavsky, Constantin, *My Life in Art*, London: Geoffrey Bles, 1962, p. 298.
5   See Littlewood, Joan, *Joan's Book*, London: Methuen, 1994, pp. 483, 497, 502.
6   Marowitz, Charles, Milne, Tom, and Hale, Owen (eds), *The Encore Reader*, London: Methuen, 1965, p. 81.
7   *The Times*, 1 July 1958.
8   Quoted in Coren, Michael, *Theatre Royal: 100 Years of Stratford East*, London: Quartet Books, 1984, p. 55.
9   Quoted in Davies, Andrew, *Other Theatres*, London: Macmillan, 1987, p. viii.
10 Marowitz, Charles, *et al.* (eds), *op. cit.*, p. 133.
11 Joan Littlewood and the Theatre Workshop Collection, Harry Ransom Humanities Research Center, University of Texas at Austin, box 2, folder 7.
12 Davies, Andrew, *op. cit.*, p. 157.
13 *Daily Telegraph*, 19 August 1963.
14 *Independent*, 23 September 2002.
15 See Goorney, Howard, *The Theatre Workshop Story*, London: Eyre Methuen, 1981, p. 123.
16 Marowitz, Charles, *et al.* (eds), *op. cit.*, p. 132–33.
17 Tynan, Kenneth, *A View of the English Stage*, London: Methuen, 1984, p. 319.
18 Marowitz, Charles, *et al.* (eds), *op. cit.*, p. 134.
19 *Theatre Workshop*, BBC Radio, 1978, tape in Ewan MacColl and Peggy Seeger Archive, Ruskin College Library, Oxford.

Chapter Fifteen

1   See Tynan, Kenneth, *A View of the English Stage*, London: Methuen, 1984, pp. 364–80.
2   Nicholson, Steve, *British Theatre and the Red Peril*, Exeter: University of Exeter Press, 1999, p. 25.
3   Tynan, Kenneth, *op. cit*, p. 369.
4   See Shellard, Dominic (ed.), *British Theatre in the 1950s*, Sheffield: Sheffield Academic Press, 2000, p. 119.
5   Shellard, Dominic, *British Theatre Since the War*, New Haven, CT: Yale University Press, 2000, p. 9.
6   Ibid., p. 10.
7   *Guardian*, 28 November 2001.
8   Marowitz, Charles, Milne, Tom, and Hale, Owen (eds), *The Encore Reader*, London: Methuen, 1965, p. 95.
9   Goorney, Howard, *The Theatre Workshop Story*, London: Eyre Methuen, 1981, p. 118.
10 Ibid, pp. 118–19.

Chapter Sixteen

1   Behan, Brendan, *The Complete Plays*, London: Eyre Methuen, 1978, pp. 83–85.
2   Ibid., pp. 117-118.

3 Ibid., p. 39.
4 Tynan, Kenneth, *Tynan on Theatre*, Harmondsworth: Penguin, 1964, p. 46.
5 Ibid., pp. 75, 76.
6 Marowitz, Charles, Milne, Tom, and Hale, Owen (eds), *The Encore Reader*, London: Methuen, 1965, pp. 94, 95.
7 Angel Lane is in Stratford East.
8 Behan, Brendan, *op. cit.*, p. 199.
9 Ibid., p. 236.
10 Chapman, Henry, *You Won't Always Be on Top*, London: Methuen, 1965, p. 103.
11 See Shellard, Dominic (ed.), *British Theatre in the 1950s*, Sheffield: Sheffield Academic Press, 2000, p. 71.
12 See Leach, Robert, *Stanislavsky and Meyerhold*, Bern: Peter Lang, 2003, pp. 27–42.
13 Delaney, Shelagh, *A Taste of Honey*, London: Methuen, 2000, p. 68.
14 Wandor, Michelene, *Post-War British Drama*, London: Routledge, 2001, p. 60.
15 *New Statesman*, 21 February 1959.
16 *Spectator*, 20 February 1959.
17 *Daily Mail*, 28 May 1958.
18 Norman, Frank, *Fings Ain't Wot They Used T'Be*, New York: Grove Press, 1960, p. 26.
19 *Queen*, 3 March 1959.
20 Paget, Derek, '"Oh What a Lovely War": The Texts and their Context', *New Theatre Quarterly*, vol. VI, no. 23, August 1990, pp. 244–60.
21 *Oh What a Lovely War*, revised and restored to the original version by Joan Littlewood, London: Methuen, 2000, p.ix.
22 Roberts, Robert, *The Classic Slum*, Manchester: Manchester University Press, 1971, p. 170.
23 Littlewood, Joan, *Joan's Book*, London: Methuen, 1994, p. 493.
24 Marowitz, Charles, *et al.* (eds), *op. cit.*, p. 231.
25 Theatre Workshop, *op.cit.*, 2000, p.28.
26 Quoted in Piscator, Erwin, *The Political Theatre*, London: Eyre Methuen, 1980, p.230.
27 *Oh What a Lovely War*, *op. cit.*, p. x.
28 *Daily Mail*, 20 March 1963.
29 Paget, Derek, *op. cit.*, p.254.
30 See Goorney, Howard, *The Theatre Workshop Story*, London: Eyre Methuen, 1981, p. 127; also Paget, Derek, *op. cit.*, pp. 258–59.
31 Fletcher, Jackie, 'A Tribute to Joan Littlewood', *The British Theatre Guide*, 20 July 2004.
32 *Guardian*, 27 July 2002.
33 *The Times*, 12 July 1961.
34 Ibid.
35 Littlewood, Joan *op. cit.*, pp.530-531.
36 Norman, Frank, *Why Fings Went West*, London: Lemon Tree Press, 1975, p. 46.
37 *Guardian*, 7 December 2001.
38 Joan Littlewood and the Theatre Workshop Collection, Harry Ransom Humanities Research Center, University of Texas at Austin, box 6, folder 6.
39 Delaney, Shelagh, *op. cit.*, p. 87.
40 Behan, Brendan, *op. cit.*, pp. 171, 172.
41 Ibid; and Joan Littlewood and the Theatre Workshop Collection, Harry Ransom Humanities Research Center, University of Texas at Austin, box 5, folders 3 and 4.
42 Paget, Derek, *op. cit.*, p. 252.
43 See *Oh What a Lovely War*, *op. cit.*, pp. 89–90; Littlewood, Joan, *op. cit.*, p. 684; Paget, Derek, *op. cit.*, pp. 252–55.
44 *Illustrated London News*, 8 April 1961.
45 Coren, Michael, *Theatre Royal: 100 Years of Stratford East*, London: Quartet Books, 1984, p. 41.
46 Goorney, Howard, *op. cit.*, p. 109.
47 Coren, Michael, *op. cit.*, p. 32.
48 Norman, Frank, *Why Fings Went West*, *op. cit.*, pp. 18, 22.

49   Samuel, Raphael, MacColl, Ewan, and Cosgrove, Stuart, *Theatres of the Left, 1880–1935*, London: Routledge and Kegan Paul, 1985, pp. 140–41.
50   Behan, Brendan, *op. cit.*, p. 225.
51   Harrington, John P., *Modern Irish Drama,* New York: W.W. Norton, 1991, p. 526.
52   Joan Littlewood and the Theatre Workshop Collection, Harry Ransom Humanities Research Center, University of Texas at Austin, box 3, folder 12.
53   Behan, Brendan, *op. cit.*, p.120.
54   See Wandor, Michelene, *Post-War British Drama*, London: Routledge, 2001, p. 61.
55   See Wittig, Monique, *The Straight Mind*, Boston: Beacon Press, 1992.

Chapter Seventeen

1   Norman, Frank, *Why Fings Went West*, London: Lemon Tree Press, 1975, p. 46.
2   Tynan, Kenneth, *Tynan Right and Left*, London: Longmans, 1967, p. 316.
3   Goorney, Howard, *The Theatre Workshop Story*, London: Eyre Methuen, 1981, p. 18.
4   MacColl, Ewan, *Journeyman*, London: Sidgwick and Jackson, 1990, p. 211.
5   Marowitz, Charles, Milne, Tom, and Hale, Owen (eds), *The Encore Reader*, London: Methuen, 1965, p. 133.
6   See Lacey, Stephen, *British Realist Theatre*, London: Routledge, 1995, p. 135.
7   Marowitz, Charles, *et al.* (eds), *op. cit.*, p. 133.
8   Barker, Clive, 'Closing Joan's Book: Some Personal Footnotes', *New Theatre Quarterly*, vol. XIX, no. 2 (*NTQ* 74), May 2003, p. 107.
9   Joan Littlewood and the Theatre Workshop Collection, Harry Ransom Humanities Research Center, University of Texas at Austin, box 3, folder 12.
10   *Observer*, 15 March 1959.
11   *The Times*, 3 December 1970.
12   Hodge, Alison (ed.), *Twentieth Century Actor Training*, London: Routledge, 2000, pp. 116–17, 123.
13   Unidentified press cutting, Victoria and Albert Archive, Theatre Museum Collections, Joan Littlewood file.
14   Quinnell, Peter, *Mayhew's Characters*, London: Spring Books, n.d., p. 225.
15   Ibid., p. 230.
16   *Oh What a Lovely War*, revised and restored to the original version by Joan Littlewood, London: Methuen, 2000, p.x.
17   Littlewood, Joan, *Joan's Book*, London: Methuen, 1994, p. 55.
18   MacColl, Ewan, *op. cit.*, p. 389.
19   *Independent*, 12 May 1993.
20   Goorney, Howard, *op. cit.*, p.194.
21   Murray Melvin, in conversation with the author, 1 March 2005.
22   Unidentified press cutting, Victoria and Albert Archive, Theatre Museum Collections, Joan Littlewood file.
23   Hawthorne, Nigel, *Straight Face*, London: BBC Audiobooks, 2004, p. 217.
24   Ibid., p. 217.
25   Goorney, Howard, *op. cit.*, p. 167.
26   *The Times* 20 March 1963.
27   *Observer*, 15 March 1959.
28   Littlewood, Joan, *op. cit.*, p.433.
29   Unidentified press cutting, Victoria and Albert Archive, Theatre Museum Collections, Joan Littlewood file.
30   *Independent*, 26 March 1993.
31   McDiarmid, Hugh, Introduction to MacColl, Ewan, *Uranium 235*, Glasgow, William MacLennan, n.d.
32   Goorney, Howard, *op. cit.*, pp. 126–27.
33   Tynan, Kenneth, *op. cit.*, pp. 316–17.
34   Littlewood, Joan, *op. cit.*, p.683.
35   Tynan, Kenneth, *op. cit.*, p. 316.

36 *Daily Telegraph*, 17 December 1958.
37 Marowitz, Charles, *et al.* (eds), *op. cit.*, p. 80.
38 Compare this with the view of most directors—e.g. that of Trevor Nunn: 'I wish I could say that I had "conducted" the play', quoted in Gottlieb, Vera, and Allain, Paul, *The Cambridge Companion to Chekhov*, Cambridge: Cambridge University Press, 2000, p. 106.
39 Tynan, Kenneth, *Tynan on Theatre*, Harmondsworth: Penguin, 1964, p. 90.
40 *Daily Telegraph*, 2 February 1973.
41 *Independent*, 12 May 1993.
42 *Independent*, 26 March 1994.
43 Joan Littlewood and the Theatre Workshop Collection, Harry Ransom Humanities Research Center, University of Texas at Austin, box 3, folder 12.
44 *Omnibus*, BBC Television, 19 April 1994.
45 Hodge, Alison (ed.), *op. cit.*, p. 123.
46 Goorney, Howard, *op. cit.*, p. 81.
47 Paget, Derek, *True Stories? Documentary Drama on Radio, Screen and Stage*, Manchester: Manchester University Press, 1990, p. 64.
48 Goorney, Howard, *op. cit.*, p. 115.
49 Unidentified press cutting, Victoria and Albert Archive, Theatre Museum Collections, Stratford East file.
50 Unidentified press cutting; *Daily Mail*, 4 September 1957; *Manchester Guardian*, 5 September 1957; *The Times*, 4 September 1957.
51 Elsom, John, *Post-War British Theatre*, London: Routledge and Kegan Paul, 1976, p. 101; Coren, Michael, *Theatre Royal: 100 Years of Stratford East*, London: Quartet Books, 1984, pp. 40, 46, 55.
52 Quoted in Shellard, Dominic (ed.), *British Theatre in the 1950s*, Sheffield: Sheffield Academic Press, 2000, p. 70.
53 *The Times*, 3 December 1970.
54 McDiarmid, Hugh, *op. cit.*
55 Littlewood, Joan, *op. cit.*, p. 404.
56 *Independent*, 12 May 1993.
57 Quoted in Tynan, Kenneth, *Tynan Right and Left*, *op. cit.*, p. 317.
58 *Guardian*, 25 September 2002.
59 Goorney, Howard, *op. cit.*, p.176.
60 Hawthorne, Nigel, *op. cit.*, pp. 217–18
61 See Goorney, Howard, *op. cit.*, p.78.
62 See Littlewood, Joan, *op. cit.*, p.467.
63 Tynan, Kenneth, *Tynan Right and Left*, *op. cit.*, p. 317.

Chapter Eighteen

1 Samuel, Raphael, MacColl, Ewan, and Cosgrove, Stuart, *Theatres of the Left, 1880–1935*, London: Routledge and Kegan Paul, 1985, p. 247–48.
2 MacColl, Ewan, *Journeyman*, London: Sidgwick and Jackson, 1990, p. 245.
3 Samuel, Raphael, *et al.* (eds), *op. cit.*, p. 247.
4 Gorelik, Mordecai, *New Theatres for Old*, London: Dennis Dobson, 1947, pp. 423, 425.
5 Littlewood, Joan, *Joan's Book*, London: Methuen, 1994, p. 288.
6 See Goorney, Howard, and MacColl, Ewan (eds), *Agit-Prop to Theatre Workshop*, Manchester: Manchester University Press, 1986, p. lii.
7 Littlewood, Joan, *op. cit.*, pp.777, 370.
8 Marowitz, Charles, Milne, Tom, and Hale, Owen (eds), *The Encore Reader*, London: Methuen, 1965, p. 85.
9 Hodge, Alison (ed.), *Twentieth Century Actor Training*, London: Routledge, 2000, p. 116.
10 *Daily Telegraph*, 15 November 2000.
11 Marowitz, Charles, *et al.* (eds), *op. cit.*, p.84.
12 *Manchester Guardian*, 16 July 1961.

13 See Goorney, Howard, *The Theatre Workshop Story*, London: Eyre Methuen, 1981, p. 70.
14 *The Times*, 27 December 1956.
15 *The Times*, 4 September 1957.
16 *Manchester Guardian*, 5 September 1957.
17 Littlewood, Joan, *op. cit.*, pp. 529, 530.
18 *The Observer*, 19 October 1958.
19 Paget, Derek, '"Oh What a Lovely War": The Texts and their Context', *New Theatre Quarterly*, vol. VI, no. 23, August 1990, p. 255.
20 *Independent*, 23 September 2002.

Chapter Nineteen

1   See Marowitz, Charles, Milne, Tom and Hale, Owen (eds), *The Encore Reader*, London: Methuen, 1965, p. 80.

Chapter Twenty

1   *Guardian*, 27 June 2005.
2   *Independent*, 23 September 2002.
3   *Guardian*, 25 September 2002.

Chapter Twenty-One

1   Barker, Clive, 'Closing Joan's Book: Some Personal Footnotes', *New Theatre Quarterly*, vol. XIX, no. 2 (*NTQ* 74), May 2003, p. 107.
2   *The Travelling People*, typescript, p. 1.
3   *The Knotty: A Musical Documentary*, Introduction and Notes by Peter Cheeseman, London: Methuen, 1970, p. xii.
4   See Itzin, Catherine, *Stages in the Revolution*, London: Eyre Methuen, 1980, p. 47.
5   Quoted in Goorney, Howard, 'Political Theatre in Britain, 1928–1986', available at Working Class Movement Library website: http://www.wcml.org.uk/culture/hgepilogue.htm
6   See *Theatre Quarterly*, winter 1979.
7   Stourac, Richard, and McCreery, Kathleen, *Theatre as a Weapon*, London: Routledge and Kegan Paul, 1986.
8   Paget, Derek, *True Stories? Documentary Drama on Radio, Screen and Stage*, Manchester: Manchester University Press, 1990, pp. 59–60.
9   See McGrath, John, *A Good Night Out*, London: Eyre Methuen, 1981; McGrath, John, *The Bone Won't Break*, London: Methuen, 1989; MacLennan, Elizabeth, *The Moon Belongs to Everyone*, London: Methuen, 1990.
10 Tynan, Kenneth, *Tynan Right and Left*, London: Longmans, 1967, p. 317.
11 Bannister, Winifred, 'New Scottish Drama', *Scottish Music and Drama*, Edinburgh Festival number, 1949.
12 *The Ballad of Ewan MacColl*, BBC Television, 14 October 1990.
13 *Theatre Workshop*, BBC Radio, 1978, tape in Ewan MacColl and Peggy Seeger Archive, Ruskin College Library, Oxford.

Bibliography

General Bibliography

Akhtar, Miriam, and Humphries, Steve, *The Fifties and Sixties: a Lifestyle Revolution*, London: Pan Macmillan, 2001.

Bakhtin, M.M., *Rabelais and His World*, Bloomington: Indiana University Press, 1984.

Barker, Clive, and Gale, Maggie B. (eds), *British Theatre Between the Wars, 1918–1939*, Cambridge: Cambridge University Press, 2000.

Bauman, Zygmunt, *Community: Seeking Safety in an Insecure World*, Cambridge: Polity, 2001.

Bell, Colin, and Newby, Howard (eds), *The Sociology of Community*, London: Frank Cass, 1974.

Billingham, Peter, *Theatres of Conscience, 1939–53*, London: Routledge, 2002.

Bradby, David, James, Louis, and Sharratt, Bernard (eds), *Performance and Politics in Popular Drama*, Cambridge: Cambridge University Press, 1980.

Branson, Noreen, *History of the Communist Party of Great Britain, 1927–1941*, London: Lawrence and Wishart, 1985.

Bridgmont, Peter, *The Spear Thrower*, Ireland: An Grianan, 1983.

Bridgmont, Peter, *Liberation of the Actor*, London: Temple Lodge, 1992.

Brown, John Russell, and Harris, Bernard (eds), *Contemporary Theatre*, London: Edward Arnold, 1962.

Chambers, Colin, *The Story of Unity Theatre*, London: Lawrence and Wishart, 1989.

Chambers, Colin, and Prior, Mike, *Playwrights' Progress*, Oxford: Amber Lane Press, 1987.

Childs, David, *Britain Since 1945*, London: Routledge, 1997.

Cook, Judith, *Directors' Theatre*, London: Harrap, 1974.

Coren, Michael, *Theatre Royal: 100 Years of Stratford East*, London: Quartet Books, 1984.

Davies, Andrew, *Other Theatres*, London: Macmillan, 1987.

Davies, Andrew, *Leisure, Gender and Poverty: Working-class Culture in Salford and Manchester, 1900–1939*, Buckingham: Open University Press, 1992.

Edwards, Ness, *The Workers' Theatre*, Cardiff: Cymric Federation Press, 1930.

Elsom, John, *Post-war British Theatre*, London: Routledge and Kegan Paul, 1976.

Goodwin, John (ed), *British Theatre Design: The Modern Age*, London: Weidenfeld and Nicholson, 1995.

Goorney, Howard, *The Theatre Workshop Story*, London: Eyre Methuen, 1981.

Goorney, Howard, and MacColl, Ewan (eds), *Agit-Prop to Theatre Workshop*, Manchester: Manchester University Press, 1986.

Gorelik, Mordecai, *New Theatres for Old*, London: Dennis Dobson, 1947.

Greenwood, Walter, *Love on the Dole*, Harmondsworth: Penguin, 1969.

Gusfield, Joseph R., *Community: A Critical Response*, Oxford: Basil Blackwell, 1975.

Hannington, Wal, *Ten Lean Years*, London: Victor Gollancz, 1940.

Hannington, Wal, *Unemployed Struggles, 1919–1936*, London: Lawrence and Wishart, 1977.

Hawthorne, Nigel, *Straight Face*, London: Hodder and Stoughton, 2002.

Hobson, Harold, *Theatre in Britain: A Personal View*, Oxford: Phaidon, 1984.

Hodgson, John, and Preston-Dunlop, Valerie, *Rudolf Laban: An Introduction to his Work and Influence*, Plymouth: Northcote House, 1990.

Holdsworth, Nadine, *Joan Littlewood*, London: Routledge, 2006.

Innes, Christopher, *Modern British Drama 1890–1990*, Cambridge: Cambridge University Press, 1992.

Laban, Rudolf, *The Mastery of Movement* (4th edn, revised by Lisa Ullmann), London: Macdonald and Evans, 1980.

Lacey, Stephen, *British Realist Theatre*, London: Routledge, 1995.

Littlewood, Joan, *Joan's Book*, London: Methuen, 1994.

MacColl, Ewan, *Uranium 235*, a documentary play with Introduction by Hugh McDiarmid, Glasgow: William MacLennon, n.d.

MacColl, Ewan, *Journeyman*, London: Sidgwick and Jackson, 1990.

McGrath, John, *A Good Night Out*, London: Eyre Methuen, 1981.

MacLennan, Elizabeth, *The Moon Belongs to Everyone*, London: Methuen, 1990.

Marowitz, Charles, Milne, Tom, and Hale, Owen, *The Encore Reader*, London: Methuen, 1965.

Marshall, Norman, *The Other Theatre*, London: John Leyman, 1947.

Moussinac, Leon, *The New Movement in the Theatre*, London: B.T. Batsford, 1931.

Newlove, Jean, *Laban for Actors and Dancers*, London: Nick Hern Books, 1993.

Newlove, Jean and Dalby, John, *Laban for All*, London: NHB, 2004.

Nicholson, Steve, *British Theatre and the Red Peril*, Exeter: University of Exeter Press, 1999.

Norman, Frank, *Why Fings Went West*, London: Lemon Tree Press, 1975.

Orwell, George, *The Road to Wigan Pier*, Harmondsworth: Penguin, 1989.

Paget, Derek, *True Stories? Documentary Drama on Radio, Screen and Stage*, Manchester: Manchester University Press, 1990.

Rabey, David Ian, *English Drama since 1940*, London: Longman, 2003.

Roberts, Robert, *The Classic Slum: Salford Life in the First Quarter of the Century*, Manchester: Manchester University Press, 1971.

Samuel, Raphael, MacColl, Ewan, and Cosgrove, Stuart, *Theatres of the Left*, London: Routledge and Kegan Paul, 1985.

Seeger, Peggy (ed.), *The Essential Ewan MacColl Songbook: Sixty Years of Songmaking*, New York: Oak Publications, 2001.

Shellard, Dominic (ed.), *British Theatre in the 1950s*, Sheffield: Sheffield Academic Press, 2000.

Shellard, Dominic, *British Theatre Since the War*, London: Yale University Press, 2000.

Sidnell, Michael, *Dances of Death: The Group Theatre of London in the Thirties*, London: Faber and Faber, 1984.

Sissons, Michael, and French, Philip (eds), *Age of Austerity 1945–51*, Harmondsworth: Penguin, 1964.

Stanislavsky, Constantin, *An Actor Prepares*, London: Geoffrey Bles, 1937.

Stourac, Richard, and McCreery, Kathleen, *Theatre as a Weapon*, London: Routledge and Kegan Paul, 1986.

Taylor, John Russell, *Anger and After*, Harmondsworth: Penguin, 1963.

Thompson, Alan, *The Day Before Yesterday*, London: Granada, 1971.

Tynan, Kenneth, *Tynan on Theatre*, Harmondsworth: Penguin, 1964.
Tynan, Kenneth, *Tynan Right and Left*, London: Longmans, 1967.
Tynan, Kenneth, *A View of the English Stage*, London: Methuen, 1984.
Vice, Sue, *Introducing Bakhtin*, Manchester: Manchester University Press, 1997.
Wandor, Michelene, *Post-War British Drama: Looking Back in Gender*, London: Routledge, 2001.

Plays (sources for the plays discussed in this book)

Auden, W.H., and Isherwood, Christopher, *The Dog Beneath the Skin*, London: Faber and Faber, 1935.
Behan, Brendan, *The Hostage*, in *The Complete Plays*, London: Eyre Methuen, 1978.
Behan, Brendan, *The Quare Fellow*, in *The Complete Plays*, London: Eyre Methuen, 1978.
Chapman, Henry, *You Won't Always Be on Top*, London: Methuen, 1965.
Chlumberg, Hans, *Miracle at Verdun*, in *Famous Plays of 1932–33*, London: Victor Gollancz, 1933.
Delaney, Shelagh, *A Taste of Honey*, London: Methuen, 1959.
de Vega, Lope, *Fuente Ovejuna*, in *Three Major Plays*, Oxford: Oxford University Press, 1999.
Griffith, Hubert, *Red Sunday*, London: Cayme Press, 1929.
Lewis, Stephen, *Sparrers Can't Sing*, London: Evans, 1962.
Lorca, Federico Garcia, *The Love of Don Perlimplin and Belisa in the Garden*, in *Five Plays*, Harmondsworth: Penguin, 1970.
MacColl, Ewan, *Rogue's Gallery*, typescript in Ruskin College Library, Oxford.
MacColl, Ewan, *The Travellers*, typescript in Ruskin College Library, Oxford.
MacColl, Ewan, *You're Only Young Once*, typescript in Ruskin College Library, Oxford.
MacColl, Ewan, *Johnny Noble*, in Goorney, Howard, and MacColl, Ewan (eds), *Agit-prop to Theatre Workshop*, Manchester: University of Manchester Press, 1986.
MacColl, Ewan, *The Other Animals*, in Goorney, Howard, and MacColl, Ewan (eds), *Agit-prop to Theatre Workshop*, Manchester: University of Manchester Press, 1986.
MacColl, Ewan, *Landscape with Chimneys* (also called *Paradise Street*), typescript in Ruskin College Library, Oxford.
MacColl, Ewan, *Uranium 235*, in Goorney, Howard, and MacColl, Ewan (eds), *Agit-prop to Theatre Workshop*, Manchester: University of Manchester Press, 1986.
Miller, James H. (Ewan MacColl) and Littlewood, Joan, *John Bullion*, in Goorney, Howard, and MacColl, Ewan (eds), *Agit-prop to Theatre Workshop*, Manchester: University of Manchester Press, 1986.
Norman, Frank, *Fings Ain't Wot They Used T'Be*, New York: Grove Press, 1962.
Odets, Clifford, *Waiting for Lefty*, in Mann, Emily, and Roessel, David (eds), *Political Stages: Plays that Shaped a Century*, New York: Applause, 2002. (Note: *Waiting for Lefty* is included in: Odets, Clifford, *Six Plays*, London: Methuen, 1987, but this version is not complete, since it omits Scene 5, 'The Young Actor'.)
Owen, Alun, *Progress to the Park*, in *New English Dramatists 5*, Harmondsworth: Penguin, 1962. (Note: the published script varies somewhat from that used in the Theatre Workshop production.)
Rice, Elmer, *Street Scene*, in *Three Plays*, New York: Hill and Wang, 1965.
Saroyan, William, *Sam, the Highest Jumper of Them All*, London: Faber and Faber, 1961.

Sinclair, Upton, *Singing Jailbirds*, Long Beach, CA: Upton Sinclair, 1924.

Theatre Workshop, Charles, Chilton, and members of the original cast, *Oh What a Lovely War*, London: Eyre Methuen, 1967; see also, Theatre Workshop, Charles Chilton, Gerry Raffles and Members of the Original Cast, *Oh What a Lovely War*, revised and restored to the original version by Joan Littlewood, London: Methuen, 2000.

Toller, Ernst, *Draw the Fires!*, in *Seven Plays*, London: Bodley Head, 1935.

Toller, Ernst, *Hoppla, Such is Life!*, in *Seven Plays*, London: Bodley Head, 1935. (Note: this play is available in a more recent translation, under the title *Hoppla, We're Alive*, in Toller, Ernst, *Plays One*, London: Oberon Books, 2000.)

Toller, Ernst, *The Machine Wreckers*, in *Seven Plays*, London: Bodley Head, 1935.

Wilder, Thornton, *Pullman Car 'Hiawatha'*, London: Samuel French, n.d.

Wilder, Thornton, *Our Town* in *Three Plays*, Harmondsworth: Penguin, 1962.

Index